Published by Ockley Books Limited,
Huddersfield, England

First Published 2021

All text copright the identified author, the moral right of
Terry Duffelen to be identified as the author of this work has been
asserted.

All rights reserved. No part of this work may be reproduced in any
form without prior permission from the author, Terry Duffelen ©,
and the publisher, Ockley Books ©.

ISBN - 978-1910906248

Layout and design by Chris Oakley,
edited by David Hartrick.

Printed and bound by
Biddles Printing, Kings Lynn.

Borussia Dortmund
A History in Black and Yellow

Terry Duffelen

Contents

1. Handbags, Beer and Birth 7
2. Revierderby 16
3. "Der Klassiker" 37
4. Champions, European Nights and Missed Chances: 1963–66 46
5. Nothing to see here 69
6. The Cobra Strikes and Nobby's Final Hurrah 86
7. Glorious Failure 108
8. The Italian Job 128
9. "God Must Be a Borussia Fan" 141
10. "Ricken, lupfen jetzt!" 150
11. Stones and Legs 164
12. What Happened Next 202
13. Clash of Civilisations 213
Postscript 223

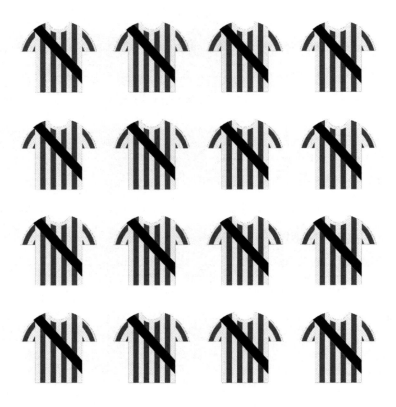

1909

Handbags, Beer and Birth
The creation of a football club in Borsigplatz

It is strange indeed that an institution so loved, so much a part of its community, so much a part the lives of so many all over the world, should be born, in part, from an angry confrontation in a bar. But our story begins with precisely that, six days before Christmas Day 1909, in a stairwell outside a room above a pub in one of the oldest districts in the city of Dortmund, North Rhine-Westphalia, Germany.

The pub in question was the Zum Wildschütz in the district of Borsigplatz, which did and still does lie in the north of Dortmund, one of the larger conurbations in the industrial Ruhr area of Germany. In this bar a group of young lads, inspired by the working men's football clubs of England, in cities such as Sheffield and Manchester, gathered to set up a club for the purposes of playing football and having a few beers afterwards. You could be forgiven for thinking that such an undertaking, while far from straightforward, would be uncontroversial. However, in Germany in 1909 social clubs of this nature were not seen as being healthy. In fact, they were regarded by some influential people as injurious to the soul.

At the turn of the 20th Century, sports in Germany were organised along political and religious lines. The *Arbeitersportbewegung* (Socialist workers movement for sports) and the *Turnerschaft* (gymnastics movement) were prominent institutions. Sport did not exist for recreation, as such; that was more of an inevitable consequence. Moreover, sports clubs were just that. They incorporated multiple sports. Many of the more historic clubs in Germany started as gymnastic clubs. Dedicated football clubs were far from common in Germany at the turn of the century and the game of football was discouraged among the upper sections of German society. Indeed, in some quarters the beautiful game was regarded as "the English disease". Eleven years prior to this meeting in Borsigplatz a gymnastics teacher in Stuttgart, Karl Planck, published the polemic *Fusslümmelei - Über Stauchballspiel und die Englische Krankheit*. In the pamphlet, he characterises football as dirty, anarchic and decidedly un-German. This view, while prevalent in the German establishment, did not stop the development of the sport in the latter part of the 19th Century.

In Britain, association football (abbreviated to soccer) had moved beyond its amateur roots in London to the industrial north. There, working men had professionalised the game under no small amount of resistance from the Football Association. Football in Britain was becoming a mass spectator sport and although the players were far from rich they were paid a wage for their labours. Professional football in Germany was decades away but the idea of football being more than a spiritual enterprise, something that people could enjoy playing and watching – especially when combined with beer – was catching on.

This would have been at the front of the minds of the young men who gathered in Borsigplatz on 19th December 1909. These men saw football as a social activity to be enjoyed among friends and they were not alone. They were far from revolutionary in this desire. No one in that room was breaking ground so much as being a symptom of social change, a reflection of the changing nature of working class agency and culture that was happening across much of Europe in the wake of the Industrial Revolution.

Moreover, they were frustrated with what they perceived as unfair treatment by the clergy. At this time football was not the most popular sport among the establishment. Other sports such as gymnastics were regarded as a healthier diversion for the young. Even then football had a bad reputation. The men who gathered in Borsigplatz were angry with the Church's attitude towards them as footballers and decided it was time to form their own club, independent of the Church. To that end they assembled. They sunk a few beers and started planning. On his way, however, was a potential obstacle in the form of a man of the cloth. Father Hubert Dewald was, according to Christoph Bausenwein in *Das Grosse Buch Vom BVB*, the local chaplain and head of the local youth group from the Holy Trinity church nearby. He got wind of the meeting and was having none of it. He hot-footed it over to the bar, prepared for an angry confrontation and with the intention of breaking up the meeting.

In 2015, a film documenting this meeting was made by Marc Quambusch. It is called *Am Borsigplatz Geboren (Born on Borsigplatz)*. In this film there is a dramatisation of that meeting and of Dewald's unwelcome intervention. The clergyman is full of righteous fury and purpose as he enters the pub and bounds up the stairs. He bursts into the room and demands that the meeting stop at once.

Some of the group allow themselves to be intimidated by Dewald who, as a man of God in a country very much deferential to the Catholic Church, represented power and demanded respect. But most in the room will not be cowed. One man – his name was Franz Jacobi – emerges from the crowd. He bustles Dewald out of the room as a nightclub bouncer would an unwelcome patron wearing the wrong shoes. There are more harsh words and some pushing and shoving. At first it was a bit of handbags, to use the modern parlance, but the confrontation escalates as neither are willing to back down. In the end Dewald's attempts to re-enter the room are halted by Jacobi, who pushes him down a short flight of stairs.

In the film there is a dramatic pause. Dewald looks up at the triumphant Jacobi, who glares down upon his defeated foe. Perhaps the moment is meant to symbolise the decline of the role of the Church in German civil society. Perhaps Jacobi is just making sure he's not badly injured a priest in a moment of beer-soaked rage. Either way, the moment passes and Jacobi turns on his heel, walks back into the room and closes the door, forever shutting the Church out of their affairs. However, Dewald's intervention was not entirely unsuccessful. There were 40 people in that room before it all kicked off. Only 18 remained afterwards.

Their names?

Franz Braun
Paul Braun
Henry Cleve
Hans Debest
Hans Kahn
Paul Dziendzielle

Hans Kahn
Gustav Müller
Franz Risse
Fritz Schulte
Hans Siebold
August Tönnesmann

Heinrich Unger
Robert Unger
Fritz Weber
Franz Wendt

Not forgetting, of course, Julius and Wilhelm Jacobi and their brother, Franz.

Some of those that departed perhaps saw the error of their ways. Perhaps others felt that the whole affair was more trouble than it was worth. More still may have thought that it wasn't worth getting into a dust-up with a priest over. What we do know is that those who stayed agreed upon a course of action and decided to form a football club. What was missing was a name for this fledgling club. It so happened that they were drinking a certain brand of local beer, and that beer would form part of the name of this new football club.

Dortmund was a city built on heavy industry: steel and coal. By the turn of the century the city's population had swelled to around 200,000 people. A significant number were immigrants from eastern Germany and Poland. Approximately 2.3 million Germans from East and West Prussia, Silesia, and Posen moved to the Ruhr, as did about 600,000 Poles. Others came from France and Great Britain. They took advantage of the demand for labour as the region industrialised and transformed both it and in turn the city of Dortmund forever. The Hoesch family set up an iron and steel works in the city in 1871. From there the firm became one of Dortmund's major employers. Indeed, Borsigplatz sits in the centre of what was known as the Hoesch Quarter, a district then populated almost entirely by immigrant workers employed by that firm. The rapid expansion of the city and the influx of workers meant many more wage packets. With that came a desire to pursue leisure activities during the workers' time off.

Beer also played a very big role in the city. Dortmunders were excellent at drinking it and exceptionally good at brewing it. Indeed, the hop is a big driver of the origins of the football club that was formed that night in Borsigplatz. In addition to iron and steel, Dortmund was a commercial brewing centre and exported beer to neighbouring regions in the Ruhr. Breweries such as Brinkhoffs, Dormunder Union and Dortmund Actien Brauerei endure to this day. However, the industry is very much past its peak as, according to the *European Beer Guide*, a number of breweries merged and consolidated in the 1990s. Although not among the most popular in Germany, the Dortmund brewing process has been replicated by other breweries as far away as Canada. One of those breweries, which sadly no longer exists, was called Borussia. It was an advert displayed in that room above the

Zum Wildschütz in Borsigplatz that was the inspiration for the name of the new venture they conceived that day:

BV Borussia Dortmund 09.

The German football writer and historian, Uli Hesse, devotes an entire chapter to the naming conventions used in German football clubs in his book *Tor: A History of German Football*. Some clubs' names were inspired by national or regional pride: names like Germania, Alemannia, Preussen, Sachsen and Westfalia were commonplace. The name *Borussia* is Latin for "Prussia". There are numerous clubs that have taken the name, including the club in Mönchengladbach some nine years earlier. However, as we know, the founders of BVB did not take the name for reasons of regional pride. Borussia Dortmund are not unique in that respect. As Hesse points out, Fortuna Düsseldorf was named after a popular bakery of the same name in that city. The founders of Hertha BSC in Berlin got the name from a boat on which they had once taken a day trip.

These names that originated for little other reason beyond expediency echo through the years and will continue to do so for decades to come. They have contributed to a multimillion-Euro international industry, attended by tens of thousands and watched worldwide by audiences of millions. Their banners and symbols are displayed with pride well beyond the communities in which they originated. I wonder if these respective groups of young lads, whose main priority was to just play football and drink beer, would have taken a little more time had they known the impact they were to have on their national culture. I sincerely hope not.

So, Dortmund's name begins with a BV which stands for *Ballspielverein*. This translates as "Ballgame club". You know about the Borussia and Dortmund part, and "09" refers to the year of foundation. Ballspielverein Borussia Dortmund 09, or just BVB for short. Now that the club had a name, what it needed next was a home in which to hang its founders' collective hats.

The white flowers of the poplar trees fell in the spring on the playing fields of Wambler Strasse in Dortmund. Because of this the field was called the Weiße Wiese or "White Meadow". It was here that Dortmund played their home fixtures. As for a uniform, some suitable striped kits were acquired with an added feature. The *Arbeiterbewegung* was a European political movement that campaigned for improved rights for worker and their conditions. Its symbol was a red sash. Many of the players were part of this movement and they elected to incorporate the red sash as part of the playing shirt for the new club. The full kit was black shorts, and blue and white shirts with the red sash.

Borussia Dortmund applied to join the West German Football Championship (WSV). However, the obstacles did not end with the pushing of a pastor down a flight of stairs. The administrators of the WSV were reluctant to admit clubs that only played football. This is not as likely to have been for political or religious reasons as much as a result to the large number of new football clubs starting up at the time. The solution was to apply as an athletics club. By so doing they gave the impression of being a well-established club with a large membership that was more likely to complete a full season.

The first officially recorded match played by Borussia Dortmund was on 15th January 1911 against VfB Dortmund at the Weiße Wiese. The game finished 9-3 to Borussia. There were a number of friendly or unofficial games that followed. The first competitive game was later in the year on 10th September against Turnerbund Rauxel at the start of the WSV C Klasse season. BVB won 1-0. Sadly, for such a momentous match, very little detail survives for posterity. Not even a goal scorer. However, according to Schulze-Marmeling in his *History of Borussia*, the line-up for the team that would go on to gain promotion to the B-Klasse that season was: Willi Jacobi, Heinrich Schaefer, Otto Hegedorn, Werth, Robert Unger, G. Pellmann, Weber, Franz Jacobi, Bohnekamp, Becker and Karl Wienke.

C Klasse was the bottom tier of the WSV and, in turn, it was at the foot of the national championship. Until 1963 the German football championship was a regional competition. Each league had its own structure and would play out its regional competition throughout the season. The top teams would then participate in a national play-off competition at the end of the campaign. All clubs in Germany were amateurs but Borussia Dortmund were truly a non-league team by comparison to the big clubs of the era, such as VfB Leipzig, Phönix Karlsruhe and Viktoria Berlin.

In the summer of 1912 BVB merged with three other local sports clubs in Dortmund: Rhenania, Britannia and Deutsche Flagge.

Although Borussia's name was retained the club's membership was given a substantial boost as a result of the merger. Britannia Dortmund's kit was black and yellow, presumably inspired by the city's coat of arms: a black eagle on a yellow shield. The following year BVB elected to adopt these colours as their own. The kit was now comprised of black shorts and yellow shirts, with a single "B" for a badge on the left breast. Borussia was not the foremost club in the city but, by adopting these new colours, they could truly claim to represent Dortmund, something that they would do in due course and with great success.

Franz Jacobi was 21 when the club was founded. A year later he became president of the club and was a decisive figure during its early years, in particular when so many of its members were away in the Great War between 1914 and 1918. Jacobi wrote to each of them while they were on the front. Jacobi himself was exempt from service. His father had passed on and as the eldest brother he was permitted to remain behind. His best friend and fellow founder was Heinrich Unger, who wrote the first ever anthem to be adopted by the club. The song was called "Wir Halten Fest Und Treu Zusammen" – "We Are Standing Together" – and it was composed in the trenches.

For all the hard work and great victories on the pitch, it is moments like these that make great football clubs. By keeping the flame alive during what must have been, at times, utterly desperate years for many of those young men, the club endured and survived the trauma of the First World War. Today, a football club can be manufactured almost from scratch, so long as there are enough moneyed interests willing to underwrite it. However, at the turn of the 20th century the story was different. Of course, many great clubs have relied upon the support of business, be it local, national or international, in order to achieve greatness. However, this support only comes when a club is established in its community and when its members and supporters really care for their club and, within reason, are willing to make sacrifices for it.

These early years determined the fate of Borussia Dortmund. Had things been different then BVB would be little more than a footnote on a statistics website. Jacobi himself would live long enough to witness the seeds he sowed come to full bloom. He would see their first final in 1949 and their first championship in 1956. He was in Glasgow in May

1966 to see Borussia make history as the first ever German football club to win a European trophy. From a few mates in a pub to the European Cup Winners' Cup within his own lifetime. What emotions must Jacobi have felt as he watched from the stands at Hampden Park?

Zum Wildschütz exists to this day as a fast food restaurant. The walls are decorated with memorabilia from the glory days of Borussia Dortmund. Jacobi died in 1979 and was interred in Salzgitter, a city in lower Saxony – south of Hannover, Wolfsburg and Braunschweig – where he and his family had relocated. It was reported in *Der Westen* that his remains were relocated to Dortmund in 2013. To show that there were no hard feelings, the memorial service for his re-burial was held at Trinity Church. No one from the Church had any objections this time.

1956

Revierderby

"My hometown is full of smurf fans!" wrote an irate fan on the Borussia Dortmund section of the hugely popular social news website, Reddit. "Guess I'm not going back for a while after 4-4 and now... this." This was posted just after Borussia Dortmund's 2-0 away defeat to Schalke 04 on 15th April 2018. The 4-4 result to which the poster referred needs little explanation, and for Dortmund and Schalke fans will not be easy to forget, albeit for different reasons. In November 2017, at the Westfalen, the Royal Blues of Gelsenkirchen engineered an extraordinary comeback from 4-0 down to square the match in the dying seconds. The result was one of a number of blows dealt to the other in what is one of the great rivalries in football. But, like all great sporting conflicts, it is an expression of a deeper social, civic and economic rivalry.

The city of Gelsenkirchen is located somewhere to the west of Herne. It is, in terms of population, smaller than Dortmund. However, its football club, Schalke 04 – named after a district of that city – is one of the most established and best supported in Germany. Its popularity goes back to before the Second World War, when Schalke were one of the best teams in the land. Gelsenkirchen and Dortmund are part of the Ruhrpott or Ruhrgebiet district of Germany, the massive industrial base that emerged in the Ruhr Valley in the 19th Century. These informal regional names vary depending on whom you ask. Some prefer 'Ruhrgebiet' because they feel 'Ruhrpott' has negative connotations due to its links with the area's industrial past. The area has gone through something of a transformation since the collapse of the iron and steel industries that were the foundations of the region's economy in the 1970s. Some of the closed steelworks and collieries that used to produce the raw energy needed to power the nation exist now as art installations, or in the region's many parks as memorials to its industrial might. In addition to Dortmund and Gelsenkirchen, Ruhrpott includes Essen – the second biggest city – Duisburg, Bochum, Herne, Oberhausen, Hamm, and a few more besides. Nearby Düsseldorf and Wuppertal could be said to be part of the Ruhr, although geographically they are not.

"When you go to the Ruhr district everything just melts into one. It's like one big city really," says Rob Turner. If you are a regular viewer of the official Bundesliga live matchday commentary or its highlights show then you'll most likely have heard his Yorkshire lilt. He is also the English language commentator of the official Borussia Dortmund stadium tour. Turner has lived in the Ruhr since emigrating from the UK in the late 1990s and has been a BVB season ticket holder since the early 21st century. "A town planner would look at the Ruhr district and think there's so much potential. There are five million people living here. If you could make yourself into one city you'd be like a super metropolis. You'd be unbeatable."

However, the Ruhr is not a place that can be tamed in such a manner. "It's made up of so many fiefdoms and the rivalry between the smaller and larger towns and their councils has always been extremely bitter," says Turner. "Everyone has always been trying to protect their own patch, which makes them a bit more patriotic about their own towns and their own industries: their own steelworks, their own collieries and their own coking plants. They each say that they are the best and the ones down the road are just upstarts. And that plays out in football as well."

A good friend of mine once described to the me the "Ruhrpott Mentality". People from the region are direct even by German standards. This is not to say that I subscribe to the stereotype of the rude German, but I have spoken to a number of English people who are taken aback by the manner of some Germans and have mistaken a natural directness for discourtesy. However, in the Ruhr they are well known for their frankness and cutting humour. If you're a nervous visitor to the Ruhr, conversing with a local can occasionally be disconcerting. The best thing to do is have another one of the region's many delicious beers and relax.

Most of the towns and cities have their own football clubs. VfL Bochum is a lovely club by all accounts, but mostly a second tier side that makes the occasional foray into the first division. However, up until the early part of this century, they were briefly an established Bundesliga club. After their relegation in 2010 they have struggled to return to the top flight. MSV Duisburg have fallen on tough times but when they played under the name of Meiderich they finished second in the inaugural season of the Bundesliga in 1964. Rot-Weiss Essen won the National Championship in 1955 and were a prominent club for many years before going into a decline from which they are yet to recover.

Unsurprisingly, with so many clubs at close quarters, derbies are a bit of a thing. Also, Ruhrpott has an integrated economy and workforce thanks to its road and public transport system. Every morning and evening workers from one part or Ruhrpott commute to another, so fans of BVB, S04, RWE, VfL and MSV will all share the same workspaces. You can imagine the banter and the amount of social capital that's at stake when these teams play each other.

"I've worked with lots of Schalke fans that came to Dortmund for work," says Turner. "I've also worked in Essen, where there's been a mix. During the week it's all good-natured but after derby day you definitely do not want to go into the office after a defeat, because you know that's all you'll hear until the next derby. So I think that gives rise to the attitude that the derby win is all that matters."

This social phenomenon is not unique by any stretch. However, given its size and the population density and mix of different club fans across the region, it is an extreme example that results in some intense rivalries, particularly between the two biggest and most supported clubs in the area. The term *Revierderby* is associated and indeed marketed as a brand to represent the rivalry between Borussia Dortmund and Schalke, but in fact it can refer to any derby in the Ruhrpott regions. "Revier" translates as "region" or "territory" but refers specifically to the Ruhr in this instance. The Dortmund v Schalke game is known popularly as the Revierderby and the derbies between the other Ruhr clubs are called *kleines Revierderby*. However, this is almost certainly a matter of opinion. In fact the term itself does not hark back to the early days of these two clubs' first meetings in the twenties and thirties. Christoph Biermann, author of *Wenn wir vom Fussball träumen: Eine Heimhreise* states that "Revierderby" was first coined in 1977 by the region's biggest newspaper, *WAZ*.

The intensity of the Dortmund v Schalke rivalry cannot be

understated. The refrain "Death and hate to S04!" is a common one among Dortmund fans. In Uli Hesse's piece on the derby for *ESPN* he recalled an incident in which a group of Borussia ultras stole some fan clothing from a group of Schalke ultras and were displaying it triumphantly within view of them. "As is the case in many other comparable youth subcultures," he wrote, "losing regalia – especially a flag – constitutes the worst possible disgrace for an ultra, who would go to considerable lengths to win it back."

Rob Turner's first experience of the derby could not have been more visceral for a young Dortmund fan not quite *au fait* with its character. "My first derby game was at the Parkstadion," he said in reference to Schalke's old stadium. In 2001 they moved to a new arena which is sponsored by Veltins, a local beer. "It was absolutely freezing," he continues, "so you needed to wear loads and loads of layers. So I thought, naively, that since I was going to Dortmund game I'll just put my Dortmund shirt on and my friends said, 'Yeah we've got tickets for the Nordkurve,' and I was like, 'Ah I'm sure I'll be fine.'" The Nordkurve section of the Parkstadion was where all the Schalke hardcore and ultras stood and it was there, at his first derby, that Rob stood in his Dortmund shirt, albeit ticked under several hundred layers of clothing. "Just stood around listening to how people were speaking about Dortmund and about the club. About the people of Dortmund and I was thinking ah, maybe it would be a good idea if I keep it really well covered up."

"It was definitely an eye-opener," he recalled. "I knew a little about Dortmund, I knew a little about Schalke, and I knew a little about the region. It was a bit similar to where I come from, Yorkshire: lots of industrial heritage and the teams and the clubs are closely intertwined with the local industry, so I was thinking it was probably going to be more good-natured really, and I found out very quickly that it's not. There is absolute hatred between the two of them."

Uli Hesse argued that the reasons why the rivalry is so forceful are not altogether clear. There is not the intense familial chemistry of a city derby in places like Manchester, Merseyside or Glasgow, where households can be separated by the colour of their shirts. There is no sign of the sectarian divide that characterises the Old Firm clubs of Glasgow, nor is there necessarily the local economic rivalry between, say, the port cities of Southampton and Portsmouth on the English south coast. There's no political or nationalist connotations such as those underlying the Real Madrid and Barcelona rivalry. Gelsenkirchen produced coal while Dortmund produced steel and beer. I am certainly not alone in comparing the rivalry with that of two great north-east English clubs, Newcastle United and Sunderland, both in port cities that generated coal during the country's industrial age.

The rivalry is also fairly recent. As Biermann says, "These days a match between Borussia Dortmund and Schalke 04 sees a spike in media coverage all around the globe, and those same old clichés about the hard-working Ruhr area clubs are trotted out time and time again. The Revierderby is sold to us as the classic rivalry between working class fan groups." However, while the animosity grew through the years, it was not always reflected by the clubs. Indeed, Biermann states that Dortmund president Reinhard Rauball said after a derby win over Schalke in 1977 that, "... his club would do their utmost to help their neighbours from Gelsenkirchen in the battle against relegation by winning their next match against Arminia Bielefeld." Ten years later such a statement would have never been made by either side.

Borussia were not a successful club in the early part of the 20th century while Schalke were very much the nation's club; the four national titles they won in the 1930s saw to that. Dortmund's growth in the years after the Second World War was during a period of relative decline for Schalke. In a sporting sense it could be argued that Köln were greater rivals to Dortmund in the 1950s and early 1960s. Perhaps the intensification of the derby grew with the decline of the region economically. Maybe the derby became an expression of civic pride at a time when life was changing beyond the cities' ability to control it, and for a great many people times were getting tough economically. Perhaps identifying themselves more with Schalke or Dortmund it allowed them a chance to affect change and – to use a modern phrase – take back control.

Football supporters are precisely that. They support the club, vocally during the games, financially through gate money and membership, through the wearing of colours, and in many cases through community activity on behalf or in honour of the club. It is a cliché but it's nonetheless true to say that football clubs are about more than football. They represent and are a part of a community, its challenges, its victories, its setbacks and its competitors. Consequently, when a club is defined so clearly in terms of its rivalry with another club, the meaning of that derby takes on extra significance. Borussia and Schalke fans don't just chant slogans, sing songs and display elaborate and spectacular tifos before the game in support of the team. They do it to assert their club's and community's identity as superior. These are matters which people can control. Of course, this happens elsewhere, but in the cultural melting pot of different municipalities that make up the Ruhr it is especially intense and, dare I say, unique.

On the final day of the 2000/01 season, BVB drew 3-3 with 1. FC Köln to secure third place in the table and qualify for the UEFA Cup. However, of greater significance that day was the very real prospect of Schalke claiming their first ever Bundesliga title and their first national championship since 1958. A win against Unterhaching and a defeat for second-placed Bayern Munich at Hamburger SV would have handed the *Meisterschale* to the Gelsenkirchen club. Schalke fought back from 3-2 down to win their game 5-3 and, when the news came through from Hamburg that Sergej Barbarez had scored for the home team in the 90th minute, there was much jubilation at a packed Parkstadion in Gelsenkirchen. The scenes at Schalke's ground were passed through a looking glass and conversely reflected at the Westfalen, where thousands of BVB fans had stayed behind to face the bad news together. Imagine the scenes, then, when Patrik Andersson popped up for Bayern deep into injury time and scored the only goal he would ever score for the club, an equaliser to clinch the title. For a brief few minutes the Schalke fans knew the ecstasy of a championship win only to have it snatched from them. There was as much despair in Gelsenkirchen as there was wild celebration in HSV's Volksparkstadion and in Munich. And, on the Südtrubune at the Westfalen, thousands of Dortmunders who had stayed behind celebrated Schalke's failure with wild abandon.

This textbook example of schadenfreude was repeated seven years later. Coming into the penultimate round of the season, Schalke were top of the table with only a point between them and Stuttgart. Dortmund were a moribund mid-table side struggling with the combined burden of the club's financial problems and being coached by Thomas Doll. However, driven by a historic opportunity to deny the Gelsenkirchen club their first ever Bundesliga title, they found an extra gear and won the game 2-0. Schalke – coached by Mirko Slomka and featuring a painfully young Mesut Özil – managed to beat

Bielefeld, but it wasn't enough. Stuttgart beat Energie Cottbus in order to wrestle the title away and lift the trophy. Not only had Schalke been denied the championship they so desperately craved but they had been denied by their most hated rivals. Such was the celebration in Dortmund that it was a mild surprise that there was no civic reception in Borsigplatz.

It is possible that onlookers might feel that this is a little too much, that preoccupation bordering on collective obsession with a club that isn't yours lacks class, or is more than a little sad, that the kind of hatred instilled is unhealthy. In some cases this is unquestionably true, with the rivalry taking on characteristics normally associated with gangland culture. The atmosphere around the stadiums before and after the Revierderby is one of febrile hostility and hatred. Almost the entire local police force is mobilised on matchday at a not inconsiderable cost to the clubs and the local authorities. There has been extreme violence between rival fans and there will be again. Such violence is small by comparison to the tens of thousands that travel to the stadium but is so devastating to those affected that it would be wrong to be dismissive or shrug it off as irrelevant.

However, for many it is an opportunity to parse these feelings in a relatively safe space. Consider that many Dortmund and Schalke fans work together and live in each other's communities. A Dortmund fan shouting "Death and hate to S04!" may well be convivially sharing an office with a Schalke fan later that week. It is not uncommon to see fans of Dortmund sitting in the Schalke end during a derby and vice versa (although it is not as likely as in other fixtures) and there are plenty of BVB and S04 fans that live in the other city, often because work and life outside football has taken them there. They live perfectly happily and even wear their colours. This is a rivalry with nuance and is part of the lives of normal human beings who live at close quarters. It would be a simplification to dismiss it as just hatred and violence. Indeed, I spoke with one fan who told me that he had been a Schalke fan at an early age but had switched allegiances on the basis that a player living locally had been rude to them. In fairness, they had only been four years old.

In the 1920s, Schalke was the biggest club in the Ruhr. The Royal Blues were at the forefront of a region that was teeming with emerging football clubs. Schulze Marmeling said that football "promoted significantly the self-esteem of the workers", not to mention the image of the area, a place associated with carbon and soot. As the popularity of the sport grew, so did the revenue raised through the turnstiles by the clubs. Although sport was strictly amateur, players were often rewarded by their employers with light duties and time off for training. However, with the extra money that clubs could raise, there was pressure to compensate players financially.

Football had its amateurism defended by the local leagues but it could not have been easy to enforce those rules. After all, league officials were themselves part-timers and did not have tremendous resources. Moreover, there was hardly a consensus about these regulations among football clubs. Sport by its very nature is competitive, and clubs will do what they can to gain an advantage and to win. Not only that, but there was a moral aspect to the payment of players. Life for working class families in the industrialised Ruhr was tough, with long hours and back-breaking work in harsh and dangerous conditions for frankly very little pay. Any player for a popular football club, seeing all this money coming in while they struggled to make ends meet, would not be satisfied by time off for training. They would want paying too, and rightly so.

It was inevitable therefore that this led to financial payments and, in turn, over-payments. In August 1930, Schalke were found guilty of professionalisation and were relegated by the WSV. There was outrage and protest at the decision, which was considered extremely harsh. The WSV represented an amateur sensibility that simply was not present among a community of players and administrators who knew first-hand what it was like to be on the wrong end of industrialisation. The decision was reversed and the rules were changed to allow players to be better compensated.

During this time Borussia Dortmund were playing in the second district league and were working their way up. The club played at the Weiße Wiese, located near Borsigplatz, and watched it grow from what was essentially a playing field into a proper football ground. From 1924 the ground was expanded, first with railings and terraces, until it became a stadium capable of holding 12,000 spectators (although by modern safety standards that would be considerably less) known as the "Borussia-Sportplatz". It was a tidy facility for an ambitious football club. However – and this may be the start of a pattern – the club very nearly fell victim to its own ambition. In 1928 it laid out huge sums of cash to recruit players of the quality that would do justice to its fine new stadium. In so doing they broke football association rules. There was a cash shortfall as a consequence and BVB president Heinrich Schwaben was forced to intervene at the last moment to pay the insurance costs and stop the club from going bankrupt.

In 1937, two years before the start of the Second World War, the Nazis mandated the Hoesch Corporation to expand their facilities as part of the rearmament of the German military. Borussia were forced to leave the Sportplatz, a stadium on which they had spent around 50,000 Reichsmarks down the years, not including the materials and countless hours of construction labour donated by club members. For this outlay the club received no compensation after the enforced eviction. The club's groundskeeper, Heinrich Czerkus, had to stand by and watch his pride and joy get demolished in the service of war and conquest. Czerkus was a communist and noted resistance leader during the war, and distributed illegal anti-Nazi propaganda, partly using duplicating equipment owned by the football club. He was murdered by the Gestapo in April 1945, mere weeks before the Nazis surrendered. A fan club is named after him and every year a charity run is held in Dortmund in support of anti-racism and anti-Nazism. In 2012 a street was named in his memory.

Borussia's new home was in Strobelallee, at a stadium called the Rote Erde – "Red Earth". The Rote Erde was built as a track and field venue in 1926 and had a running track around the pitch. BVB would play their matches there until 1974. In reality they never really left. The new stadium, built for the 1974 World Cup, sits right next to the Rote Erde; Borussia's reserve teams still use the ground for their home games.

When the Nazis won power in Germany they sought to influence every aspect of German society, including sport. In 1932 the German FA had resolved to create a national league. The plan for this new Reichsliga was cut short by the Nazis. The idea was revisited in 1939 but not implemented. Any prospect of further professionalisation and nationalisation of the game was ended. Germany would have to wait until 1963 before its football fans could watch national league football. In 1933 the leagues were restructured and renamed as Gauliga.

Originally there were 16 leagues across Germany, a number that grew larger upon the annexation of Austria and parts of France, the Czech Republic, Yugoslavia and Poland. Borussia Dortmund and Schalke were in Gauliga Westfalen, although BVB did not gain promotion to the first division until 1936. That division was made up of 10 different clubs, expanding to 12 in 1940 and dropping back to 10 the following season. The final season in this format was in 1944/45 and was divided into three parts before it was dissolved in the final stages of the War.

The same name sat at the top of the league at the end of every season in the Gauliga Westfalen: Schalke 04. The winner of each regional league would progress to what we would now call a post-season and play-offs for the national championship final. Schalke competed in eight such finals and won six of them. The Royal Blues dominated national football during this time, also appearing in five German Cup finals, albeit emerging only once as winners. The team was well known for its short passing style, which was on a different level to their opponents. Only Hannover in 1938 and the Austrian team Rapid Vienna could beat them in championship finals. The former needed a replay while the latter squeezed past them, 4-3. Needless to say, the Gelsenkirchen club made short work of Borussia whenever they played.

The first meeting between them was in 1925 and Schalke won 4-2. The inaugural derby game in the Gauliga came after BVB were promoted in 1936. Schalke won 4-1 and 7-0 in the first two Gauliga derbies. There was a brief respite the following season when Borussia managed a 3-3 draw, but from then on it was Schalke all the way and they won handsomely most times. In 1939 the Royal Blues won 9-0. The following year they beat Borussia 10-0. BVB's first win did not happen until the final full season of the Gauliga, when they finally beat Schalke by a solitary goal to nil. These results serve to illustrate Schalke's dominance during this time rather than Borussia's failing. After having been promoted to the first tier of the Gauliga, the Dortmunders consolidated their position and maintained their status until the league was dissolved. When competitive football resumed in the late 1940s BVB were in a good place to capitalise and went on to enjoy a period of success of their own, crucially succeeding Schalke as the force in the region and occasionally at national level too. This was thanks, in part, to the club's first ever superstar player: one August Lenz.

If you are familiar with the sight of the Südtribune – the south stand at the Westfalenstadion – in full flow, then you will have seen the banners and logo of The Unity, one of the largest and most prominent fan groups that populate that stand. Incorporated into the emblem found on their flags, walls, lamp-posts, public benches and various other places throughout the city in the form of stickers and stencils, is the stylised image of August Lenz. It is possible that Borussia would not have risen to the prominence that it enjoys today had Lenz not joined them. A Dortmund native, he played as a goalkeeper for numerous local clubs in exchange for a case of beer. In time, he joined Borussia and made his debut between the sticks against a team called TBV Mengede. During the game, striker Hannes Jakubowitz sustained an injury and had to leave the field. There were, of course no substitutes back then, so Lenz was quickly converted from goalkeeper to striker. The reports of how many Lenz scored of the 14 BVB goals that day range between nine and eleven. The Borusseum (the official Borussia Dortmund museum, situated in the Westfalenstadion) says that it was nine, so let's go with that.

There was no looking back for Lenz after that. In 1935 he became the first Borussia Dortmund player to play for the German national team. He scored nine goals in his 14 appearances and it is said that he could have played in the 1938 World Cup, had Germany not been obliged by the Nazi powers to incorporate into their post-annexation ranks many of the Austrian Wunderteam that had so very nearly won the World Cup in 1934.

In the same year Lenz was offered the chance to move to Schalke. The opportunity would almost certainly have meant a substantial rise in income and the chance of more major honours. The modern equivalent would have been an EFL League Two player moving to a top four Premier League club. However, Lenz chose to remain with his home-town club and thus his status as club legend was sealed. What's more, when BVB beat Schalke for the first time in 1943 it was Lenz who scored the only goal. He also played a significant role in their second win over Schalke, a 3-2 victory in the Westfalen championship final in 1947. By the time he retired at the age of 38, Lenz had made more than 1,000 appearances. Sadly, he hung up his boots just before Borussia's first ever national championship final. BVB lost the game 3-2 to VfR Mannheim in Stuttgart. He spent more than three decades of his retirement running a pub in Dortmund and continued to attend games and support the club until his death in 1988. A club legend who turned down Schalke to continue to play for Borussia; small wonder that his image lives on in supporter culture all these years later.

The Battle of the Ruhr took place between March and July of 1945 and all the major cities and towns in the region were heavily bombed. Dortmund suffered the worst. In March 1,108 aircraft dropped 4,851 tonnes of bombs on the centre and south in a raid that stopped all production for months and effectively flattened the city. In 2015, just days before the Revierderby at Dortmund, an unexploded British bomb was found in the car park outside the west stand of the stadium. Dortmund was rebuilt but not restored. Only a few of the original buildings were reconstructed. The city was regenerated using post-War architectural principles, what we would call modernist architecture. Thanks to the so called *Wirtschaftwunder*, Dortmund – and the region – enjoyed a post-War boom. The "Economic Miracle", to use the English term, created plenty of employment opportunities and generated enough income for ordinary working people in the city to enjoy some leisure time, including, of course, attending football matches.

After the War, West Germany had been dissuaded by the controlling US authorities from pursuing nationalist culture and identities, especially militaristic ones. The reasons for this are obvious. It was a heightened sense of nationalism that the Nazis had exploited when in power and, anxious to avoid the re-emergence of similar sentiments, emphasis was placed on the value of local communities and regions. Football played an important role in this. As the German historian Wolfram Pyta said, "... the commitment to regions as a focal point of identity gained new significance, and in this way football clubs became more and more important as figureheads of regions."

Massive social changes took place in West Germany, a nation transformed by the influx of refugees after the War; the levelling out of income between the middle and working classes; and an economic boom that introduced a consumerist economy. As a region where the raw materials of industry were produced and, in Dortmund's case, where a vast amount of beer was brewed and exported, these were good times. From 1950, the city's population grew as workers arrived to fill the labour requirements. Pretty soon the working men of Dortmund wore smart hats and waistcoats. They also wanted something to do on their days off. Needless to say, this prosperity was reflected in the success of their football club, which truly came of age in this time.

Despite its growth, only one Borussia Dortmund player was included in the West Germany World Cup squad that travelled to Switzerland in 1954. Goalkeeper Heinz Kwiatowski was born in Gelsenkirchen and played for Schalke as a schoolboy. He joined BVB in 1952, via Rot-Weiss Essen. He made close to 300 appearances for the club, winning two national titles. Widely recognised as an outstanding goalkeeper, his international career was marred by his participation in the 8-3 defeat to Hungary in the group stages of the 1954 World Cup. He did not feature in the tournament again. West Germany played that great Hungary side again in the final and incredibly beat the Mighty Magyars 3-2 to lift the World Cup, their reward for winning a game that became known as the Miracle of Bern. Kwiatowski is also associated with the world champions' 6-3 defeat to France in the third place play-off in the 1958 World Cup. The Dortmund player had been the back-up goalkeeper who had been given a run-out in a game of little significance. Perhaps Kwiatowski wished they hadn't bothered.

Of course, it takes more than mere favourable economic conditions to make a football club a success, and in 1952 there was a change of management. The new president was Werner Wilms, a lawyer, and Egon Pentryp was the chairman. The club strengthened their squad with the addition of Kwiatowski and the returning Adi Preißler. Another player with a street named after him, an iconic image of Alfred 'Adi' Preißler holding the Meisterschale aloft with one hand after the 1956 final against HSV can be found adorning one of the walls propping up the Westfalenstadion. It is also used to point the way to the Borusseum, a worthwhile visit if you're ever planning on going to a game. The image is in its own way as enduring as that of August Lenz. His bald pate gleams with almost the same ferocity as the championship trophy in his clutch, his smile like the proverbial cat with the cream. It is difficult to assess his abilities as a player beyond the raw stats: 78 games in his first stint with Borussia from 1946 to 1950, and 211 games upon his return to Dortmund from Preußen Münster in 1951. For the next eight years the Duisburg native battered opposition defences.

His style of play – what little there is to see in the archives – was that of a determined and direct attacking player with a hunched shoulder. His gait and receding hairline, and his dynamism, made him stand out from his team-mates. When he stopped playing for Borussia in 1959 he had 174 goals to his name, a record that has yet to be beaten. Frankly, it is highly unlikely that any BVB striker will stick around long enough to break it. Sadly, his feats were not acknowledged at national level, and he made just two appearances for West Germany, due in part to a troubled relationship with the national team coach, Sepp Herberger. That disappointment aside, Adi Preißler is and probably always will be Borussia Dortmund's all-time greatest goalscorer.

The list of BVB's top ten highest goalscorers is populated with footballers that will be celebrated later in this book, names like Timo Konietzka, Lothar Emmerich, Mannie Burgsmüller (who remains BVB's all-time Bundesliga goalscorer), Michael Zorc, Stéphane Chapuisat and some guy call Pierre-Emerick Aubameyang. There also are two names that are contemporaries of Preißler: Alfred Kelbassa and Alfred Niepieklo. Together, this trio of attacking talent were dubbed the "Three Alfredos". Kelbassa was a supreme athlete and won the German Youth Pentathlon championship in 1942. Born in Buer, a suburb of Gelsenkirchen, he graduated with a sports degree from the University of Cologne. Fredy Kelbassa was blessed with lightning pace. It was reported that he could sprint 100 metres in under 11 seconds. He was described by a former teammate as running like a horse, with "small tufts of grass flying high" in his wake. Before moving to Borussia he played at Preussen Münster and STV Horst-Emscher. In 1954, having made his name at the Gelsenkirchen club, he made the move to Dortmund, took a job as a clerk, and signed for Borussia on the standard terms of DM 360 per month plus bonuses.

His pace and athletic discipline gave him the ideal engine to compete on the high intensity, stop-start, ankle-breaking sport of soccer. However, Kelbassa also had great technique which gave him the ability to score goals – lots and lots of goals. He retired just before the formation of the Bundesliga having scored 104 times in 183 appearances between 1954 and 1963. Kelbassa scored a brace in the 1956 National Championship Final win in Berlin and was top scorer with 30 goals in the following season. He made only six appearances for the national team with an untypical return of just two goals.

To say that there were strong family ties in this team would be no exaggeration: Kelbassa's son married the daughter of Alfred Niepieklo. The pair were strike partners as players and eventually grandparents to the same child. Niepieklo played as the third striker in the W-M system pioneered in England by Herbert Chapman of Arsenal and still in use at this time in Germany. He was born in Castrop-Rauxel, not far from Dortmund or Gelsenkirchen. Niepieklo joined BVB in 1951 and remained there until 1960. He scored 107 goals, including one in each of the 1956 and 1957 finals. Described by current club president, Reinhard Rauball, as "one of the great Borussens", Niepieklo was a member of the club's council of elders until his death in 2014 at the age of 86.

It is easy to downplay the significance of winning back-to-back national championships during this time. After all, the game was semi-professional and the spectrum of talent between the players would have been quite wide. Clubs like Dortmund, Hamburg and Kaiserslautern, with lots of money to pay the best players, made short work of smaller clubs in their respective regions. However, this was after the Miracle of Bern, Germany's extraordinary World Cup, and only a few years before the establishment of the Bundesliga. Consider also that Dortmund won these two titles in succession with the same 11 players. The full line-up was: Kwiatowski, Burgsmüller, Sandmann, Schlebrowski, Michallek, Bracht, Peters, Preißler, Kelbassa, Niepieklo, Kapitulski. The coach of this team was Helmut Schneider, who began his coaching career at the age of 33 at Mainz, not unlike a certain other Borussia coach. He earned his qualifications at Sepp Herberger School in Cologne. After spells at Fürth, Mannheim, FC Köln and Pirmasens, he arrived at Dortmund in 1955.

Borussia qualified for the national championship post-season tournament as winners of the Oberliga West. They were placed in Group 2 along with Hamburg, VfB Stuttgart and Viktoria Berlin, who faced the prospect of a final in Berlin should they top their group and face the winners of Group 1. Sadly for them they only managed two points in the group after the teams had played each other home and away. BVB won their group on goal difference. A thumping 5-0 win over Hamburg was the difference maker in the group and they could easily have met Schalke in the final. The Königsblauen missed out on top spot in Group 1 by goal difference. This was controversial because Schalke's goal difference was, in fact, greater. However, there was a peculiar rule in place at the time that weighted the value of goals scored against the Gelsenkirchen club. Dietrich Schulze-Marmeling reported that Schalke ended up missing out by a goal difference of 0.07 – a Revierderby national final in Berlin would have been a match for the ages. As it was, Borussia had to settle with a clash with the Swabian club Karlsruher SC. The official attendance was 75,000, with 5,000 travelling to West Berlin from Dortmund. Once there, a number of fans unfurled a banner expressing solidarity with Schalke and the injustice done to them in not progressing to the final. The banner claimed that "Doom and evil spirits come after Westphalia!" and that Borussia would lift the trophy for the region. This is a moment of solidarity with Schalke, whereby intra-regional rivalries were set aside in favour of standing up for the honour of Westphalia. Were the situation reversed, the Schalke fans would have done the same. Probably.

Heinz Kwiatowski drew the accolades for his goalkeeping heroics in the final. He was, however, unable to prevent Max Fischer of KSC putting his team ahead after 10 minutes. Borussia stormed back though, and took an unassailable 4-1 lead with goals from all three Alfredos. First Nieplieko, then Kelbassa, then Preißler. Before the game the latter had tried to negotiate a pay rise for the players that the club refused on the grounds that it would be breaking the law. Interestingly, the players were offered cars as reward for winning the championship but would never receive them. Wilhelm Burgsmüller was unfortunate to put the ball into his own net on 66 minutes but the Dortmund players closed the game down in the final stages and, at the second time of asking, lifted the Meisterschale, affectionately known today as the Salad Bowl. The reception from the fans demonstrated the scale of the achievement in bringing real sporting success to the city of Dortmund. 250,000 people lined the streets to welcome the team and its entourage on two flatbed trucks. These were truly the best of times in the city: a booming economy, disposable income and a winning football team. The only thing that could have made it sweeter was to have beaten Schalke in the final.

The title win afforded Dortmund the opportunity to enter the European Cup. Borussia were obliged to play a qualifying round before entering the first round proper. They did make it through but they needed a replay to beat Spora Luxembourg. Helmut Bracht,

Nieplieko and Preißler put four past the Luxembourg side at the Rote Erde in the first leg, only for Marc Boreux to score a hat-trick for Spora. Dortmund took the one-goal lead to the Stade Josy Barthel but were defeated 2-1. There was no away goal rule back then so a replay was required, and order was restored with a resounding 7-0 win for the Black and Yellows. Their good fortune continued as Borussia were drawn against the great Manchester United team of the 1950s. The Busby Babes, so named after their manager Matt Busby, were the first English team to enter the competition. Busby was a vigorous supporter of the European Cup and insisted that his team participate despite the protestations of the somewhat parochial English Football League. Manchester United supporter and historian, Tom Clare, attended the first leg at the old Maine Road stadium and has written about his experiences: "The roar that greeted the two teams was like nothing I had ever heard before and it must have frightened the life out of the Germans."

The visitors were overwhelmed in the first half, going down 3-0. When the players took to the field for the second half the home crowd were anticipating a repeat performance. What they got was a spirited comeback. Clare continues, "The Germans tightened up considerably in the second half." Helmut Kapituluski and Preißler scored in the last 10 minutes to silence the crowd and keep the tie alive for the second leg. According to Clare, a sizable portion of the 44,450 crowd at the Rote Erde for the away leg were British soldiers and airmen on National Service in the area. "The ground inside the stadium was like a skating rink – bone hard and very icy. To compound United's problems for this game, the box containing the rubber studs that would have replaced the normal studs mysteriously went missing on the day of the match. Nor could Tom Curry find replacements for them in any outlet in the Ruhr area! They took to the field wearing the normal leather stud in their boots." Despite this handicap, the English team prevailed by holding out for a scoreless draw.

This Dortmund side marked a sharp change away from the more cultured, passing game epitomised by Schalke and towards a game based more on power and pace. The approach was to use superior physicality and speed to overwhelm the opposition, some of whom were wedded to a more considered strategy. Tilkowski, Michallek, Kelbassa, Nieplieko and Preißler were the immovable basis of the team. Even young tyro Aki Schmidt struggled to replace any part of the attack. His time would eventually come.

Curiously, for a team that dominated the club scene, Borussia players were still largely overlooked for the national team. Sepp Herberger, the coach who had steered the team to their Miracle of Bern in 1954, had his preferred players, and it is said that he did not favour players from the Ruhr. Schulze-Marmeling quoted Helmut Bracht as saying that, "We knew that Sepp did not like us... the national team had no importance for us. Maybe he did not like us because we were from the Ruhr area. Maybe we were too loud for him." This remark, although no doubt sincerely expressed, is a little unfair given that Helmut Rahn – the scorer of the winning goal for West Germany in Bern – was from Essen.

The following season Borussia encountered stiff opposition in the Oberliga West in the shape of Duisburger SV, not to be confused with MSV Duisburg, who also played in this league (under the name of Meiderich SV) and in a few years would become the main club in that city and the third club in the Ruhr to found the Bundesliga. Eventually, BVB proved too strong for the rest of the league and would enter the national finals as champions. Kelbassa was the league's top scorer with 30 goals. The championship format was altered for the 1957 season. Instead of teams from each group playing each other home and away, they would play each other only once at a neutral venue. Dortmund travelled to Ludwigshafen in the south to play and beat Kickers Offenbach 2-1 in front of 55,000 spectators. There were 75,000 people watching Borussia's 3-2 win in Hannover against Kaiserslautern. Finally the Black and Yellows were confirmed as finalists in front of only 15,000 fans at Braunschweig, against a poor Hertha side. Perhaps the Dortmund fans were confident enough in their team to not make the journey north. Those that did travel would have to make a similar trek back to nearby Hannover and the Niedersachsenstadion for the final against Group 1 winners HSV and their own young star: one Uwe Seeler.

In front of 82,000 fans, Borussia lined up with exactly the same 11 that had played in the previous season's final in Berlin. Before the start of the match, as the two sets of players faced off against each other before kick-off, Seeler – at the tender age of 19 – tried to banter off (as modern parlance would have it) the 34-year-old veteran Max

Michallek. "So, Grandad" said Seeler, "Still here are you?" to which Michallek replied, "I'll keep you in check even when I'm 70." Needless to say Seeler was taught a lesson. Borussia were comfortable 4-1 winners with Nieplieko and Kelbassa scoring a brace each. BVB were crowned champions twice in successive years. Once again, fans lined the streets of Dortmund to welcome home their heroes and celebrate a feat that would not be repeated by the club for decades.

The following season saw the departure of Helmut Schneider and a few changes to the squad. BVB's period of domination was over as the team changed from one influenced by Michallek, Kelbassa, Nieplieko and Preißler *et al* to players like Jürgen 'Charlie' Schütz, Aki Schmidt and Friedhelm 'Timo' Konietzka. Following the tragic passing of Schneider's successor, Hans Tauchart, Max Merkel was appointed coach. The people of Dortmund would have to wait a few more years but, in time, the 1960s would prove to be a fruitful decade for their football club.

Meanwhile, the characteristic of the rivalry between Schalke and Dortmund in the 1960s was quite different to what it became. Schalke were experiencing something of a decline while Borussia were in the ascendancy. Perhaps more pertinently, the region was still enjoying the effects of the post-War economic boom. The employment rate was high and, while the work was hard, the wages were decent and life was good. Football was a pastime in which folk indulged. It was a leisure activity. It was fun, particularly in Borussia's case because they kept winning. However, there was not necessarily the edge to the rivalry that would follow. Football was not quite a way of life yet and consequently, the intensity of various rivalries were low. "In the fifties, when industry was the high point of the region, football was just a thing to take your mind off your work," says Rob Turner. "But since the decline football has filled that vacuum and become the centre of the week."

As Axl Rose once sang, "Nothing lasts forever", and neither did the boom. The economic decline that began in the 1970s did not have any immediate effect on Borussia, who would remain a successful and high-profile club throughout the decade. However, the resultant job losses and lowering of wages did have an effect on civic society in the region. Support for your football club became a lot more important and, as a result, the Revierderby became much more intense during this decade.

We are living in an age where football has become the basis of a lifestyle. People identify themselves by their love of the game, its culture and traditions. An entire global industry now exists and some of the bigger league and clubs attract the attention of audiences around the world. Indeed, this book is a testament to that. For a significant portion of the planet's population football matters in a way that it has not mattered before. In the past, derby games would be a local matter, of concern only to the towns and cities of those clubs. With the advent of television coverage these derbies took on a national significance. As the sport media market matured we saw leagues selling TV rights to other countries, and with each passing season the importance of selling those rights becomes greater still. The internet and social media allow football fans to watch and engage with big games like the Revierderby in a way that could not have been conceived of when these two clubs first faced off against each other back in 1925. At that time supporters of those clubs rarely left the confines of their own neighbourhoods.

Assuming this level of interconnectedness and access continues and intensifies, it is unlikely that interest in these matches will diminish. When Borussia and Schalke players line up for each Revierderby they do so knowing that the consequences will be felt well beyond the seething mass of visceral humanity in the stadium itself. The currency of winning the derby now goes well beyond planting your flag on your neighbour's turf or the banter in the office the following Monday. This hitherto strictly local matter has taken on global proportions. The Schalke fan in Connecticut sits there and quietly seethes while the Dortmund fan in London celebrates on his Twitter timeline. A year later he is the one laughing it up as he watches BVB fans go into social media meltdown because Dortmund have surrendered a four-goal lead under absurd circumstances. That is why this derby – and it is not the only derby, just the one that concerns us now – will continue to be more important than any other game. Perhaps it's more important than winning the league. It's certainly of greater significance than the somewhat *faux* modern rivalry with Bayern Munich.

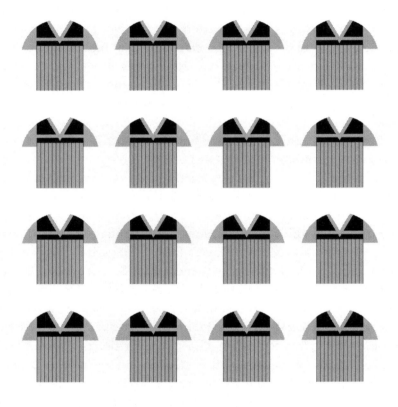

1983-84

"Der Klassiker"

It was October 2015, early in the first season in charge for Thomas Tuchel, and his first encounter as Borussia Dortmund's new coach with the old enemy, Bayern Munich. Tuchel was so highly thought of as a coach for his tremendous success at 1. FSV Mainz that he was almost regarded as an *auteur*. During the match Twitter was alive with images of Tuchel's touchline antics, constantly making shapes and signals with his arms, trying to convey his complex and well-considered tactics to his friends. In that respect he was the equal of the grandmaster himself, Pep Guardiola, who occupied the opposition technical area. However, in one key respect there was a divergence: Bayern's players were better and they won the game 5-1.

Despite all the pre-match hype about the two best teams in Germany and most progressive coaches in modern football going toe to toe, it was a fairly convincing win for the champions. Bayern would by no means have it all their own way during this time but the performance illustrates the most problematic element of Dortmund's rivalry with Bayern: most of the time, it's pretty one-sided. The first draft of this chapter was written just days after Borussia's 6-0 humbling at the hands of Jupp Heynckes' Bayern Munich, a team that itself is arguably on its last legs. The result was the culmination and realisation of the rarely spoken truth that this Dortmund team was finished and needed significant restructuring. Bayern can do that to clubs in Germany; they chasten them into confronting the ugly truth and compel them to act on things they should have addressed months earlier.

It should be obligatory for every history of every German football club to have one chapter about that club's relationship with FC Bayern Munich. Every club that has spent any significant amount of time in the Bundesliga has a deep and meaningful one. Every fan will be able to recount tales of bitter defeat to the red menace or, from time to time, sweet victory over an organisation that seems to revel in its own infamy. Every single club has their local rivals, then Bayern. These are the clubs they look for when the fixtures are published. Every game Bayern play is a national derby. Every stadium they visit is a cauldron. The bunting always comes out for those moustache-twirling Bavarian villains. Bayern are everyone's deadly rivals and to elevate one rivalry is to cheapen the others. This is the mistake that the Deutsche Fußball Liga (DFL) marketers make when applying the ill-conceived tag of *Der Klassiker* to the bi-seasonal fixture between Bayern and Borussia Dortmund.

"Der Klassiker" is a very recent term and is used predominantly for the English-speaking market. There have been references to a "Classico" in some German media, and I recall hearing a German commentator referring to it as such as early as 2012. However, it does not have the weight of tradition as say the Clasico in Spain or the Old Firm in Glasgow, although the term has clearly been invented to ape those traditions. Since their rise to prominence in the late 1960s Bayern Munich have enjoyed many great challenges in their quest for silverware, notably from Borussia Mönchengladbach in the 1970s, Werder Bremen in the 1980s, and Borussia Dortmund in the 1990s and early part of the 2010s. Of course, if Dortmund had their way they would always be at least the number two club in Germany, unable to match them in terms of income but at least able to keep pace and enjoy the rivalry, able to capitalise when the Munich club have off-years or go through periods of transition. This is another reason why the concept of Der Klassiker is so attractive to many; it helps to elevate Dortmund to a level above the rest of the Bundesliga, particularly Schalke.

That is not to say that Borussia Dortmund and Bayern Munich have not had their moments. Indeed, some of these moments have had ramifications that went beyond the parochial to the truly international. Bayern Munich were late entrants to the Bundesliga in the 1960s. They were a very popular and well supported club at this time but were still recovering from Nazi rule, which had been unkind to what used to be known as the "Jewish Club". That term stems from the club's president at the time, a man by that name of Kurt Landauer, who was head of advertising sales for a daily Munich-based newspaper – and Jewish. Consequently the club was singled out by the Nazi regime. Landauer, a veteran of the First World War, was arrested in 1938 and lost three brothers and a sister to the Nazi concentration camps.

Their city rivals, 1860 Munich, were regional champions in 1963 when the Bundesliga was formed and were awarded a place in the national league at Bayern's expense, and despite their appeal. This proved to be a blessing in disguise as the short time spent in the second division allowed their crop of talented young players, such as Sepp Maier, Gerd Müller and Franz Beckenbauer, to mature away from the harsher Bundesliga spotlight. By the time Bayern rose to prominence Dortmund's star was on the wane. That said, the first meeting between the two sides ended in a 2-0 win for Borussia at the Stadion an der Grünewalder Strasse in October 1965. Reinhold Wosab scored both goals against a Bayern team that included the aforementioned Maier, Müller and Beckenbauer. Bayern would return the compliment later that season in the DFB-Pokal (the German Cup) by knocking Dortmund out and going on to win. That cup win was to become the turning point in their story. From there, Bayern played in the European Cup Winners' Cup and beat Rangers to lift the trophy in Nürnberg in 1967, one year after Dortmund had done the same in Glasgow.

Their cup and European success set off an era of silverware. During Dortmund's wilderness years in the seventies and eighties Bayern amassed nine Bundesliga titles, four German Cups and three European Cups before BVB finally tasted glory again. In 1971 came Dortmund's heaviest defeat at the hands of the Bavarians, an 11-1 thrashing in their relegation season. When looking for classic matches to contribute to the mystique of Der Klassiker, this one-sided bloodbath of a result is lost in the midst of time. Let's just keep it there, shall we?

When the Black and Yellows returned to the first division of the Bundesliga in 1976, Hans-Werner Hartl snatched a late equaliser in a 3-3 draw. Wolfgang Vöge and Erwin Kostedde scored the other two for Borussia. Gerd Müller and Karl-Heinz Rummenigge (twice), netted for the Bavarians. During the 1970s and 1980s it was pretty much advantage Bayern. There weren't many thrashings in this time, though, and occasionally Dortmund would catch them at a bad moment, for example in May 1983 when the great Marcel Raducanu bagged a brace in a cracking 4-4 draw at the Westfalen. Then, in November 1987, Dortmund won 3-1 in the Munich Olympic Stadium. This was the team emerging under coach Reinhard Saftig and included Michael Lusch, Murdo MacLeod and Nobby Dickel. Daniel Simmes scored a brace.

MacLeod was not the only Celt on the field; lining up for Bayern was Mark Hughes. The Welsh international spent that season at Bayern on loan from Barcelona and played 27 games, scoring seven goals.

It was in the 90s that the rivalry took on an intensity worthy of the description. This was when Dortmund were in the ascendancy and Bayern were, by their standards, off the pace. In the 1995/96 season Bayern tried to sign Matthias Sammer, Stefan Reuter and Steffen Freund. There was also a big row with Borussia's kit supplier, Nike, who objected strongly to Sammer appearing in a Dortmund kit in an Adidas brochure, with the Nike emblems on his boots airbrushed out. Adidas, of course, has a longstanding relationship with Bayern, and the publication of the brochure coincided with a protracted tug-of-war between the two clubs for Sammer's signature. The assumption was that Bayern were indulging in a "Cold War" against Borussia in the hope of destabilising them, turning their better players' heads with transfer bids and asserting economic influence to disrupt their opponents. From the outside there is a whiff of conspiracy theory about this but, interestingly, it is something that Bayern are not quick to deny.

One of Bayern's best players in that period was Lothar Matthäus. "I saw Dortmund actually move past us two years in a row," he told *Deutsche Welle* in 2013. "But in the end that was no more than a phase – they just benefitted from a temporary weakness at Bayern." This view is perfectly consistent with the narrative of Bayern Munich's attitude which, to those who don't support them, can be pretty insufferable and condescending. The they're-only-winning-because-we're-shit train of thought might apply sometimes but it doesn't hold up when you take Borussia's Champions League win in 1997 into account. In the face of Dortmund's dominance, Bayern responded with all the weapons at their disposal. "We knew we had to react to the Dortmund challenge," said Matthäus. "We had to drive the message home to them: You had your bit of fun, but now it's over."

After two seasons of the Bundesliga title taking up residence in the Ruhr, the Bavarians hit back hard to reclaim the Meisterschale in 1997. I feel it necessary to point out that despite the big words, Matthäus and his colleagues were unable to actually beat Dortmund in either Bundesliga match that season, both games ending in a draw. Also, while it's true that Bayern won the Bundesliga, inferences that they were the better team are mitigated by the fact that Dortmund had a lengthy and ultimately successful Champions League with which to contend in addition to the league fixtures. And so it was that a series of hotly contested duels took place in the late 1990s and early 2000s before Dortmund's abrupt and almost catastrophic fall from grace. Bayern even had their say in those events (more on that later). One of the great figures in these battles was the Bayern goalkeeper Oliver Kahn. The German international's reputation for excellence is as well founded as his competitiveness. His on-pitch persona was, for Bayern fans, befitting of the spirit of a great and successful club. To everyone else he could be some way north of obnoxious. Needless to say, Kahn revelled in those matches between Bayern and Dortmund and did not shirk the battlefield. In one glorious game in April 1999 – I say glorious because no one was seriously injured –he performed an extraordinary Kung Fu-style kick on Stéphane Chapuisat and attempted to bite his fellow striker, Heiko Herrlich.

It was a game of high stakes. Dortmund were in fifth, one point away from Champions League qualification, and Bayern were closing in on the Bundesliga title. During the match Herrlich competed for a high ball which Kahn claimed. However, the striker allowed himself to barge Kahn, almost pushing him over the line. "I remember that Jürgen Kohler had said to me that Olli was easy to provoke among the high balls," Herrlich told *Der Spiegel* in 2006. Kahn's notoriously short fuse blew once again and, with the ball tucked under his arm, he pushed his nose onto Herrlich's neck and made a biting gesture. "When he came to me and put his nose on my neck I was surprised, but at the same time I felt an inner joy because I knew now he shows weakness."

"Of course, that's madness," said Kahn immediately after the game. "When you look at the game today you'll recognise fight, aggression and commitment." A few minutes later Kahn came charging out of the penalty area to claim a ball and launched himself into the air with a flying kick that was aimed at the oncoming Chapuisat, who looked more bemused than outraged. Perhaps by that point nothing could shock him. "It looks bad and stupid from me," said Kahn, again after the game. "But I didn't want to injure him." Well, that's OK then!

The game finished 2-2 with Herrlich scoring both for Dortmund. Both teams had a player sent off but, perhaps surprisingly, Kahn was not one of them. In fact, he saved a penalty from Lars Ricken on 77 minutes to rescue the point. Referee Bernd Heynemann's decision to keep Kahn on the field did much for the overall entertainment value of the match but from a sporting perspective it was peculiar. However, decisions of this nature are attributed to what is known in Germany as *Bayern-Dusel*. It is at this point that any Bayern fans reading this and looking for alternate perspectives will roll their eyes in exasperation. The expression "Bayern-Dusel" refers to a perception that Bayern Munich are the beneficiaries of undeserved luck. Most supporters and historians of other German football clubs will probably point to numerous examples of games decided by such luck against Bayern. The failure to dismiss Olli Kahn is an example, although much of it is associated with late drama involving last-minute penalties. Bayern fans will argue that such good fortune is earned in the same way that Manchester United used to earn all that added "Fergie Time" at the end of their football matches. Others will simply say that Bayern-Dusel is a myth, used by the club to troll fans of other clubs from time to time. My theory is that it is a statistically proven fact that luck plays a major role in the outcome of many football matches. All teams experience luck but the best teams are the best at exploiting it. Bayern Munich, sadly from this writer's point of view, are forever one of the best teams in Germany and Europe.

By 2001 Bayern's mini slump was in the past and the two clubs were fierce competitors. A season before Borussia would win their third Bundesliga title in six years, the Bavarians had a commanding 15-point gap between themselves and second-placed Bayer Leverkusen. With the prospect of another championship in the offing, Munich, now under the stewardship of one Ottmar Hitzfeld, travelled one April afternoon to the Westfalen to face a Dortmund team fifth in the table and looking to overhaul Hertha BSC in fourth and claim a European spot. The game ended 1-1 but three players were sent off: Evanilson for Dortmund, and Bixente Lizarazu and Stefan Effenburg for Bayern. The latter, the very picture of charm, blew kisses at the home fans who were giving him the bird as he departed for the dressing room. Bayern's general manager, Uli Hoeneß, was furious, and demanded that the referee who had the temerity to dismiss two Bayern players be sacked. Looking back, it all seems pretty funny. But at the time… well, in truth it was probably pretty funny back then as well.

These clashes lit up Bundesliga seasons and there were indeed greater duels that followed, some of which will be chronicled later. However, while there has not been too much said about this, as it is still a very recent wound, it is widely acknowledged that the rivalry between the Dortmund and Bayern players who made up a large bulk of the German national team at EURO 2012 was such that it could not be reconciled. The clubs went hammer and tongs at each other during this time and things got personal. It has been suggested that it had a deleterious effect on the spirit in the dressing room. Many of these players are still active and have yet to commit their memoirs to print. When this happens we may gauge to what extent this conflict was responsible for Germany's relatively poor performance in Ukraine and Poland that year.

Amid the rivalry, rancour and fierce competition came the ultimate insult from Bayern Munich to Borussia Dortmund: an act of kindness and generosity. As we shall see shortly, Dortmund's golden era in the nineties and noughties yielded a hangover from which the club nearly did not recover. In the deep financial crisis of 2004, when the club were around €200 million in debt, Borussia received an interest-free loan of €2 million to help pay the players wages. This revelation was announced at a 2012 Bayern supporters' meeting by Uli Hoeneß at the height of yet another ding-dong title race (which Bayern would ultimately win). Later that season the two would meet in the Champions League final at Wembley.

"It was a critical situation for Borussia Dortmund," said Hoeneß. "When they couldn't even pay their salaries we thought we should help. I'm a big fan of tradition in sport and I think it was the right thing to do." In 2014 it was reported in *Bild* that the loan was paid back in June 2005. "It was very honourable from Bayern Munich, helping other clubs in critical situations," said Dortmund's chief financial officer Thomas Tress, as reported in *The Guardian*. "It was a critical situation for Borussia Dortmund. But it was not to save Borussia Dortmund because we are talking about €2m. If you realise the financial debt was roughly €200m, so €2m does not solve the whole problem, but it helped. It was an honourable step and what's more to say?"

Did Hoeneß share this news in an attempt to undermine Borussia by taking the moral high ground? In 2014, Hans-Joachim Watzke stated that "we have come too close to Bayern in the past few years," implying that the revelation was designed to let some of the air out of Dortmund's balloon. Such machinations are not beyond the now-retired Bayern Munich President, but he had ample opportunity to reveal his piece of hidden history in the previous years when Dortmund were in the ascendancy. Tress was right to point out that the loan was small compared to the scale of the overall debt. This was really the equivalent of a mate lending you a tenner until payday; a generous act but perhaps not to be overstated.

And I suppose that it is this honourable act that ultimately prevents Bayern and Dortmund's relationship from becoming the eternal rivalry that the marketers would like it to be perceived as being. The Bavarian club is by some margin the wealthiest and most successful at maximising its return in the form of wins and silverware. With acts of decency to Dortmund, and indeed other clubs such as FC St. Pauli and even their cross-city rivals 1860 Munich, there is an aspect of paternity about Bayern that elevates them. It is certainly possible to hate Bayern and resent their success, but can Dortmund or any club truly be their rivals? To do that they would need to reach their level on and off the pitch, like a Liverpool, Manchester United, Real Madrid or Barcelona. Given the gap between them this seems like an eternally forlorn ambition. This is why Der Klassiker lacks the tangibility of a true rivalry.

1966

Champions, European Nights and Missed Chances: 1963 – 66

By the early 1960s the transition from the fifties team dominated by the Three Alfredos was complete. Borussia Dortmund would go on to enjoy a period of great success and notoriety, if perhaps not complete dominance. The new heroes in black and yellow were names like Konietzka, Kurrat, Schmidt, Schulz, Wosab and Emmerich. This team would go on to win the German Cup in 1965 and the UEFA European Cup Winners' Cup the following season, but first came the title that got the ball rolling: the German National Championship of 1963, by way of the final Final before the formation of the Bundesliga the following August.

The team was coached by Hermann Eppenhoff. A native of the Ruhr, Eppenhoff was born in Röhlinghausen, Wanne-Eickel and moved west to nearby Gelsenkirchen to play for the Schalke club in 1938. As a winger he won three national championships in 1939, 1940 and 1942. One of the German game's leading lights during the Second World War, Eppenhoff was part of an all-star exhibition team, the *Rote Jäger* (Red Hunters), along with the eventual 1954 West German World Cup-winning captain, Fritz Walter, and the coach, Sepp Herberger. In 1943 and 1944 the Rote Jäger toured the country and in their final game they thrashed a Luftwaffe XI, winning 14-0 in front of 3,000 spectators. The Red Hunters may have dodged the fighting but they did not escape the War. Eppenhoff was captured by Soviet Forces in 1945 and did not return until 1949. He continued to play for Schalke until 1955 and his last appearance was in the German Cup Final, where his team lost 3-2 to Karlsruher SC. A coaching career began the following year at TuRa Bergkamen and then Sportfreunde Gladbeck. He replaced Max Merkel as coach of Dortmund in 1961.

Merkel, a former Austrian and German international, went on to have a successful managerial career and had taken Dortmund to the 1961 championship final in Hannover, where they lost 3-0 to Max Morlock's 1. FC Nürnberg. Merkel's style of play was regarded as somewhat cynical. His final season was punctuated by some standout performances against Duisburger SV, where they won 7-0, and in a madcap 6-4 win against Rot-Weiss Essen, both at the Rote Erde. However, there were two disappointing draws against Schalke.

When Eppenhoff arrived it was like a breath of fresh air. He introduced a more fluid style, making use of the versatility of BVB's forward players. Eppenhoff also converted Wolfgang Paul from inside forward to defender-cum-libero. Students of the 1966 World Cup may know Paul as a member of the West Germany squad that finished runners up in England. Given that his role was very similar to Franz Beckenbauer's, it is not surprising that he was second in line to Der Kaiser. However, it is a surprise – at least when applying a modern football filter – that he did not earn a single cap for his country. Paul's lack of international credentials should not take anything away from his ability as a player. The Olsberg native was an elegant defensive midfielder who worked hard on the field. He had good anticipation and excellent timing in the tackle. He could also accurately pass the ball out of defence.

The road to the championship final started in 1962 with the beginning of the Oberliga West season. Dortmund kicked off the campaign with a barnstorming 11-1 win over TSV Marl Hüls. Jürgen 'Charly' Schütz scored three goals and Reinhold Wosab scored two. However, it was Friedhelm Konietzka, with five goals, who kept the match ball, so to speak. Konietzka, a prolific striker who sits third in Borussia Dortmund's list of all-time top goalscorers, joined the club as a youngster in 1958. His nickname, 'Timo', came from his permacropped hair that resembled Semyon Timoshenko, a Martial of the Soviet Union of some prominence. Konietzka strike partner Schütz scored 41 between them in the 1962/63 season, Schütz's final season before departing for AS Roma in Italy. In total, Borussia scored 77 goals in the campaign, bettered only by Viktoria Köln who let themselves down somewhat by conceding 69 to Borussia's 39.

Two defeats against 1. FC Köln (2-3 and 2-1) prevented BVB from claiming top spot and it was the Billygoats who won the Oberliga

West, with Dortmund finishing as runners up. Both teams progressed to the national final stages. The Black and Yellows were in Group 2 with Hamburger SV, Borussia Neunkirchen and 1860 Munich. The post-season didn't start too brightly. They lost 3-2 to 1860 in Munich and then could only muster a 0-0 draw at home to Neunkirchen. Their fortunes turned with a 3-2 win against the Hamburg club, thanks to a goal from Aki Schmidt – who scored at both ends – along with one from Schütz and Alfred Kelbassa's last for the club. The result looks narrow on paper but Dortmund took a 3-0 lead and conceded two late goals, one from Uwe Seeler and Schmidt's own goal.

Eppenhoff's team followed this up with a 1-0 win in Hamburg, Schütz scoring the only goal. Konietzka scored twice in a 5-2 win at Neukirchen and top spot was finally secured with an emphatic 4-0 win in Munich. Konietzka scored another brace and so did Schütz. Dortmund's opponents in the final were 1. FC Köln, who had seen off Nuremberg, Kaiserslautern and Hertha BSC, so it was an all-west encounter in front of an official attendance of 75,000 at the Neckarstadion in Stuttgart, where they had lost their first war final against VfR Mannheim in 1949. They returned to the south against what must be acknowledged as a great Köln side who were the defending champions and would go on to become the first Bundesliga champions the following season. This makes the result and performance by the men in black and yellow all the more impressive. Dortmund played outstandingly in the final.

The game was won 3-1 and has the distinction of being one of the few football matches in which Timo Konietzka did not score. BVB took the lead just before the 10-minute mark. Gerhard Cyliax won a corner by outpacing the full back, Leo Wilden. The corner was short and the ball came to Dieter 'Hoppy' Kurrat, who scored from outside the area with a daisy-cutter that somehow found its way through the Köln defence and underneath the diving goalkeeper, Fritz Ewert, whose flat cap fell off his head to reveal a despondent bald pate. Kurrat was not known for his goalscoring prowess and spent most of his career outside the opposition penalty area. His timely goal was one of only 17 in his 312 games in black and gold.

The remainder of the half was combative and Köln very nearly scored when Bernhard Wessel made a point blank save from Hans Sturm and Konietzka saved the follow-up shot on the line with his chest. Hans Schäfer managed to get behind Dortmund's deep back line only to blaze over the bar. Wolfgang Paul was immense in the first half, dispossessing players, putting his body on the line and bringing the ball out of defence.

Willi Burgsmüller collided with Heinz Hornig and there was a nasty clash of heads. Back then, head injuries were not taken as seriously as they should have been and he continued in the second half with his head wrapped in a bandage. In spite of Köln's attacks Dortmund were a frequent menace, particularly on the counter. In the second half they fully capitalised to win the game. Dortmund's second came on 57 minutes from the outstanding Wosab. He picked up the ball from the left back position, played a rapid one-two with Paul in midfield, drove into the middle and caught the Köln defence cold. He sailed past Karl-Heinz Schnellinger and fair larruped the ball into the back of the net. The third arrived eight minutes later as Dortmund were keeping up the pressure, seeking to kill the game. A disastrous sideways pass from a Köln player found Konietzka just outside the area. He played in Schmidt and the game was all but over.

Schnellinger then grabbed a consolation goal after Paul failed to deal with a long punt up the field – embarrassing for Paul, but it made no difference. Dortmund were convincing winners and the final national Oberliga champions. "It was a very special feeling," said Burgsmüller in an interview with *11Freunde*. "The fans stormed the pitch and there was an indescribable hubbub." It was not lost on the players that they had won the last ever championship final before the title would be decided by a national league with no post-season. "We knew exactly that this title had placed us in the history books," declared Burgsmüller.

Finally, some 30 years after the ill-fated Reichsliga had been proposed, the formation of a national league of 16 teams – the Bundesliga – was announced. The decision was made by the West German FA at their annual conference just up the road from Dortmund's Rote Erde stadium in the Westfalenhalle. With only 16 berths in the new league, many well established clubs of the day missed out, including Bayern Munich, who were trumped by their city rivals 1860. There was a distinct slant towards the North Rhine Westphalia region, where Dortmund is located, and both BVB and Schalke were admitted. Of course Borussia were the national champions so even if they had not met the FA's somewhat arbitrary criteria then they surely would have taken their place in the new league in order to defend their crown.

Before the Bundesliga kicked off there was an early setback for Dortmund as they lost the DFB-Pokal Final 3-0 to HSV. The game featured two of German football's hottest strikers in Konietzka and Seeler, and it was the latter who took the honours by scoring all three goals in front of 68,000 fans in Hannover. This was to be the last final to be played prior to the start of a league season. With the launch of the national league structure, the German Cup would be played throughout the season and culminate in a final at the end.

The inaugural Bundesliga season kicked off on 24th August 1963 and Dortmund's first ever national league fixture was up north at the Weserstadion against Werder Bremen. They lost 3-2 but the honour of scoring the first ever Bundesliga goal went to Timo Konietzka. The goal came in the first minute of the match, which proved too early for the camera crew who had not set up in time. From the right Emmerich collected a pass from Franz Brungs and squared the ball to Konietzka. "All I had to do was put my foot on the ball and it went into the goal," Konietzka recalled in an interview with *11Freunde*. "Granted, there are prettier goals. I would have preferred to score with a hammer shot from 30 meters."

Borussia's home opener was against 1860, coached by former BVB boss Max Merkel. They needed a penalty save from Hans Tilkowski and an 80th minute equaliser to salvage a point in a 3-3 draw with the Lions at the Rote Erde. The following week was a disaster as Dortmund lost the first derby against Schalke in the Bundesliga. The game was played at Schalke's Glückaufkampfbahn stadium (their home until 1973) and finished 3-1 to the home side. Dortmund took the lead with a goal by Wosab but missed chances from Cyliax and Schmidt proved costly when Manfred Berz equalised on the stroke of half time. Schalke rallied in the second half and took the lead through Waldemar Gerhart only six minutes after the restart. Another six minutes later Lothar Geisler faced the embarrassment of scoring an own goal in a derby game. In mitigation, BVB were missing Paul and Kurrat through injury, while Bracht took a knock during the game and was sent to play out of position and away from danger on the wing. Coach Eppenhoff was not prepared to use that as an excuse.

It took until the fourth matchday for BVB to register their first win in the Bundesliga, a 2-1 victory at home against Saarbrücken. Willi Sturm was played as a makeshift defender in the absence of Paul. Bracht was playing but still carrying an injury. He swapped positions with Schmidt, again to avoid trouble. The opposition were poor and eventually relegated that season but Dortmund went a goal down and laboured to a 2-1 win thanks to two late goals from Wosab and Konietzka. Arguably it was their poor start to the season that cost Borussia their shot at the title. After the Schalke defeat the season progressed well and they finished fourth behind Eintracht Frankfurt, Meiderich and champions Köln.

On their way to fourth Dortmund registered their first derby win in the Bundesliga, a 3-0 win against Schalke. All the goals came in the second half, starting with Emmerich on 51 minutes and followed by Konietzka, who pounced on the ball which was dropped by Schalke goalkeeper Horst Mühlmann after 65 minutes. Emmerich rounded off the result with his second. At the end of the season there was a 12-point gap between Dortmund and Köln in first. The highest position they reached was second, for a couple of weeks in November, and they never dropped below fifth. With three games remaining Dortmund lost 5-2 at home to Köln on 18th April and the result sealed the championship for Köln. It must have been a sweet moment for the Billygoats to win at the home ground of the team that beat them in the Championship Final the year before. Had Borussia got a little more from their first three games then perhaps they could have come closer to being the first Bundesliga champions and back-to-back title winners. Another factor that mitigates Dortmund's disappointing league campaign was a superb run to the semi-final of the European Cup.

They were packing into the ground early doors for this evening kick-off at the Rote Erde on 4th December 1963. Despite being 2-1 down from the first leg the Dortmund players knew that this European Cup quarter-final was still wide open. Benfica's best player, the immaculate Eusébio, was injured and would not play. By the time the players took to the field the "House Full" signs were up and the atmosphere under the floodlights was the stuff of legendary European nights to come.

This Benfica side were European football royalty, having won the European Cup in 1961 and 1962 under the legendary coach Béla

Guttmann, and then finishing runners up earlier in 1963. Despite the absence of Eusébio their team was packed full of champions and world class players such as Santana, Cavem, Cruz, and Coluna. There were five rounds of the 1963/64 European Cup, including the final. Dortmund qualified, as every team that played in this competition, as national champions. Characteristically it was Timo Konietzka who scored two goals in the second leg of their 7-3 aggregate win against the Norwegians FK Lyn in the preliminary round, which set up this tie against the previous year's losing finalists. Lining up alongside Konietzka was the birthday boy, Franz Brungs, 27 that day. Brungs was a tall, blond and somewhat lanky striker, full of energy. Frankie was on fire. He gave himself and his team the best possible present, a hat-trick in a 5-0 win. It was probably his greatest night in his two-season stint in black and yellow.

Brungs was born in Bad Honnef, near Bonn in the Rheinland. His home town had its own football club and it was there that Brungs began his career. He moved to FC Köln in 1958 and scored five goals in 24 appearances, picking up a DFB-Pokal winner's medal along the way. Before joining Dortmund in 1963 he spent three years at Borussia Mönchengladbach, scoring 41 goals in the Oberliga West for the Foals. His time at Dortmund was relatively short but he scored 23 goals in his 54 appearances, including the three in this emphatic win that propelled him into the limelight across the continent. His exploits in Europe earned him the nickname 'Goldköpfchen' or 'Golden Head'.

Willi Burgsmüller was the club captain and a career Dortmunder. He played in the youth team and was brought into the seniors in 1955, one of a number of other young players that would form the backbone of the title-winning team. A full back, his career was sadly cut short by injury in 1965 with three championship medals to his name. Burgsmüller's fellow defender, Theodor Redder, was also a one-club man. He played 115 times for Dortmund between 1962 and 1969 and played a crucial role in the 1966 European Cup Winners Cup Final. Dieter Kurrat was another ever-present and Dortmund lifer. From 1960 to 1974 he played just in front of the defence. A top class deep midfielder, 'Hoppi' was only denied a chance at the national team because the coach, Helmut Schön, considered him to be too short. Completing the back line was Lothar Geisler, who played 117 games for BVB after starting his senior career at nearby Bochum. An unspectacular and uncompromising defender, Geisler was very much the professional's choice. He played between 1959 and 1967 and won a national championship and one DFB-Pokal.

Making comparisons with modern midfield roles is unwise but I suppose Wilhelm Sturm could be described as holding midfielder. He made 239 appearances for Dortmund and joined the one-club club. Partnering Sturm in the middle of the park was Aki Schmidt, a prolific scorer from midfield who would star for Dortmund, scoring 76 goals in 276 games. He played for the West German national team 25 times, scoring eight times, and was the first Dortmund player to captain the national team. While nominally a 4-4-2, in actuality the team was set up with a front four, with Brungs and Konietzka being supported by Lothar Emmerich and Reinhold Wosab. Like many others in this side Wosab was at the beginning of his career at Dortmund. He would go on to score 83 goals as a supporting striker, including the third in the 3-1 championship win against FC Köln in 1963, in his nine years at the club.

Emmerich became a player so entrenched in Dortmund lore that they named a mascot after him. 'Emma' scored 126 goals in 215 appearances for BVB. Astonishingly he only made five appearances in a West German shirt. A tall, lithe forward, he was capable of both delicacy and brute strength when required. Over time he came to lead the line and his intelligence and positioning would make him one of the most prolific strikers in the Bundesliga.

It was a cold and wet evening in Dortmund when BVB welcomed their opponents from southern Europe. The pitch was ice and, as Brungs recalled in an interview with *11Freunde*, he had hoped that the conditions and the atmosphere would work in their favour. "Back then there was no undersoil heating," he said. "The pitch was hard and would not run smoothly." Figuring that the conditions would not favour the technical players, coach Hermann Eppenhoff set his team up to disrupt the silky skills of the Benfica team who, even without Eusébio, were heavy favourites to win.

Dortmund started the game in positive fashion by closing down their Portuguese opponents almost everywhere on the pitch. After five minutes the home side made two decent chances, with Konietzka the closest to getting on the score sheet. While primarily a front man, Konietzka was happy to play deep when his team were not in possession. On the flanks he was supported by the equally energetic Brungs and Emmerich. After 13 minutes Konietzka's arms were up in celebration after combining with Brungs and unleashing a powerful shot from outside the area that hit the crossbar and, in the Dortmund striker's eyes at least, crossed the goal line. The referee, a Sheffield native by the name of McCabe, ignored it and the game continued at what was by this point a ferocious pace.

It was this ferocity that blew Benfica away in the first half. The Eagles were not given the chance to breathe. Serafim was largely ineffective and their first meaningful effort came on 20 minutes after António Simões was allowed a run through the middle. However, Serafim, José Augusto and Santana were nullified for the most part by Burgsmüller, Kurrat and Geisler. The spirit was encapsulated after approximately 30 minutes when Serafim picked up a stray ball in the Benfica half. He waltzed past one man and got as far as just outside the centre circle before a yellow and black shirt was on him and, with a meaty tackle, sent the ball flying for a throw in. The commentator didn't spot the player and it's difficult to discern on the grainy video who it was for definite, but I would speculate with a level of prior knowledge that it was Geisler.

The assault on Benfica's goal continued with the visitors having to clear a shot off the line and then defend a succession of corners. The opening goal finally came on 33 minutes, when Konietzka met Burgsmüller's cross and headed past Zé Rita in goal. The old cliché about floodgates was probably coined for games like this because within four minutes the single-goal lead became three. Brungs scored his first with a shot using the outside of his foot, taken first time from Konietzka's through ball. His second arrived just a minute later when Brungs met Emmerich's short pass, swivelled past his man and unleashed a beauty into the bottom right corner. By now the crowd were on cloud nine and the press photographers were running onto the pitch to capture Brung's moment of celebration with his teammates.

As the second half came to a close Emmerich was punishing his full back and Benfica were desperate. Emmerich almost scored himself after combining with Brungs, but was thwarted by Rita. Half time may have brought respite but it did not bring salvation. Goal number four was scored just after the start of the second half from a corner, Brungs completing his hat-trick with a header at the far post. The fifth came from Wosab just before the hour mark. Rita's palms were stung by a long range shot, Wosab stopped the ball from going out for a corner, jinked inside, and beat the keeper at the near post. To coin a phrase, some people were on the pitch, such was the excitement at the Rote Erde after the fifth goal. Confident of victory before the match and magnanimous in defeat, Benfica coach Lajos Czeisler told the French sports magazine *L'Equipe* that, "I am the loser but consider myself lucky to have seen such magnificent football. Benfica were executed by Borussia." This victory was a high point in the story of this golden generation. While they would not go on to achieve European success this performance marked the team out as an emerging European powerhouse.

The next round drew Dortmund against the Czechoslovakian team Dukla Prague. The first leg was a *tour de force* for the Dortmund attackers; Wosab was the main man with a brace to secure a 4-0 away win. However, it was Brungs and Konietzka who broke the back of the Czech champions in the first half. The second leg was considerably trickier, with Dortmund conceding three at the Rote Erde. Burghard Rylewicz only stayed for one season, playing just 11 times, but it was his goal that was enough to make the tie safe. Just as well, since Dukla staged a late offensive to win the game 3-1 on the night but lose 5-3 on aggregate.

So, for the first time ever, a German team made it as far as the semi-final of the European Cup. The journey was to end there as they encountered the 12 men of Internazionale. This was the legendary *Grande Inter* team that was managed by the great Argentine coach Helenio Herrera. Already a star trainer at Atlético Madrid and Barcelona, his maligned but much misunderstood *Catenaccio* tactics provided the basis for three Serie A titles, two European Cups and two Intercontinental Cups (the forerunner of the World Club Cup). Inter's path to the final of their first European Cup first took them to Dortmund. Initially there had been a desire from the board to move the game to Hannover's much larger Niedersachsen Stadium in order to cash in on the huge interest in tickets. The idea was quickly dismissed once the fans made it clear that this would not be a popular decision, so they packed into the Rote Erde and, while the board members wondered how great it would be to build a really big stadium, the fans watched Inter take the lead with a near-post diving header by Sandro Mazzola after just four minutes. The home side fought back and Franz Brungs latched onto a through ball for the equaliser. He then made mincemeat out of the centre half and slotted past Giuliano Sarti to score another first-half brace, just as he had against Benfica. Borussia could not hold the lead until half time, however. The 'Mandrake' Mario Corso levelled the match after rounding Tilkowski to score from a very tight angle.

That's how the game finished and Inter had the advantage of away goals going into the return leg at San Siro. This Inter side had some great players that would leave a lasting legacy, including Luis Suarez (not that one) and Armando Picchi. However, it seemed that for Inter this was not enough. The second leg finished 2-0 to the home side but there was a moment of controversy when Kurrat was kicked out of the game by Suarez. The referee took no action against the player and Dortmund were reduced to ten players for the rest of the match. In an interview with *11Freunde*, Aki Schmidt said that the referee, Branko Tesanic, had been bought. Shortly after the game, while holidaying in the Adriatic (paid for by Inter), he admitted that he fixed the game. The German FA appealed the result to no avail. Tesanic received a lifetime ban.

It would be unwise to assume that BVB would have gone to win that tie without the referee's interventions, much less go on to beat Real Madrid in the final. But it is perhaps a back-handed compliment that Inter felt it necessary to take additional precautions. There was a bizarre postscript to this match and Dortmund's exit from the tournament. After the game, BVB coach Hermann Eppenhoff made some remarks to the press which some members of the club's board found to be overly critical. In a fit of pique they fired the man who had only delivered them the title the season before.

It was not the end of Eppenhoff's career at BVB. After consulting his lawyer, it transpired that club president Kurt Schoienherr's election to his position was not legally binding. With the dressing room in uproar, Eppenhoff was immediately reinstated and Schoienherr stepped down along with the rest of the board. It truly would have been a tragedy had the former Schalke player been ousted. The style of play he developed was more than just fun to watch, it was also extremely effective. Eppenhoff eventually stepped down, but not before bringing more silverware to Borsigplatz.

Only 1860 Munich scored more goals than Dortmund in the 1964/65 Bundesliga season. In total Dortmund hit the back of the net 67 times – 56 of those coming from the forward four of Brungs (14), Emmerich (10), Wosab (10) and Konietzka with a mammoth 22 strikes. Joining the club for the start of the season was Rudolf Assauer, a defender. He would play in black and yellow for six years and go on to manage Schalke with distinction.

BVB finished third behind Köln and a Werder Bremen team that dominated the league for most of the season. By far the most satisfying results were the 10-2 aggregate Revierderby wins over Schalke. The first was on Matchday 6, when Aki Schmidt's long range strike kicked off the hijinks in what would finish as a 6-2 drubbing in front of a packed house of mostly grumpy Schalke fans at the Glückaufkampfbahn. Brungs, Konietzka twice, Emmerich and Brungs again all scored in the first 36 (thirty-six) minutes. The DFL's archive footage of the game shows what appear to be Schalke fans trying to leave the stadium only to be thwarted by a closed gate blocking the exit. Perhaps because of this the house was still packed until the end and they were rewarded with two consolation goals from Werner Grau and a certain Reinhard Libuda. More on him shortly.

In what turned out to be a wretched season for Schalke, the Gelsenkirchen club were hammered 4-0 the following February at the Rote Erde. Sadly (for Dortmund fans at least) there is no surviving footage of this match, a genuine shame because it is the match in which midfielder Hermann Straschitz had the game of his short career at Dortmund. He scored two of his four goals for the whole season in that one game. Straschitz was signed from Fortuna Düsseldorf in the preceding summer and would only play for two years. He had a reputation for truculence having once refused to train before a Dortmund game against Borussia Mönchengladbach in 1965. Straschitz was out of the team and reluctant to participate in training for the game until coach Willi Multhaup assured him that he would play. Multhaup then went back on his word and refused, leaving him out. Dortmund won the match 5-4.

Clashes with former Oberliga West rivals Köln were very much a feature during this period and a 3-3 draw in Cologne was particularly memorable. The home side dominated the game and took the lead through Heinz Hornig, whose shot made its way in right after the Dortmund defence had cleared two off the line immediately before. Köln doubled the lead on 55 minutes with a penalty from Hans Sturm. Wolfgang Overath looked to have put the game out of reach on 65 minutes with his shot from just inside the penalty area but a tactical change turned the tide. Eppenhoff moved Cyliax into attack, which altered the game. Konietzka scored BVB's first three minutes after Overath's goal. The revival was completed by a pair of goals from Emmerich in the 80th and 83rd minutes. His first was a curling shot which beat Köln goalkeeper Anton Schumacher at his far post, his second a bullet header from a cross by Brungs. Other extraordinary results included a 6-3 win against Hertha BSC, in which Konietzka scored a hat-trick, and a 5-4 win against Eintracht Braunschweig.

Borussia competed in European competition, the Fairs Cup to be precise. After overcoming FC Girondins de Bordeaux they were hammered by Matt Busby's Manchester United, 6-1 at the Rote Erde and 4-0 at Old Trafford. But while their European dreams were shattered, Dortmund would experience success domestically by winning their first ever DFB-Pokal at the Niedersachsenstadion in Hannover at the end of the season. Dortmund's path to the final began at nearby Preußen Münster, where Wosab scored the only goal of the game. Tennis Borussia Berlin were the next opponents in a half-empty, snow-covered Olympiastadion. Wosab and Schmidt were on the mark in a 2-1 win. It was a double from Emmerich that did for Eintracht Frankfurt in the next round and set up a semi-final (at home for the first time in the competition) against Nürnberg.

The home side blew the visitors away in the first 10 minutes. Emmerich's bullet header came after just one minute. Konietzka made a rampaging run from the inside left position and scored his first cup goal of the season despite the Nürnberg players' claims that he handled the ball. It is said that the DFB-Pokal was not as prestigious a trophy back then as it is now. However, this game was played in front of a big crowd at the Rote Erde and Nürnberg were certainly not giving up their place in the final without a fight. Dortmund goalkeeper Bernhard Wessel had to make a couple of top saves in the first half, and in the second the visitors stormed back to 2-2 with goals from Manfred Greif and Tasso Wild. The game was settled in the 72nd and 75th minutes. Wosab was free at the far post to hook the ball in from close range with a spectacular volley. Konetzka's second was a sucker-punch. He rounded the goalkeeper and walked the ball into the net.

The final against Alemannia Aachen was held on 22nd May but a couple of departures had been confirmed beforehand. Firstly, Eppenhoff resigned after four years in charge. His final game would be the cup final. Also leaving was Konietzka. After seven years, 163 appearances and 121 goals, he was transferred to 1860 Munich to join his old boss and former BVB coach, Max Merkel, much to the consternation of the Dortmund fans. In fact it was to be a double swoop for the lions of Bavaria. Joining Konietzka at 1860 was that season's second top goalscorer for Dortmund, Franz Brungs.

Before the final some of the players took issue with Konietzka's selection, questioning his commitment. There was also a fierce argument between the two goalkeepers. Bernhard Wessel had been between the sticks for Dortmund's cup run but Hans Tilkowski was selected for the final. Eppenhoff also dropped Brungs – favouring a lone striker – from what would have been his final game, and both he and Wessel threatened to walk out. BVB took to the field in unfamiliar white shirts. Both teams played (and still do) in black and yellow and so an arrangement was made whereby BVB would wear white while Aachen played in red with white pinstripes. The game was won in the first 20 minutes. Aki Schmidt lifted the ball over the goalkeeper for the first. Lothar Emmerich cracked in the second and final goal from the left-hand side, just outside the area.

What followed after was a whole bunch of nothing. Former Germany coach Sepp Herberger was in the stadium and said, "The best thing about the match was the army music ensemble, and the weather was nice too. There's nothing else I can say about this game." Aachen were set up to defend and could not offer much once they'd gone two goals down. Dortmund, after a long season and with their coach on his way out the door, took it easy. The crowd were frustrated at times but the game was won and, as Eppenhoff said after the game, "Who's going to be asking in three weeks how we won the match? The main thing is that we won the cup and that we'll be in Europe next season." He was quite right, of course, and this now largely forgotten match proved to be the catalyst for Dortmund's and Germany's first ever European club success.

Generally speaking, Glasgow does not suffer the worst of its weather in May. That being said, on 5th May 1966 the rain was so hard as to be positively biblical. It was the day that the city was set to host the 1966 European Cup Winners' Cup Final. The reputation of the weatherproof Glaswegian was put to the test at this largely uncovered ground. The year 1966 is well known for a certain ball that may or may not have crossed a goal line between an English and a German team (it definitely did) in a huge final, and a similar scenario occurred between another English and German team earlier in the year. The former is of course the World Cup Final at Wembley. The latter was a few months earlier, 400 miles to the north of the Empire Stadium, during the European Cup Winners' Cup Final between Liverpool and Borussia Dortmund.

Dortmund had five rounds to navigate in order to get to the final. As semi-finalists in the European Cup the season before, they would have expected to have done well in this competition, which was by no means easy but did not pose too many stiff challenges in the earlier rounds. FC Floriana of Malta were dispatched 5-1 in the first leg and 8-0 in the second at the Rote Erde. Lothar Emmerich scored six goals in the latter match. CSKA Sofia of Bulgaria were next and Borussia took a commanding 3-0 lead, which proved enough despite losing 4-2 in Sofia.

Emmerich scored in both legs of the quarter final against Atlético Madrid. This was a considerably tougher encounter but Dortmund squeezed through 2-1 on aggregate to leave them in the final four with three British teams: Glasgow Celtic – looking for a place in the final in their hometown – along with Liverpool and West Ham United. Dortmund can consider themselves somewhat fortunate to have drawn the east London club. The Hammers were not a top side in the English First Division but any team that featured Geoff Hurst, Bobby Moore and Martin Peters, a trio who would go on to win the World Cup later in the year, was not to be taken lightly. Indeed, it was Peters who scored the opening goal of the tie at Upton Park, just after the start of the second half. Thankfully for BVB the goal machine, Emmerich, scored a quickfire brace in the 86th and 87th minute to hand the advantage to the Germans. In the second leg Emmerich gave the Londoners a mountain to climb when he scored in the first minute. His header came from his own rebounded shot which had struck the post. Knowing that the tie was effectively over, some fans and press photographers – eager to capture the moment – charged onto the pitch. They did it again after Emmerich's second on 29 minutes, which came from a free kick just on the edge of the West Ham penalty area. On both occasions some rather irate-looking security personnel in mackintosh coats escorted the interlopers off the pitch with the help of their German shepherds. Dortmund's final goal was scored by Cyliax, a deflected long-range shot that left West Ham goalkeeper, Jim Standen, stranded. Former Crystal Palace legend Johnny Byrne's header afforded the Hammers some consolation but Dortmund's place in the final was sealed and Liverpool were to be their opponents, having denied Celtic their own date with destiny.

Both teams were playing in their first European final in a half-full stadium on a rainy night in Glasgow, before a crowd mostly made up of Englishmen but with a significant portion of locals who had adopted Dortmund for this game. Aki Schmidt recalls that, "We were the complete outsiders. Willi Multhaup told us that we would probably lose nine out of ten games against Liverpool, but the one time when we do beat them it would have to be in the final."

The playing surface was far from ideal given the weather conditions and both teams struggled with passing combinations. While there were chances at either end, both sets of players needed the first half to come to terms with the wind, rain and cut-up pitch. The second half was a different story. After kick-off there was only one team in it. The Liverpool players took the initiative and played with a good deal more pace, putting the Dortmunders on the back foot. It could be said that BVB played a deliberate counter-attacking style but such was Liverpool's vigour as they came out for the second half that it's as likely that Dortmund were caught unawares by their intensity. Eventually a goal came and it went against the run of play. Running in between the two Liverpool centre backs and picking up a through ball from Emmerich, Siggi Held let loose a half volley and sent the ball past the Liverpool goalkeeper, Tommy Lawrence.

Sigfried Held had joined Borussia from Kickers Offenbach in the preceding summer. He was born in the Sudetenland in 1942, and he and his family were relocated after the Second World War, when that region became part of Czechoslovakia. Held spent his early years in a refugee camp, where he started to play football. He began his playing career at Offenbach, close to the army base in which he was stationed for his national service. An outstanding attacker for his club, his move to a Bundesliga club was inevitable when Kickers did not make the step up to the national league. Held was and would remain for some seasons the only "foreign" player at the club, that being defined as someone not from the Dortmund area.

The Merseysiders contrived an equaliser from Roger Hunt. He received the ball from a cut-back from Peter Thompson; as the Englishman centred the ball, some of the Dortmund player's hands had risen in protest as they believed that the ball had crossed the goal-line. Hunt had enough time and space in the penalty area to take an extra touch and slotted the ball home for the leveller. Amid the exuberant Liverpool fans who had ran onto the pitch to celebrate Hunt's goal, the Dortmund players protested to the linesman, who had originally flagged for a goal kick. The referee overruled him and the goal stood. Neither side could muster another in 90 minutes so the game went to extra time.

The winner came on 109 minutes and was both inspired and absurd. Aki Schmidt's long ball was met by Held. Goalkeeper Lawrence rushed off his line to meet him and blocked his shot and the ball was deflected into the path of Reinhard Libuda on the right wing. His first time shot from between 35 and 40 yards out looped over Lawrence and the covering defender, Ron Yeats. It was a beautiful long-range chip but not quite good enough to find the net, and the ball bounced off the post. However, Libuda's technique and audacity merited some good luck. The ball rebounded off Yeats and into the net to win the match and the first piece of European silverware for Borussia Dortmund. The records show Libuda as the scorer but the truth is his shot hit the post and it was Yeats' final touch that was telling. It is, however, unlikely that Liverpool statisticians will be petitioning UEFA for a correction. There is also a case to be made for awarding the goal to Libuda for having the brass balls to give it a try. In any event, Libuda was mobbed by his team-mates and Dortmund became the first German Club to lift a European trophy.

As memorable and significant as it was, the goal was a bittersweet moment for Libuda. Nicknamed 'Stan' because of his similarities to Stanley Matthews, Libuda was a reluctant Borussia Dortmund player having been transferred from local rivals Schalke 04 in 1965, the same summer as Held had signed. The Gelsenkirchen club needed to cut back on the budget at the time and Libuda was sacrificed. He played 74 games for BVB between 1965 to 1968 before returning to the club that he had joined as a youngster in 1954. Described by his Schalke and West German national teammate Klaus Fischer as the best right winger he had ever seen, Libuda was a long-legged and prodigious dribbler of the ball who often enjoyed playing with opposition full backs with his tricks. At times this was too much of a preoccupation and Aki Schmidt remarked that it could be frustrating waiting for Libuda to cross the ball. Perhaps this is why he only played 26 games for the national team. He did, however, enjoy the dubious distinction of having scored for both Dortmund and Schalke in the Revierderby.

A somewhat withdrawn chap who made few friends and rarely gave interviews, Libuda later made no secret of the fact that he was a Schalke man at heart and that his successes with Dortmund did not resonate with him. In the modern era, a player of his talent who needed to be sold on for financial reasons would go to another big club such as HSV, Stuttgart or perhaps even Bayern Munich, rather than local rivals. Relocating to another part of Germany was not always practicable in 1965 and it made sense for Libuda to stay local even if it meant playing for his club's enemies. In truth this was far from uncommon. It remains one of the game's ironies that Dortmund's first tangible success in Europe came to be thanks in large part from a reluctant hero. He returned to Gelsenkirchen in 1968 but his career was curtailed after his embroilment in the bribery scandal in 1971. He lived in Gelsenkirchen until throat cancer took him in 1996.

Back in Glasgow, that cup final defeat seemed to hit Liverpool manager Bill Shankly pretty hard and he criticised his opponents' tactics. "We were beaten by a team of frightened men," he said after the game. "I am quite sincere when I say they are the worst team we met in the competition this season." His reaction was understandable, if uncharitable and inaccurate. Shankly was a supremely confident man and his team were to win the English championship that season. He had been dismissive of Dortmund before the game and was confident his players would prevail on the night. To lose out on his first European title was a blow. In fact, the Scot would only win one UEFA trophy in his time on Merseyside. The fact is that while Liverpool enjoyed the greater possession and purpose, Borussia defended well and played a good counter-attacking game, and perhaps that was suitable for the atrocious conditions.

In Dortmund, no one cared about Shankly's sour grapes. The team were given a parade on the way back from the airport and a reception at the Neuen Markt (now Friedensplatz), where thousands gathered to greet the players. This proved to be the high water mark for this Dortmund side. The European Cup Winners' Cup of 1966 was Borussia Dortmund and Germany's first European trophy, only three years after the formation of Germany's first national league. This mighty achievement was somewhat overshadowed by a heartbreaking league campaign. For 10 weeks towards the end of the season Dortmund occupied the top spot in the Bundesliga but, after a disastrous run of three defeats, they missed out on what would have been their first championship in the new national league.

The season had started badly with a 4-0 defeat to the Eintracht Braunschweig. The Brunswick club were a big deal back in the sixties and would go on to win the title the following season. That loss was to be one of only six that season and would set up a run of 14 games without defeat, 10 of those victories, including an extraordinary 5-4 win against Borussia Mönchengladbach and a satisfying 3-2 defeat of Schalke in Gelsenkirchen the following week. The next loss, however, was significant. Despite Borussia's run there was one better team so far and that was 1860 Munich, coached by former Dortmund manager Max Merkel and home to ex-Dortmunder Timo Konietzka.

On the final day of the Hinrunde (the first half of the season) before the winter break, the top two teams in the Bundesliga met at the Grünwalder Stadion in Munich. The game was reportedly a high-tempo affair in which 1860 were the better side for the first half. After 29 minutes Alfred Heiß opened the scoring from a through ball by Rudolf Brunnenmeier. The second half saw a galvanised Dortmund denied a strong penalty claim early on. Shortly thereafter Siggi Held was fouled in the area by Wilfried Kohlars and Emmerich equalised on 72 minutes. Parity was fleeting, however, as Hans Rabelle scored thanks to a lay-off from Konietzka and the game ended 2-1.

Unbowed by the defeat Dortmund rallied in the Rückrunde, the name given for the second half of the season, and went on an unbeaten run of 13 games including an even more satisfying 7-0 win over Schalke. After that they finally overhauled 1860, who had been top of the table since October. They would stay there for 10 weeks but that proved to be two weeks too short. The wheels fell off on 23rd April 1966 – five days after the second leg of West Ham game – against Meidericher, when the home side beat the leaders 2-1 in Duisburg. The 3-2 win at home to Köln was their last; BVB lost their remaining three games. Defeat to Werder Bremen by a goal to nil was the result of a hotly disputed penalty in the 89th minute. However, the clincher was the penultimate game on 21st May in Dortmund against 1860. The winner would all but win the league with a game to spare. It finished 2-0 to the visitors. The Lions' Peter Grosser was the star on the day with an assist for Rudi Brunnenmeier on 66 minutes and a reportedly superb individual goal in the 89th minute. Deflated, Dortmund lost their final match at Frankfurt 4-1.

Few would argue that the Cup Winners' Cup victory wasn't a more significant achievement at the time than the national league. Success in Europe meant international recognition. The English press referred to Emmerich and Held as the "terrible twins" after the final against Liverpool. Dortmund's profile as a club was inevitably raised by that sort of notoriety. That being said, the final stages of the cup may have affected the players' league performance and ultimately cost them their first Bundesliga title. Certainly, that was Multhaup's view. "It was simply too much," he said. "The double effort for weeks on end was not without consequences."

Of course it was easy for Multhaup to say this. He was after all the coach and responsible for the results. But his argument is entirely plausible. Even at the time of writing modern football clubs struggle with the rigours of domestic and European commitments. With the comparatively smaller squad of the era it is reasonable to think that fatigue would play a part, not to mention a loss of concentration after the victory in Glasgow. Dortmund's first match after the final was a trip to the Weserstadion and, although the game was decided by a controversial penalty, it was a subpar performance, with Emmerich and Libuda singled out as being particularly disappointing.

Nevertheless, the European win represented a giant leap forward for a club that had rapidly grown in stature since the end of the War. Being the first German club to lift a European trophy is an unassailable benchmark. It also lifted Borussia Dortmund above Schalke – in the eyes of the club and its fans, at least – as a club that had achieved greater feats than their traditionally more illustrious neighbours.

However, as we are about to discover, the Bundesliga title was to elude Borussia Dortmund for well over two decades. One can't help but wonder what would have happened if Dortmund had lifted the "Salad Bowl" in 1966. Given the size of the support base and knowing what we know now about the construction of a new stadium right next to the Rote Erde, Dortmund fans can allow themselves to imagine what this great club would have achieved with a Bundesliga title under its belt. That being said, Dortmund were not the only well-followed team to miss out on becoming champions in the early years of the Bundesliga, and not all of them went on to achieve the greatness BVB would eventually enjoy. While it is lamentable that players like Held, Kurrat, Wosab, Schmidt, Paul and Emmerich never won the league title they perhaps deserved, their European exploits meant their names will be writ large in Borussen and German football history for all time.

Willi Multhaup resigned after just one season in the summer that followed. FC Köln, anxious to restore the glory days, made a move for him and he headed south. Nicknamed 'Fishken' throughout his career because of his family trade in fish, Multhaup had been a successful coach at Werder Bremen before joining Dortmund. His spell in the Ruhr was short but eventful. Replacing Multhaup for the 1966/67 season was Heinz Murach, a native of Gelsenkirchen. Murach steered Dortmund to a disappointing third-place finish. After having won a European title and coming so close to winning the league in the season before, BVB were fancied to go one better and lift the Bundesliga trophy. Their defence of the Cup Winners' Cup began and ended in defeat to Glasgow Rangers. This was the beginning of the end of the golden period. Sadly, while the memories are worn and the trophies glisten under the lights, there was no lasting legacy. Dortmund, like the rest of the Ruhr, was coming down from its trip and Borussia would not find itself immune from the economic difficulties of the region. It would not be long before those great moments both at home and abroad would feel like distant memories. Mediocrity and failure were around the next corner.

The 1966/67 season was notable, however, for an extraordinary game in Bavaria against 1860 Munich. Tensions between the club were high following the controversial transfer of Konietzka. The game was to end in acrimony and violence. Moreover, it would have a far-reaching effect on Konietzka's career after he was sent off in the 81st minute for an assault on the match referee. *Kicker* magazine called it "Skandalspiel der Giganten" (scandalous game of the giants). Tensions began to mount in the first half after a full-blooded challenge on Brunnenmeier by Wolfgang Paul that resulted in a penalty. The Dortmund skipper hotly contested the decision but the referee, Max Spinnler, was unmoved. The replay suggests (in so much as 1960s TV replays can suggest anything) that there was a lot more ball than man and that it was a decent tackle, particularly in the context of the physicality of football at the time. Irrespective of the correctness of the decision however, Brunnenmeier missed from the spot to much celebration from the Dortmund players. Their celebrations were quickly snuffed out when Brunnenmeier slotted home at the far post on 38 minutes.

The game really kicked off, so to speak, in the 75th minute. Emmerich took Held's cross on his right foot, switched it to his left, and equalised. 1860 stormed back but were sucker-punched by Siggi Held. The number 9 met a through ball from Kurrat just inside the area and, according to the home players, controlled the ball with his hand. The referee did not see it and allowed the goal to stand. The 1860 players and touchline stiff mobbed the linesman in a futile attempt to persuade him to change the referee's mind. The home fans were furious and threw cans onto the pitch. It was in the aftermath that Konietzka is alleged to have assaulted the referee with what *Kicker* reported to be a "bump to the chest, a kick against the shinbone and punching his whistle away."

Unsurprisingly, Konietzka was sent off, as was his team-mate, Manfred Wagner, for manhandling the linesman. The former Dortmund striker protested his innocence but was banned for six months, a punishment that he considered to be too harsh. When he returned from his ban he was booed and heckled by fans in every stadium in which he played. He later admitted that it was this experience which partly informed his decision to leave Germany and transfer to the Swiss second division team, Winterthur. His career as a frontline player in a league emerging as one of the strongest in Europe was over before his 30th birthday. He did return to Dortmund as head coach for a short spell in 1984 but most of his coaching career was in Switzerland, a country that he would soon adopt as his own and where he would die in 2012, at a euthanasia clinic in Brunnen, after suffering from cancer.

1977-78

Nothing to see here
Defeat and relegation in the 1970s

1971/72 was a wretched campaign for Arminia Bielefeld. The North Rhine-Westphalia club began the season at the bottom of the Bundesliga table and there they stayed. You might have heard of the "Bielefeld Conspiracy", which satirises conspiracy theories by falsely claiming that the city does not actually exist. Well, in this season that may as well have been true about its football club. They were relegated after having won a derisory six games against hapless opponents. One of them was Borussia Dortmund.

In fact, Arminia's fate was already sealed. They were to be relegated from the Bundesliga irrespective of their performance after being found guilty of fixing three matches the season before. They were allowed to play the season but they would drop down to the Regionalliga regardless of the outcome. Needless to say, the team's heart was not in it. Dortmund had no such excuses as former national champions, European Cup Winners' Cup winners and, until recently, contenders for the Bundesliga. However, the landscape of the German game was changing and a new force was emerging in the shape of Bayern Munich. Nothing illustrated this more than Bayern's 11-1 demolition of Dortmund in November 1971.

The Bavarians had missed the cut for the inaugural Bundesliga season in 1963 and had taken four seasons to hit their stride. Their first title win had come in 1968/69. When they played Dortmund in the Grünwalder Stadion of November 1972 they were on their way to their second Bundesliga title. The starting eleven reads like a who's who of German football. Sepp Maier, Uli Hoeness, Paul Breitner, Gerd Müller and Franz Beckenbauer were in the line-up against a Dortmund team that was a shadow of its former self. Bayern played as though the opposition weren't there. Contemporary reports say without exaggeration that they could have scored 20 goals and it would not have been an unfair reflection of the difference between the sides. After the game, a number of the few Dortmund fans at the match are reported to have joined the players on the pitch, not to berate them but to console them. They understood that this was no contest and that sympathy and solidarity were required. Believe it or not, this hammering was not to be BVB heaviest defeat. More on that later.

In the intervening years the great team of the mid-sixties drifted apart. In the heart of the defence, Wolfgang Paul's influence had declined to the point where he made no appearances in the league the season before. One-club men Gerhard Cyliax and Theodor Redder left in 1968 and 1969 respectively. Rudolf Assauer moved to Werder in 1970. Up front, Lothar Emmerich's distinguished career at Dortmund came to an end in 1969. Siggi Held returned to Offenbach in 1971; ditto the great number 7, Reinhold Wosab, to Bochum. Stan Libuda only stayed at Dortmund for three seasons before returning to his beloved Schalke in 1968, the same year that Aki Schmidt retired.

Such changes in a squad over a period of four or five years are hardly uncommon but Dortmund struggled to manage them correctly, which resulted in the sorry state they found themselves in prior to the game against Bayern. In fact, the inability of clubs to reinvent themselves is common in Germany for everyone not called Bayern Munich. Dortmund's decline was down to more than poor recruitment. To a certain degree the club's economic fortunes can be tracked with those of the region. While Dortmunders laughed up their sleeves about Schalke's poor form a few years earlier, BVB later became beset by the difficulties reflected in the area. Like Schalke, Dortmund's decline led to relegation and a trough so deep that it would take nearly two decades for them to climb out.

After the "Economic Miracle" there was a perhaps inevitable slowdown which affected the industrial Ruhr. Things would eventually improve but there would be consequences for football clubs and the leisure industry in general. Moreover, as Uli Hesse points out, there was an additional local economic issue. Dortmund's beer industry also went into an irreversible decline. For a club that identified itself with the golden ale this was a huge psychological blow as well as a monetary one.

In February 1968 there was an almost complete overhaul of the club's supervisory board. Earlier that season, the club's president, Willi Steegmann, was under pressure after a run of poor results. Steegmann became president in 1965 and the club enjoyed a golden era. The tenure of his successor, Dr Walther Kliemt, was anything but. The squad still had the benefit of 'Hoppi' Kurrat's experience and Jürgen 'Charly' Schütz was returning from his Italian sojourn. But the new squad was not a patch on the great teams of previous years and succumbed to relegation. The manager was former Schwarz-Weiss Essen coach Horst Witzler, who took over from Hermann Lindemann in 1970. Witzler was the man in charge for the Bayern thrashing, one of 24 defeats in 51 league games. Such was the pessimism around the club that Witzler had offered his resignation before the season began. The board declined, confident that the club could endure. After 36 years in the top flight or the regional equivalent thereof it was easy to imagine the board's complacency. Given their recent successes it was perhaps easier and more comfortable to regard the club's malaise as a temporary blip rather than the long-term decline that it turned out to be.

Witzler remained in his post until the end of 1971 when he was replaced by Herbert 'Budde' Burdenski. As a player, Burdenski won two national championships with Schalke in the 1940s. As a coach, his career was less impressive. Both Dortmund and Rot-Weiss Essen were relegated under his stewardship. No doubt he would argue that he had a rough deal with both clubs, and he would have a point. Like Dortmund, the Essen club were subject to the economic storms sweeping the region. Unlike Dortmund, they would not return to prominence.

As the season ground along attendances dropped and fans found other things to do with their time rather than watch the glory fade, and the black and yellow paint flake. Consider also the broader implications. The 1971 Bundesliga match-fixing scandal had occurred the season before. Borussia were not implicated (although Stan Libuda who had returned to Schalke was banned) but there had been an overall drop in attendances and interest in football in West Germany.

Overall it was a crappy time to be a *Fussball* fan and an even worse time to be a Dortmund one. BVB lost 20 games, including both derby matches against Schalke. They were thrashed 5-1 at home to Werder,

6-0 at Kaiserslautern and 7-1 at Mönchengladbach. But it was the 11-1 defeat that will remain symbolic of Borussia Dortmund's debagging. The club finished the season with 20 points and an horrific goal difference of -49. Their time out of the Bundesliga would be brief but their real return to prominence was years away, and it would also be years before the club won another trophy. In the meantime, Borussia Dortmund were to become a beneficiary of the upcoming 1974 World Cup. Before they were relegated, plans for a new stadium were already on their way, a stadium that would massively increase the scope of the club and provide them with a home beloved by their fans and envied around the world.

Dortmund were relegated from the Bundesliga to the Regionalliga West. There was no national second tier in 1972 and so, after less than a decade of traveling to far-flung places such as Hamburg, Munich and Stuttgart, BVB were back to local games at much smaller clubs. Joining BVB in the league were –amongst others – SG Wattenscheid, Sportfreunde Siegen, Eintracht Gelsenkirchen, DJK Gütersloh and some club called Bayer Leverkusen, who were terrible at the time. There is no modern equivalent to compare. The modern German league structure is national for the first three divisions. The notion of a big club such as Dortmund suddenly being relegated to a regional league in a single summer is remote, if by no means impossible.

However, Dortmund were not alone in being a big-name club in reduced circumstances. Their 1965 DFB-Pokal Final opponents, Alemannia Aachen, were participants in the Regionalliga West, as were Rot-Weiss Essen. This 18-team league competed for two play-off spots that were awarded to the first- and second-placed clubs. Those two teams would go on to a promotion tournament for entry to the Bundesliga. It was a tournament to which Dortmund would never progress. They came close in their first season but finished in fourth. The following season was the last one for the old regional structure and Borussia finished sixth. In August 1974, the 2. Bundesliga was formed. Still based on a regional league format there were two regional divisions: northern and southern. Borussia Dortmund were in the northern section.

It was clear that the club needed time to lick its wounds before returning to the Bundesliga. The squad assembled was balanced, with only a few players under the age of 21. There was experience in the form of Branko Rašović, by now a four-year veteran in yellow and black. Foreign players were still a rarity in Dortmund but the Montenegrin – a Yugoslavian international who played 210 games for Partizan Belgrade – travelled to Dortmund in 1969, just in time to observe the club's demise at close quarters. Joining the club from Hannover was Horst Bertl. He stayed for two seasons before moving to Hamburger SV, where he would win a European Cup. The Bremerhaven native scored 10 goals in 40 games for Dortmund. The seventies were the age of Der Kaiser and almost every team in Germany employed a libero. Dortmund's was a former Bayern Munich team-mate of Beckenbauer, Helmut Nerlinger. If the name is familiar then it's because his son, Christian, played for both Bayern and Dortmund before "enjoying" a brief and less than successful stint as general manager of the Bavarian club. Nerlinger the elder would give Dortmund his best years between 1972 and 1978, bringing the ball out of the BVB defence with varying degrees of success.

Saying a protracted farewell in the first season in the second tier was Kurrat, who had made his debut in the old Oberliga in 1960. The stalwart midfielder was the last link to the great mid-sixties team. He retired as a player but his time at the club was not over. The following season, Kurrat would stand in as coach for four months as the managerial merry-go-round whirled at the Westfalenstadion. Also leaving the club after its first season in the second flight was Theo Bücker. The midfielder joined the first team in 1969 and made 62 appearances in black and yellow, scoring 13 goals. He left in 1973 to spend five seasons in Duisburg and then another four at Schalke. Married to a Lebanese woman, Bücker coached the Lebanon national team and became the first coach to take them to a World Cup qualifier.

Czech defensive midfielder Miroslav 'Mirko' Votava joined Dortmund as an 18-year-old and played there for eight seasons. Most of the historical data websites put Votava in the defence but, having seen highlights packages of Dortmund's games in the 1970s, he looked more like a midfielder. That was certainly how he played later in his career. He moved to Atlético Madrid in 1983 and then Werder Bremen in 1985, where he stayed for 12 seasons, winning five trophies with the northern giants. Mirko had a brother, Josef, who also played at Dortmund, albeit for only four games. The two played together in all four of those matches but Josef only started one: a 4-0 win against VfB

Stuttgart's amateur side in the DFB-Pokal in 1975. Mirko marked the occasion with a beautiful lob to beat the VfB goalkeeper to open the scoring.

Joining the squad for this inaugural 2. Bundesliga season was a player disgraced in Germany but remembered well in Aberdeen. Zoltán Varga was a Hungarian inside forward who was described in his obituary in *The Scotsman* as "naturally gifted and technically outstanding". Varga would have played more games for the Hungarian national team had he not defected in 1968, and he would have had a far more celebrated career had he not received a two-year ban for involvement in the match-fixing scandal of 1972. As a Hertha BSC player he took a bribe from Arminia Bielefeld to underperform in a game between the two clubs, which Hertha lost 2-0. The Hungarian played 31 games for Aberdeen while in exile and is fondly remembered by Dons fans for performances that, "lit up grounds all over Scotland with his refined skills that had punters and pundits alike drooling," according to *The Scotsman*.

Varga returned to mainland Europe and was given the onerous and ultimately fruitless task of replacing Johan Cruyff at Ajax. Finally, he made his way back to Germany and Borussia Dortmund, where he gave the Black and Yellows two seasons and 10 goals from the midfield. A tall-to-the-point-of-spindly central midfielder with a mop of blond hair and an agreeable ranginess to his stride, Varga was described by Schutz-Marmeling as, "One of the most brilliant players to ever wear a BVB shirt." A languid and accurate passer over distance, he helped Dortmund eventually return to the Bundesliga. The few clips that have surfaced from his time at Dortmund reveal a player with good positional awareness, close control and an eye for the imaginative free kick. His little feints and tricks were not for nought and he was able to reliably pick out a team-mate with his passing. This player seemed well suited to the 2. Bundesliga Nord, a league in which football was played at a more civilised pace at the time. This would be among the numerous reasons why he was unable to fill Cruyff's shoes at Ajax. However, for Dortmund, he was a rare and unexpected gem, deserving of a place among its pantheon of classy players.

Otto Rehhagel was the coach who decided to let Varga go. He was something of a free spirit whose style was considered to be passé. However, the footage also reveals that he wasn't always on the same wavelength as some of his team-mates. Often you would see misplaced passes which had more to do with Varga's speed of thought being too quick for the legs of his team-mates. He moved on to Augsburg and then Gent before enjoying a decent stint as a coach back in Hungary. Sadly, he died suddenly at 65 while playing a veteran's football match in Budapest.

Klaus Ackermann was another arrival for the new season. The striker was by then a veteran Bundesliga player taking the drop to 2. Bundesliga. The previous five seasons had been spent at Kaiserslautern, playing 157 games for the Red Devils. Prior to that he spent two seasons at the top level with Borussia Mönchengladbach. Lothar Hüber was also drafted in from Kaiserslautern and would stay at Dortmund until the end of the 1986/87 season.

The 1974/75 season saw Dortmund finish in sixth place having fallen away in the last three weeks after dropping points to Mülheim, Uerdingen and Wacker 04 Berlin. The highlight was a run to the semi-final of the DFB-Pokal, where they were knocked out by MSV Duisburg of the first division, losing 2-1 after extra time. The financial problems that had beset the Dortmund club since their sixties heyday were coming home to roost. By 1974 bankruptcy was a very real possibility. There was, however, a silver lining in the shape of a brand new stadium constructed right next to the Rote Erde: the Westfalenstadion.

Cologne withdrew as a host city for the World Cup in 1974 and Dortmund dusted off the previous decade's plans for a new stadium, with the money originally allocated for the redevelopment of the stadium in Cologne was redirected to Dortmund, supplemented by taxpayers in the city. The new facility was originally intended to be a multi-purpose stadium with a running track around the pitch; mercifully, cost-cutting measures meant that the track was abandoned and Borussia fans would get much closer to the action when their team moved in. The keys to the stadium were handed over in April 1974 and, after the World Cup, BVB played there for the first time. 'Stan' Libuda returned with Schalke for a friendly and spoiled the party, winning 3-0.

Dortmund's successful 1975/76 season was not without luck. One of the worst penalty decisions I have ever seen was given in favour of BVB against Aachen, when an Allemania defender blocked a shot on the line. While the ball clearly hit his arm it was placed in front of his torso and he couldn't have avoided contact without either stepping aside or cutting off his arms; an absurd decision. The resultant penalty gave Dortmund a 2-1 win in a match that Aachen had largely dominated.

The season was also punctuated by a welcome return for the Revierderby. The loss of this previously perennial fixture would have been a sad loss to the fans and accountants of both clubs during Dortmund's exile in the second tier. The pair were drawn together in the second round of the DFB-Pokal at the Parkstadion in Gelsenkirchen. Schalke were coached at the time by none other than Max Merkel and had a fair to middling league season that year. Perhaps unsurprisingly the game ended with a 2-1 win to the first division side. Schalke missed a barrel-load of chances, including one that had to be cleared off the line, and scored twice in the first half with goals from Hannes Bongartz and Manfred Dubski. Dortmund's Hans-Werner Hartl pulled one back just after half time.

As the season progressed, and with Dortmund on the fringes of the two promotion slots at the top of the table, coach Otto Knefler was sacked after 21 matches. It was rough justice for a man who had put together the side that would go on to be promoted. The decision created something of a rift in the dressing room, with goalkeeper Horst Bertram – by then the longest serving member of the squad – unhappy that the decision had been influenced by some of his team mates, Helmut Nerlinger and Zoltán Varga among them.

Knefler's replacement was Horst Buhtz, previously of Besiktas in Turkey. Buhtz was only intended to be a temporary coach until the end of the season but Dortmund's fortunes improved to the point where they qualified for the Relegation Play-off with Nürnberg. Contrary to what the name implies, the play-off winner would be promoted to the first division for the next season. Matters were complicated by the fact that Buhtz had agreed to join Nürnberg from the start of the following season. Under the circumstances it was decided to let Buhtz go before the play-off and Rehhagel, then a young coach, was drafted in as his replacement. The decision to replace Buhtz so close to such a vital pair of games seems bizarre today. However, one has to consider that the Bundesliga match-fixing scandal loomed large over the football landscape and conflicts of interest would have been uppermost in the minds of the supervisory board at Dortmund. Nürnberg's outgoing coach was former Dortmund goalkeeper Hans Tilkowski. A champion and European trophy winner with the Westfalen club, few would have blamed Nürnberg fans for questioning the commitment of their coach in the knowledge that he was on his way out. That being said there is no suggestion that Tilkowski did any favours for Borussia.

Sadly there is very little footage of the two-legged play-off that took place on two Saturdays in June. The Nürnberg stadium, at that time a concrete bowl, was basking in the sunshine as the youthful Rehhagel took his seat in the Dortmund dugout. His opposite number, Tilkowski, was his polar opposite in terms of each coach's career trajectories. Egwin Wolf scored the only goal for Dortmund in the first leg and, despite spirited resistance from Nürnberg, BVB won the second leg 3-2, Peter Geyer, Hans-Werner Hartl and Lothar Huber – in the 89th minute – scoring the goals. A jubilant Borussia crowd invaded the pitch at the final whistle to celebrate their promotion. Huber had checked with the referee with a minute to go, but unlike many of his team-mates and the Nürnberg players, was on the far side of the pitch from the tunnel when the final whistle blew. "I needed half an hour to get to the dressing room," he recalled in an interview in 2012. "My jersey, socks, short, shin pads – everything was gone. Except my underpants. Nobody wanted those."

Rehhagel stayed at the Westfalen for another two years. He would go on to win Bundesliga titles with Werder Bremen and Kaiserslautern, and the European Championships with Greece at EURO 2004. At Borussia, however, he would suffer one of the greatest indignities as a coach. It called his reputation into question and brought shame on him, his players, and the club.

It's the final day of the 1977/78 season. Dortmund have only just survived another difficult campaign in the Bundesliga. Their opponents for the finale are Borussia Mönchengladbach, at the Rheinstadion in Düsseldorf, the temporary home of 'Gladbach while their own stadium, the Bökelbergstadion, undergoes renovation. 'Gladbach start the final day of the season level on points at the top of the table with their local rivals, 1. FC Köln. However, the Cathedral City club have an unassailable goal difference advantage of +10; barring a freak result they should claim the Bundesliga title with a win at home to St Pauli.

Köln did claim their title in the end but it was in spite of the aforementioned freak occurrence nearly happening. Indeed, it was freakish to the point of suspicious, in truth, and a result that would stigmatise a group of players and cost the coach his job. The match was the last in charge for referee Ferdinand Biwersi, who was interviewed by a camera crew in the centre circle seconds before kick-off. He graciously accepted his place in the limelight for a few moments and it is unlikely that he considered that he would have the best seat in the house for one of the most extraordinary football matches ever played. Before the game Dortmund coach Rehhagel had a minor selection issue in goal. First choice goalkeeper, Horst Bertram, had recovered from a back injury and was fit to play, but Rehhagel elected to stick with the stand-in goalkeeper, Peter Endrulat. This was despite the fact that Endrulat had been told on the eve of the game that his contract would not be extended.

"St Pauli! St Pauli! St Pauli!" chanted the 'Gladbach supporters after their team took the lead almost straight from kick-off with a looping header from their forward player, Jupp Heynckes. The early goal had heralded a renewed sense of optimism. At 5-0 some of the crowd were singing, "We are the champions!" in English. Dortmund enjoyed plenty of possession and, in the ten minutes between the first and second goals, they managed a couple of attempts of their own. However, the more they conceded the more haphazard their possession became. Surging individual runs from deep were easily crowded out. Increasingly Dortmund resembled the little guy swinging his fists at the big fella nonchalantly holding him out of arm's reach.

Referee Biwersi showed no interest in prolonging the first half and blew up a few seconds early. In the dressing room, amidst the hundred-yard stares, Endrulat was asked if he wanted to be substituted. It was reported in *11Freunde* he declined on the basis that it could not get much worse. He was wrong.

When the excellent number 5 for Mönchengladbach, Carsten Nielsen, scored the eighth goal of the match (his second), the home side's players had stopped celebrating. The crowd, on the other hand, had not. A number had brought transistor radios with them and they were hopeful that their team may yet grab an unlikely title win from Köln. Needless to say, from a tactical point of view the game had descended into farce. Dortmund, clearly humiliated, tried to grab a consolation, thereby leaving space at the back for Mönchengladbach's now-hungry attackers to ruthlessly exploit. The 'Gladbach defence were playing as though they were defending a one-goal lead in order to preserve their goal difference.

The Dortmund club captain was striker Manfred 'Manni' Burgsmüller. He recalled in *Spiegel Online* that by the time the score reached 9-0 there were no ball boys. As the shots rained in from the 'Gladbach players there was an understandable reluctance on the part of the BVB players to continue the game, with referee Biwersi forced to retrieve the ball when it was kicked out of play. In fact the ball boys were there but the pitch was surrounded by an athletics track and the ball would often travel beyond its boundary, presumably too much of a journey for their little legs.

The game finished 12-0 and, understandably, it was investigated for possible match-fixing. It is possible to construct a conspiracy theory based upon the selection of Endrulat, a player who barely featured between the sticks throughout his time at Dortmund, despite the availability of Bertram, not to mention the fact that he knew he was out the door the following day. It could be argued that his selection would be part of a fix by the player, his coach and Borussia Mönchengladbach. But one could just as easily argue that Endrulat was picked by his coach in a meaningless game for Dortmund in order to provide a shop window and an opportunity to show potential new clubs what he could do. If that was the case then it backfired completely. The stand-in Dortmund goalkeeper was probably at fault for 'Gladbach's sixth, when he went to ground too early and spilled a shot for Heynckes to stab home. Endrulat himself recalls that he was at fault for the tenth goal. However, he defended his performance to a point. "Most people forget that I made a lot of saves," he told *11Freunde*. "At least the ones that could be saved."

In any case, the situation for Gladbach was surely not so desperate that they needed to resort to match-fixing to such an extreme degree. After all, Köln could quite conceivably have dropped points in their game against St Pauli, in which case goal difference would not have been an issue. That is, unless there was some grand conspiracy in which the entire Dortmund team were out to throw the game and they all got so carried away with the task that they ended up conceding 12 goals.

I suspect that 'Gladbach, who were then the current Bundesliga champions, were simply determined not to mess up the outside chance they had at retaining the title and went out all guns blazing. With their attacking line-up they were more than capable of blowing away a team like Dortmund, described by Heynckes to RP Online as, "mentally already on holiday". On a normal day 'Gladbach may have eased off and invoked the Mercy Rule. However, the 'Gladbach players saw an opportunity to redress the goal difference between themselves and Köln and, according to Heynckes, they were being encouraged from the sidelines to push forward and score more goals. "Whilst the scoreline was 9–0, they wanted three more, to which I replied, 'Have you gone crazy?'"

Manfred Burgsmüller caught a lift home off the coach, Rehhagel. During the journey Rehhagel told Burgsmüller that he would be sacked the next day. It should come as no surprise to anyone that the coach, dubbed 'Torhhagel' in the media after the drubbing, was indeed given his cards, ending what had been a moderately successful stint at Borussia Dortmund in the worst possible manner. Since taking over for that play-off game against Nürnberg, Rehhagel had succeeded in establishing Borussia Dortmund as a first division club, albeit not the force they were in the fifties and sixties. The club's finances were poor and Rehhagel, still an inexperienced coach in the late 1970s, kept the club's head above water.

Born in Essen, Rehhagel had played for his local club, Rot-Weiss Essen, for the three years leading up to the formation of the Bundesliga in 1963. When the national league was formed the young defender moved to West Berlin and Hertha BSC. His best work was at Kaiserslautern, where he spent the majority of his playing career. As a coach he did not find his feet until after he left Dortmund. He enjoyed great success at Fortuna Düsseldorf, Werder Bremen and Kaiserslautern, and developed a football philosophy called *kontrollierte offensive*, or controlled offense, a style of play that emphasised power and pace over flair. Rehhagel's teams were defensively strong but flexible enough to attack on the counter. As a coach he won a DFB-Pokal (with Fortuna) and two league titles, two cups and a European Cup Winners' Cup (with Werder Bremen). He took Kaiserslautern from 2. Bundesliga to the the 1. Bundesliga title in consecutive seasons in the late nineties and, of course, he won the European Championships in 2004 with Greece playing the kind of football that only the Greeks would love. All of this must have seemed impossible that night in 1978 when he and Manni Burgsmüller headed home from a 12-0 beating in Düsseldorf.

When Dortmund returned to the 1. Bundesliga in 1976 they reinforced their forward line with two experienced attackers, Erwin Kostedde and Willi Lippens. Kostedde had already made the last of his three appearances for Germany when he joined Borussia Dortmund in 1976. He was the first black player to play for the national team. On his day he was one of the best strikers in the country and his international call-up came at the recommendation of none other than Franz Beckenbauer.

Kostedde was born in Münster. His father was an American soldier whom he never knew. His career began at Preußen Münster and then Meiderich (now MSV Duisburg) before he moved to Belgium and Standard Liege, where he scored 43 goals in 52 games. In 1971 he returned to Germany with Kickers Offenbach and it is there that he did his best work: 80 goals in 129 matches between 1971 and 1975. During this time he answered the call of his country. His signature move was the "Erwin Shuffle" which he described as a double stepover, old hat these days but noteworthy at a time when German football was a little more utilitarian than it is today. Dortmund paid Offenbach 600,000 Marks for Kostedde in 1976. This was no small sum for a club under financial pressure and sadly the 30-year-old was not able to reproduce his earlier form. He scored 11 goals in the 1976/77 season but only seven the next year. He did not play in the 12-0 defeat and did not return to Dortmund the following season. He retired in 1983 after briefly returning to Liege and having a healthy spell at Werder Bremen.

Throughout his career Kostedde encountered prejudice and racial abuse from the stands. In 1990 he was arrested for the armed robbery of an amusement arcade in Coesfeld, Westphalia. He spent six months in prison before the case went to trial and was almost instantly acquitted. The experience took its toll on his health. Sadly, the most recent reports suggested he was out of work and left embittered by his career. When he recalled his prison experience in Stern.de he said the only man from his playing days to visit him was Lippens.

Willi Lippens was born in Bedburg-Hau near the Dutch border. His father was from the Netherlands and moved there before the Second World War. His mother was German. His waddling gait earned him the nickname of 'Die Ente' – The Duck. Lippens played 172 games for Rot-Weiss Essen before joining Dortmund. An attacking midfielder with a sublime touch, Lippens was probably one of the greatest players you've never heard of. Beyond his excellent ability on the ball he had a sharp wit to match his intelligence. He frequently tormented both opponents and referees with his lip. In one famous instance he was sent off for correcting a referee on his grammar while the official was warning him about his conduct. It was all in good spirits, however, and he was known for being one of football's nice guys.

Lippens enjoys the distinction of being the only native German speaker to play for the Dutch national team. He only made one appearance and was not made welcome. Helmut Schön had offered to make him a German international but, in deference to his father, who suffered greatly under the Nazis and did not like Germans, he declined. Had his father been more sanguine it is likely that Lippens would have lifted the World Cup in 1974. It is also likely that he would have moved to a more successful club than Dortmund.

Kostedde and Lippens were both absent for the hammering against Gladbach, another factor to throw into the mix. However, Burgsmüller was present. Another native of Essen, Burgsmüller joined Dortmund in 1976 from Bayer Uerdingen. His 20 goals were an essential contribution to Dortmund's survival in their first season back in the 1. Bundesliga. He played 223 games in black and yellow before departing in 1983 and later working with Rehhagel again, at Werder in the late 1980s. He was a prolific goalscorer, never getting less than double figures in a season, and those 20 goals in the 1977/78 season were probably the biggest single reason why Dortmund managed to stay afloat in the Bundesliga. It is sad that this career highlight should be overshadowed by a horrific 12-0 result at the end of the campaign. However, while he played in an underwhelming period of Borussia Dortmund's history, no one has scored more Bundesliga goals for the club than Burgsmüller. A true Borussia Dortmund legend, his passing in May 2019 was keenly felt and the Südtribüne honoured his memory with a magnificent tifo.

Also in that team on the final day of 1977/78 was one Wolfgang Frank, who had joined the club that season. Frank made only nine appearances. He stayed for two more seasons but did not make that much of an impact. Frank did however go on to become something of a revolutionary coach who, as we shall discover in due course, would have a profound albeit indirect influence on one of the greatest times in Borussia's history.

Dortmund's new coach was Carl-Heinz Ruhl, who had enjoyed a successful season getting MSV Duisburg into the UEFA Cup. As a player, Ruhl was a teammate of Rehhagel at Hertha Berlin. He also won a DFB-Pokal medal with 1. FC Köln. Ruhl's time at Borussia could not have got off to a better start than a 1-0 win at home to Bayern Munich on the first day of the 1978/79 season. Who else but Burgsmüller scored the goal? Making his debut at the tender age of 17 was Eike Immel, a goalkeeper. Immel's first clean sheet was not his last and he would eventually succeed Horst Bertram as first choice and make 247 appearances for Borussia over the course of eight seasons. The result proved to be a false dawn, sadly, as Dortmund had another poor year, once again finishing 12th. Particularly hard to take were a 5-1 defeat to Schalke and 5-0 thumpings at the hands of Köln and HSV. There was also a somewhat outlandish score line in which Borussia and Werder Bremen shared eight goals and a point each.

To coincide with the new coach a new president was elected after the club had been without one for six months. At 32, Dr Reinhard Rauball was the youngest president in the league; there were four players in the squad who were older. Rauball was a prominent lawyer in Dortmund and a member of the German Social Democratic Party. He would remain as president of Borussia Dortmund until 1982 but that would not be his last stint at the top of the club. Ruhl's time at Dortmund, meanwhile, was short lived and uneventful. Eventually, under pressure from the players, he was let go in April 1979 and replaced, temporarily, by Uli Maslo. In an ambitious move, Dr Rauball hired one of the most successful coaches in German football of the time, Udo Lattek, coach of the Borussia Mönchengladbach side that so narrowly missed out on winning the Bundesliga in 1978 despite that almighty final day thrashing. Before 'Gladbach, Lattek had coached Bayern Munich to three consecutive Bundesliga titles and a European Cup. Hiring such a high profile and obviously successful coach was a signal of intent for an ambitious president. Sadly for Borussia there were no Allan Simonsens, Paul Breitners or Franz Beckenbauers for the Polish-born thoroughbred coach to work with at Dortmund. Unfortunately, their return to greatness would need considerably more effort if it was ever to be achieved. Sadly for Lattek, personal tragedy struck and his time at Dortmund was cut short.

1988-89

The Cobra Strikes and Nobby's Final Hurrah
Desperation and Glory in the 1980s

Erdal Kaser was 10 years old when his family moved from Turkey to Hagen in the Ruhr. Turkish immigrants were still relatively uncommon in Germany in the 1970s. They crossed over to fill labour shortages and faced the same challenges that almost all new communities do with integration. Kaser managed by playing football. He began playing with the other youngsters at SSV Hagen before graduating to nearby Borussia Dortmund. He was 19 when he made his debut for Dortmund as a 62nd minute substitute in a 2-2 draw at Fortuna Düsseldorf in February 1981. He was the first Turk to play for the club.

"Because foreigners were so rare, eyes were automatically directed towards me," he told *11Freunde* in 2011. He was relatively well received at the Westfalen but endured "Turks out!" calls at away grounds. He insists that this did not bother him: "These calls only motivated me more." In fact, he says that he frequently blew kisses at opposition fans. Even in front of his own fans it was not easy: "I was popular because I could decide matches. But I was always judged on a different scale. I had to be better than the Germans. If I had played an average game, I was bad." Kaser spent four seasons at Borussia Dortmund and returned for one more after a brief spell at Galatasaray. In all competitions, he played 116 matches for Borussia, scoring 30 goals.

The 1980/81 season also proved a landmark for Manni Burgsmüller, who scored a mammoth 27 goals during the campaign. Amongst those were three hat-tricks, in a 5-0 win against Arminia Bielefeld, a 5-1 thrashing of Duisburg, and another five-goal haul against Leverkusen. He also scored twice in a 5-3 defeat to Bayern Munich at the Olympiastadion in Munich, and again in a 6-2 mauling of HSV.

If not for his exploits at Dortmund, Burgsmüller might be a familiar name to Gridiron aficionados, as he played for Rhein Fire in NFL Europe in the early 2000s. The striking blond midfielder was at his most prolific as a goalscorer from midfield but in his dotage in the late 1980s he was played up front as an orthodox striker by Otto Rehhagel at Werder Bremen. Beginning in 1986 he spent four seasons by the Weser and won a Bundesliga title in 1988. It was quite the Indian summer.

The season started optimistically and with something of a landmark. Atli Edvaldsson's close-range poke against Bayer Uerdingen was the first goal scored in the Bundesliga by an Icelander. Edvaldsson only played 30 games for Dortmund before moving to Fortuna Düsseldorf. That goal against Uerdingen was the first of 11. He scored again in the derby against Schalke in Gelsenkirchen and again against Die Knappen in the reverse fixture at the Westfalen, which ended 2-2. Edvaldsson played 70 times for his national team and went on to become a successful coach in Iceland. Sadly, he was taken from us by cancer in September 1989 at just 62 years old.

Another somewhat unusual addition to the squad – this time mid-season – came from the unlikely location of FC Schalke 04. Rolf Rüssmann, a defender, played his last game for the Gelsenkirchen club in a 2-0 defeat at Nürnberg at the end of November 1980. Less than a fortnight later he was turning out in the black and yellow of Borussia Dortmund against Borussia Mönchengladbach. Rüssmann had made 304 appearances for Schalke. A promising German international youth player, there were expectations that he would graduate to the senior squad. That was before he was found guilty of perjury during the *Bundesligaskandal*. He took a bribe from Arminia Bielefeld in 1971 and was subsequently banned from playing in Germany in 1973. He served his ban in Belgium with Club Brugge before returning to Schalke. His prospects of a long international career were effectively blown by that point, although he did go on to make 20 appearances in the late seventies.

Schalke were experiencing financial problems in 1980. They elected to sell Rüssmann and Dortmund were the obvious choice, given their location. Rüssmann would spend the next four-and-a-half seasons at the Westfalen before retiring with 453 games and 48 goals on his bedpost. He went on to have a distinguished career in management, most notably with Borussia Mönchengladbach, where he won a DFB-Pokal. However, Rüssmann was another to die too young, of prostate cancer just before his 59th birthday.

After years of mediocrity the 1980/81 season was a welcome relief. Yes, there were some heavy defeats against Bayern and Bayern Leverkusen, but the good memories outweigh the bad. Dortmund's season was punctuated by impressive results against Arminia Bielefeld (5-0), 1860 Munich (4-1), MSV Duisburg (5-1) and HSV (6-2).

Tragedy struck coach Udo Lattek later in the season when his son passed away from leukaemia at the age of 15. Grief-stricken, he left Dortmund and eventually quit Germany to take up the coaching reins at Barcelona. He led the Catalans to victory in the European Cup Winners' Cup and eventually returned to Germany to coach Bayern for a second time. There, he won three Bundesliga titles and two German Cups. At BVB Lattek was replaced by a caretaker coach, Rolf Bock. Dortmund were a whisker away from qualifying for Europe in the form of the UEFA Cup. A 3-0 defeat at the hands of Lattek's former club Borussia Mönchengladbach scuppered things, however, and Dortmund finished the season in seventh place. Given his record before arriving at Dortmund it is possible that BVB might have done enough to qualify for European competition had Lattek stayed. Indeed, the club could conceivably have gone on to enjoy great success under his stewardship. However, given the tragic circumstances of his departure, it doesn't really matter.

In any event, two years after the humiliation at Mönchengladbach in 1979, Borussia Dortmund were at least competitive once more. The following season saw the arrival of two legends of the game, one established and the other yet to be. The first was the coach, Branko Zebec. The Zagreb-born Croatian played in the midfield for the Yugoslavian national team in the 1954 and 1958 World Cups. As a club player in the fifties and early sixties he won three Yugoslavian cups with Partizan Belgrade and a league title at Red Star Belgrade. He finished his playing career in Germany at Alemannia Aachen between 1961 and 1965 but returned home before the DFB-Pokal final against BVB in 1965.

Zebec began his coaching career at Dinamo Zagreb. He won the Inter-Cities Fairs Cup in 1967 and then returned to Germany, and Bayern Munich, in 1968. The Bavarians won their first Bundesliga title on his watch. They won the DFB-Pokal the same year. He joined Borussia Dortmund after having won another Bundesliga title in 1979, at Hamburger SV. The Croatian's departure from HSV was less about football and more to do with his drinking problem, the malaise that would do for him in the end. Nevertheless, Dortmund decided to invest in this highly regarded coach and gave him the job as head coach.

The second arrival was a 19-year-old midfielder called Michael Zorc. He made the first of what would be 572 appearances for Dortmund (463 in the Bundesliga) as a substitute in a 2-0 defeat at Werder Bremen on 24th October 1981. It would be no exaggeration to say that Zorc would go on to become one of the most influential figures in the history of Borussia Dortmund.

BVB needed four games to get their first win, at home to Duisburg. After that only Bayern Munich, Kaiserslautern and Nürnberg on the final day bested Borussia at any point for the rest of the season. By that point Borussia had qualified for the UEFA Cup – after years of misery the fans had the excitement of a European campaign to experience, or at least they would have done had they not been knocked out by Glasgow Rangers in the first round. Zebec left for Eintracht Frankfurt, Mirko Votava for Werder Bremen. The incoming coach was Karl-Heinz Feldkamp, who had been in charge at Kaiserslautern for four seasons. Joining the playing squad was one of the finest players of his generation and a player who frequently appears in Borussia Dortmund all time elevens: Marcel Răducanu.

A year earlier, West Germany had played a friendly international in Dortmund against the Romanian national team. Răducanu was the Romanian captain. The Bucharest-born attacking midfielder had won two league titles and two Romanian Cups with Steaua Bucharest in the late seventies, and was a household name in Communist Romania. Despite his success and celebrity back home, Răducanu defected after the friendly match – or, to be specific, sometime in the second half. He played as well as he could in the first in order to attract the attention of German clubs. In the second he faked an injury. "I had a thick bandage to my knee and complained about the pain," he recalled to *11Freunde*. "I was suddenly alone in the locker room. I took my small bag with my stuff and walked out of the stadium. Out there waiting for my friend in the car – and we set off."

While the Westfalenstadion was searched from stem to stern, Răducanu was safely in Hannover with his friend. "I called my wife and said, 'I'm sorry!' She wept bitterly, 'Come back!' But I couldn't, it was too late." That phone call cost him dearly. It was intercepted by Romanian internal security and his possessions were confiscated. For a while there were concerns that he might even be assassinated on the order of the brutal Romanian dictator, Nicolae Ceaușescu. As it happened he was merely airbrushed out of Romanian history. His records were expunged in Romania and he was sentenced to five years and eight months in prison *in absentia*.

The defector successfully claimed asylum and was allowed to remain. However, his playing career in Germany did not get off to a flyer. This is because he decided to sign for two clubs: Hannover 96 and Borussia Dortmund. Consequently, he received a UEFA ban for one year. There was some dispute regarding who would finally get to have Răducanu in their squad. The matter went to court and Borussia got their man but had to pay Hannover DM500,000 for the privilege. And a privilege it was, because Marcel Răducanu is remembered as one of Dortmund's finest ever players. The tragedy is that he played during such a mediocre time of their history.

Răducanu was in the starting line-up for Borussia Dortmund's record victory in all competitions on 6th November 1982, an 11-1 win in the Bundesliga against Arminia Bielefeld. Astonishingly the score was 1-1 at half time and Arminia had taken the lead with a goal from Frank Pagelsdorf. Manni Burgsmüller equalised and the game was relatively quiet. "I said that we can win here, we had more of the game," said Arminia coach Horst Köppel, remembering the interval in 2002. By the time Köppel took his seat on the bench for the second half it was 3-1 to Dortmund. Burgsmüller and Rüdiger Abramczik did the early damage.

The Dortmund coach was Karl-Heinz Feldkamp. He was somewhat downbeat in his recollections, attributing the scoreline to one of those days in which every shot went in. Burgsmüller scored five in total and Bernd Klotz scored a hat-trick. Răducanu scored once and Lothar Hübner sheepishly put away a penalty to complete the slaughter. During that mad second half, according to Rolf Rüssmann in *Die Welt*, some of the Arminia players were laughing. The coaches of both teams would swap places within the same decade and both would enjoy great success in their careers. Horst Köppel will be returning to these pages presently.

Dortmund were top of the table at the time but could not use the result as a platform. They finished the season in seventh and failed to win their final four games of the season. This run included an extraordinary 4-4 draw with Bayern Munich, a 5-0 drubbing at the hands of the eventual champions, Hamburg, and a 6-4 defeat to Borussia Mönchengladbach

The following season was a disaster. There were no fewer than four different coaches and all the changes happened before the end of November. Uli Maslo returned for a brief stint at the beginning of the season and was gone by 23rd October. In that time Borussia had suffered six defeats, including a 4-2 reverse at Bayer Leverkusen and a 7-0 mauling from Fortuna Düsseldorf. Helmut Witte was Maslo's assistant and stuck around long enough to preside over a 4-1 loss to Waldorf Mannheim before Hans-Dieter Tippenhauer took charge. Tippenhauer had enjoyed unexpected success by leading Fortuna Düsseldorf to the DFB-Pokal in 1979 and subsequently to the European Cup Winners' Cup Final, where they lost in extra time to Barcelona. Tippenhauer was brought in from Bayer Uerdingen, at the cost of DM100,000, with a remit to do more than coach the team. He was expected to professionalise the back office and modernise the dressing room but neither were for turning. Tippenhauer lasted two games before he was off; a 1-1 draw with Bochum and a 2-1 defeat to Borussia Mönchengladbach.

In not unrelated news, this season also saw the end of Manni Burgsmüller's career at Borussia Dortmund. He spent a season at Nürnberg and then another at Rot-Weiss Oberhausen before transferring to Werder Bremen, where he would win a Bundesliga title with fellow BVB alumni Mirko Votava and coach Otto Rehhagel. The club also said goodbye to Rüdiger Abramczik, another exile from Schalke who spent three seasons in the Dortmund attack, scoring 30 goals. The departure of players of this calibre had an effect on the results and consequently on attendances. Under coach Horst Franz, Dortmund limped to thirteenth place at the end of the season, shorn of their more popular players and without any direction from the men at the top.

At the start of the 1984/85 season an old face returned to the

Westfalen as manager. Timo Konietzka had previously been coaching Bayer Uerdingen, who at this time appeared to be an accidental feeder club for Borussia Dortmund. The former BVB hero only took charge for nine league games and two cup matches. Only Bochum and Leverkusen succumbed in that time, as well as SC Dudweiler in the Cup. Konietzka was ousted by the new supervisory board at the club. The president at the time was Frank Roring, who had presided over a financial crisis and was extremely unpopular with the supporters. Reinhard Rauball was the fans choice but Roring was reluctant to move on. Matters came to a head in the home game against Karlsruhe, when the fans staged a sit-in on the Westfalen pitch. Roring relented and quit, taking most of the board with him.

Up next on the coaches carousel was Erich Ribbeck, fresh from a stint as West Germany's assistant coach. Ribbeck would go on to coach Bayern Munich and the German national team but he was unable to revive Dortmund. It was yet another dreadful season for them both on and off the pitch. There had to be fundraising activities and corporate intervention to help the club address its debts. The DFB even expressed concern that the club might not be able to fulfil the criteria required to participate in the league, and that they could lose their licence. The club survived. In fact, in Rauball's return as president, one of the seeds was being sown for the long-term recovery of the club.

Despite having won two Bundesliga titles and a German Cup with Bayern Munich, Pál Csernai was not the easiest coach to get on with and departed Bavaria in May of 1983. At a loose end, he was taken on by Borussia Dortmund for the following season. The former Hungarian international's style of play would be familiar to football audiences in the early 21st Century. Csernai was a flamboyant coach with a penchant for wearing a silk scarf. His tactical approach of high pressing and swift counter-attacking was, in the words of Reinhard Reibull, as relayed on the BVB website, "Many years ahead of its time. Many of his ideas are now among the tactical foundations of every professional team."

Sadly Csernai's methods proved too much for this Dortmund team. The club embarked upon another disastrous run in the 1985/86 season. Despite a memorable 1-0 win at the Olympiastadion against Bayern Munich, the season was pretty horrific, the worst being a 6-1 defeat at Bochum and another to Schalke by the same scoreline. Amid the league chaos was a run to the semi-final of the DFB-Pokal. Three of the five rounds they played were against lower league opposition and the most eye-catching result was a 9-2 win at SC Neukirchen. Wins at Paderborn, Homburg and Sandhausen followed before they ran into high-flying Stuttgart. The cup dream ended there with a 4-1 defeat.

Less than a month later Dortmund would face Stuttgart again and lose once again, this time by four goals to nil. It was the third to last game of the season and Borussia Dortmund were third from bottom. It was also Csernai's final game as coach. Unlike many of his predecessors, Csernai came to Dortmund with pedigree and a well-defined philosophy. It is a great sadness that the dressing room could not respond. His successor was Reinhard Saftig who had been assistant to Csernai, Ribbeck and Konietzka. The former Bayern assistant's task was immediately clear: keep Dortmund in the first division.

With two fixtures remaining Borussia were still third from bottom. If they stayed put then there was a chance of a reprieve with a relegation play-off but, if they lost what little ground there was left, the Westfalenstadion would be hosting second division football once again. Indeed, given the club's frequent problems managing its financial affairs the consequences in the longer term could have been much darker. BVB's penultimate game was at home to Schalke. Olaf Thon gave the visitors the lead in the first half but Michael Zorc popped up after 78 minutes with a precious equaliser and the game finished as a draw. Dortmund were unable to creep out of the bottom three but crucially had not dropped into the automatic relegation zone. The final game of the regular season was at Hannover 96. Fortunately for the away side, the 96ers were bottom and already relegated. With only a shred of pride to play for and no doubt anxious to hit the beach, the Hannover players put up little resistance. Dortmund won the game 4-1. Răducanu and Zorc were on the score sheet. The season's top scorer, Jürgen Wegmann, bagged a brace.

Nicknamed 'The Cobra', Essen-born Wegmann enjoyed two spells at Borussia Dortmund. He started his career at Rot-Weiss before settling at BVB. The nickname comes from a quote of his: "I am more toxic than the most venomous snake." Wegmann was one of the game's characters and later enjoyed a successful spell at Bayern Munich, where he won a Bundesliga title. He also won the 1988 Goal of the Year with a spectacular overhead kick for the Munich club against Nürnberg.

The win against Hannover had been enough to keep Borussia from dropping into the bottom two and they had a chance to retain their first division status in a relegation play-off against Fortuna Köln. It was a chance that they seemed to have spurned after losing the first leg 2-0 on 13th May. The second leg took place on a sweltering hot afternoon on 19th May at the Westfalenstadion. A few days before the match it was revealed that Wegmann was going to leave Dortmund in the summer – for Schalke 04. "They [the fans] called me Judas," recalls Wegmann in an interview with *11Freunde*, "and whistled at me when I entered the field. But the cat calls motivated me more."

Wegmann said in the dressing room before the game that he felt the match might be settled in the final minute. He wasn't wrong. However, the second leg got off to the worst possible start for BVB when Fortuna opened the scoring through Bernd Grabosch on 14 minutes. The revival was unlikely but began in the second half with a penalty scored by Michael Zorc after 54 minutes. On 68 minutes Răducanu wheeled away in celebration after scoring Dortmund's second. Fortuna tried to game-manage their way over the line by slowing down the play, but Dortmund were not to be denied. It was Wegmann who bundled the ball over the line in the 90th minute. Once again Dortmund had lived to fight another day. Had the away goal rule been in place for this play-off then Fortuna would have been promoted there and then. As it was, Borussia's 3-1 win was enough to level the tie on aggregate and force a one-off replay at a neutral venue. The Westfalen was pandemonium. A stray fan climbed the barriers and ran on the pitch to embrace Wegmann, his impending defection to Schalke temporarily forgotten.

The Fortuna players were understandably crestfallen. They were seconds away from an historic promotion to the 1. Bundesliga, a feat they had only achieved for one season prior to this moment and have yet to achieve again since. The replay was held in Düsseldorf, of all places, a city that for centuries has been a rival to nearby Cologne. Moreover, the match was also delayed until 30th May due to illness in the Fortuna squad. It is likely that this was a major contributor to their performance; Dortmund slaughtered them 8-0. Zorc scored twice in the game. Wegmann also scored on his swansong, although he would return before the end of the decade. In the meantime, his parting gift to Dortmund had been to score that precious goal in the play-off second leg that saved the club from oblivion. Who knows what would have happened to this debt-ridden club from the Ruhr had they lost that game and been relegated in 1986.

This season marked the end of the career of a true great of the Bundesliga, albeit not at Borussia Dortmund. Horst Hrubesch scored 96 goals in 159 games for Hamburger SV between 1978 and 1983. He won three Bundesliga titles with HSV and won a European Championship winner's medal with West Germany in 1980. He was also a runner-up at the 1982 World Cup. After two seasons in the Belgian second division he was recruited by Dortmund for the 1985/86 campaign. Hrubesch was restricted to just 17 appearances and two goals, and left at the end of the season. Dortmund also said goodbye to Eike Immel. The goalkeeper had stood guard between the sticks for eight years and endured all kinds of punishment for his trouble. His reward was a move to VfB Stuttgart and he would go on to win a Bundesliga title in 1992. Like Hrubesch, Immel was a squad regular in the West German national team and has a Euro '80 winner's medal.

Reinhard Saftig was retained as head coach of Borussia. Born in Uersfeld, Saftig's frontline coaching career began as an assistant to Uli Hoeneß at FC Bayern Munich at the age of 27. He was 34 when he sat down on the bench as head coach of Borussia Dortmund. After half a decade Dortmund had arrived at a coach who would keep his job for three seasons.

Despite a promising 2-2 draw with Bayern Munich on the opening day of the 1986/87 season, BVB did not register their first Bundesliga win for five games. The scorers in this 4-2 win at Bayer Uerdingen were both new arrivals to the Westfalen: Frank Mill and Norbert Dickel. The former scored a hat-trick.

Frank 'Frankie' Mill would go on to become a fan favourite, captaining the team and scoring 47 goals in the eight seasons he spent at Dortmund. He was a classic poacher with a penchant for keeping his socks down and shirt untucked in the style of many maverick players of the time. He joined his hometown club, Rot-Weiss Essen, in 1976. The club were relegated from the first division and Mill found his touch in the 2. Bundesliga North, scoring 85 goals in 149 games over five seasons. Most extraordinarily, in his final season at Essen he notched 40 goals in 38 matches. Needless to say he made the move back to the Bundesliga, albeit with another club: Borussia Mönchengladbach, coached by Jupp Heynckes. More goals and a call-up to the national team and Olympic team followed. At the end of the 1985/86 season a fee was agreed for the 28-year-old to move to Borussia Dortmund. There was some doubt about the transfer because of Dortmund's protracted relegation play-off but the deal was finally done.

However, Mill's first taste of Bundesliga action in a Borussia Dortmund shirt was very sour indeed. His debut was at the Munich Olympiastadion in the aforementioned game against Bayern. With BVB a goal down he had the chance to level the match after latching onto the ball following a calamitous defensive error. In the final third of the pitch with only Bayern goalkeeper Jean-Marie Pfaff for company, Mill expertly side-stepped the goalie's attempt to retrieve the ball for his team. Bearing down on the open goal, well inside the six-yard box, Mill slightly overtook the ball and had to check his stride. There was still plenty of time and space to score but Mill managed to find the foot of the post. It would and should have been easier to miss. "I was in a bit of an awkward position," he said immediately after the game, "and I tried to hit the ball too precisely."

Norbert 'Nobby' Dickel's career was a short one. Injury put paid to it in 1990 but his legacy can be heard even today on matchdays; Dickel is the stadium announcer and presenter of Borussia's in-house online channel, *BVB Total*. Dickel's on-field contribution to the Dortmund we know today is even greater, as we shall discover shortly.

Further back in the team, BVB made two further key signings. Between the sticks was Wolfgang 'Teddy' de Beer from MSV Duisburg, who replaced the Stuttgart-bound Eike Immel. Thomas Helmer arrived from Arminia Bielefeld. Helmer is a household name in Germany and a familiar one to many international football fans. He made an immediate contribution by shoring up the defence in what was a big season for Dortmund. Breaking through was *libero* Frank Pagelsdorf who cemented his place in the first team squad.

Saftig's team produced some juicy results in a season that would signal their return to the big time. There were two 2-2 draws with Bayern, a 7-0 win against newly promoted Blau-Weiss Berlin and a 6-0 thumping of Waldorf Mannheim. It was honours even in the Revierderby, Schalke 04 winning their home game 2-1 only for BVB to respond with a 1-0 home win later in the season thanks to a goal from

Dickel. In total Dickel scored 20 goals in the 1986-87 season. Frank Mill scored 17 and Michael Zorc 14 from midfield. Borussia did find themselves on the wrong end of some results including a 5-0 defeat to Werder Bremen (former BVB player Manni Burgsmüller scored a brace) and a 6-1 loss to Borussia Mönchengladbach in the DFB-Pokal, but these were unhappy blips in an excellent season. Dortmund finished fourth and qualified for the UEFA Cup.

In 1987 the Celtic player Murdo MacLeod received a phone call from a German club called Eintracht Frankfurt. They expressed an interest in signing him. The Scotsman thought it was a joke. "I thought it was just people taking the mickey, one of my team-mates putting on a German accent on the phone," he told the *Sunday Herald* in 2016. "And then another phone call came from my agent and it was Dortmund."

McLeod had been at the Glasgow club for nine years and was due a testimonial. However, Celtic did not offer to extend his contract, so he was open to new opportunities. He embraced the change of club and the new life in Germany for himself and his family with open arms. The Scottish international's stint in the Ruhr lasted for three highly productive seasons and his three appearances in the Scotland 1990 World Cup team were as a Dortmund player. Truth be known, McLeod's debut season for his new club was not a vintage one in terms of the Bundesliga. They finished thirteenth. The campaign was punctuated by a memorable 4-1 win over Schalke and a less than memorable 3-0 loss against the same team. The really interesting work, however, was done in the cups, both foreign and domestic.

The Oberliga Baden-Württemberg was a regionalised fifth tier amateur league of which FV Offenburger was a member. In 1987 they qualified for the first round of the DFB-Pokal. As is the custom in this competition teams from the lower leagues are seeded to draw home ties with clubs from higher up the leagues. In this case they drew Borussia Dortmund. Astonishingly, the tie went to a replay after a 3-3 draw. Unsurprisingly Dortmund were able to recover some dignity with a 5-0 win at the Westfalen but the second round was only moderately less troublesome for BVB. FSV Salmrohr were going through a high point in their modest history. This tiny club from the Rhineland had just spent a season in the 2. Bundesliga and, while they were relegated, they were still a tough side and had knocked out Osnabrück in the first round. Dortmund overcame a difficult encounter with a 1-0 win at the Salmtalstadion. The next round saw Borussia drawn at Bayer Uerdingen. This game also went to extra time after Dirk Hupe scored an 87th minute equaliser to make it 2-2. That was one of three goals from the midfielder in what was to be the final of his three seasons at Dortmund. Stefan Kuntz retook the lead for Uerdingen in extra time but Günter Kutowski forced a replay that Dortmund lost 2-1. Kuntz was on the scoresheet for the visitors again.

In Europe, Borussia travelled to Glasgow and Parkhead, the home of Celtic. Frankie Mill's wonderful strike secured a vital away goal in a 2-1 loss to the Scottish team. In the second leg, the home crowd at the Westfalen needed to wait until the 74th minute before their team turned the tide of the tie. Nobby Dickel's opener gave Borussia the advantage and his second, 12 minutes later, settled matters. In the next round, Dickel was a scorer again along with Dirk Hupe at home to Velež Mostar, taking a 2-0 lead to what was then Yugoslavia. In front of a packed home crowd Meho Kodro took the lead for the home side and the tie was very much alive. Fortunately for Dortmund, Mill equalised on the night in the 88th minute and, despite Predrag Juric's strike a minute later, Borussia were in the hat for the third round. Hopes of an extended run in the competition were high when BVB took what should have been a commanding 3-0 aggregate lead to the second leg at Brugge. However, the away side were blown away to the tune of 5-0 and that was the end of that.

In the winter of that season there was a further addition to the squad from Eintracht Frankfurt: one Andreas Möller. And, as many people will tell you, there *is* only one Andreas Möller, for all manner of reasons. For many years, my recollection of Möller was of his infamous celebration after scoring the winning penalty in the shoot-out in the Euro '96 semi-final at Wembley. However, like Diego Maradona and his hand of God, this is a decidedly narrow English perception of one of the best ever players ever to come from Germany. Much has been said about this attacking midfielder's approach to the game but what strikes me about him was his ability to anticipate the movement of the ball and allow it to come to his foot, even when striking on goal. Möller's relations with the Dortmund fans are complicated. On the one hand he is arguably one of the best midfielders to ever play the game in any colours. On the other hand one of those colours was the blue of Schalke, to whom he transferred from Dortmund. However,

Frankfurt-born Möller was a key member of the team that would bring silverware back to Strobelallee and would be present at almost everything great that happened to Borussia Dortmund for the decade, starting with the DFB-Pokal.

It is not easy to express the feeling of anticipation and anxiety that comes with being so close to attaining a goal that has for so long been out of reach, yet is so very nearly yours. This feeling is complicated, in the case of the sports fan, by the attainment of that goal being beyond your influence. Of course, supporters of a club at a ground or stadium can play a role in the performance of the team they are supporting. It is not for nothing that players praise or lament the part the fans played in their latest victory or defeat. They are not just platitudes. But, to many fans, at least certainly to this fan, the feeling of being an active participant is not present. Standing or sitting on the sidelines watching on is inactive, bearing witness rather than being involved. So often in these ultra-tense moments it is only the ultras that have the dedication and commitment to keep singing, keep encouraging their players to fulfil those dreams. Everyone else just waits in desperate anticipation, praying to the football gods that they be kind.

For supporters of Borussia Dortmund there was indication of another day of glory after such a barren spell from the late 1960s. Many great players and beloved characters had passed through but, since the failed title bid and European win in 1966, it had been pretty much downhill. Then came the cup run in the 1988/89 season, a run that was not so much out of the blue but a welcome distraction from what had been a moribund couple of decades. The 1989 DFB-Pokal Final was to be significant not just for Dortmund but for their opponents, Werder Bremen. It was the first of three consecutive arduous trips through Communist East Germany to the Olympiastadion in West Berlin; the journey to the beleaguered West German enclave surrounded by the antagonistic German Democratic Republic would become considerably less problematic for subsequent finals. The following November, after the 1989 final, the Berlin Wall came down and its rubble formed the path to the reunification of Germany.

The DFB-Pokal was inaugurated in 1953, although its roots go back to the mid-thirties. As we know from earlier, it was a summer tournament with the final taking place just before the start of the season. The last summer final was in Hannover, where Dortmund beat Aachen in an otherwise forgettable match. From the 1950s all the way through to 1985 the final was played in a variety of different stadiums in West Germany. Borussia had come close to appearing in the final in 1983, when they reached the semis only to lose 5-0 to second division Fortuna Köln. In fairness, it was an appropriate result: Fortuna played city neighbours 1. FC Köln at the Müngersdorf Stadium in Cologne in the final. Dortmund would exact no small measure of payback for that semi-final loss in the relegation play-off final three years later.

In all likelihood there was a strong political element to taking the cup final to West Berlin. In May 1989 Germany was divided into two different countries: the Federal Republic of Germany, otherwise known as West Germany, and the German Democratic Republic, or East Germany. The West was born in 1949 out of the allied occupation zones controlled by France, the United Kingdom and the United States of America after the Second World War. The system of government was set up along the lines of what we would understand to be western liberal democracies. East Germany was created in the same year from the zone controlled by the Soviet Union and was set up very much under their system of government, which it's fair to say was very different to what people in the west are used to. Berlin is located in East Germany but the west side of the city was still under the control of the western allies. The division was clearly marked by a heavily fortified wall which became a symbol of this divided country and – in a broader sense – of the Cold War between the US and her allies, and the Soviet Union and hers, which took place in the second half of the 20th Century.

In order to get the Olympiastadion in West Berlin, fans from West Germany had to travel through not just another country, but a country that was antagonistic towards them. They had to take designated roads from the west, through the GDR, and into the city. Down the years there had been stories of embittered GDR Polizei arresting or harassing exuberant football fans on their way to the finals. One of the fans making the trip through East Germany was Uli Hesse – journalist, author and Borussia Dortmund fan, man and boy – whose writings for numerous outlets both English and German will be well known to most readers.

"They were distributing leaflets at Dortmund about what you

should not do on those East German motorways," he told me one Saturday afternoon from his flat in Berlin. Hesse is the editor of *11Freunde* magazine and spends most of his time in the capital city. "They said, 'Don't stop the car' and, 'Please don't break down'. And also on the leaflet it said, 'Don't have scarves outside of the windows' and, 'Don't honk your horn'. That's because the East German police were notorious because they wanted western currency. Just for the slightest reason they would stop you."

Hesse recalled his experience on those roads in the east: "There's cars and cars and cars with people in them who are in black and yellow. We get to the border and it's our turn and the guy looks at our passports for what seems like half an hour. And finally he says, 'Are you going to the football game?' And you wanted to say, 'Look at us?' I think he said something like good luck or whatever. The way you sort of imagine East German border police, you know?"

Accompanying Hesse on the road to Berlin were his brother and a giant inflatable gorilla. To abuse an old English phrase, if you remember the late 1980s then you weren't there. It was an era of japery on the football terraces, where giant inflatables were a common sight. The custom began in England (at least that's what we say in England), probably with Manchester City back when their fans compensated for their teams erratic performances on the pitch with humour that may or may not have been connected with the growing club and music rave scene of the time. The practice was soon adopted on the continent and various inflatables could be seen at the Olympiastadion on that sunny afternoon in May.

The metaphorical road to the final also has its own roadblocks along the way. Two home wins against Eintracht Braunschweig (6-0) and FC Homburg (2-1) were straightforward enough. However, for the third round BVB were drawn against none other than Schalke 04. These were dark days for the Gelsenkirchen club, who had been relegated from the 1. Bundesliga the season before after finishing bottom of the table. The 1988/89 season was one of transition and mediocrity in the second tier. After the draw was made the anticipation grew, with Norbert Dickel pronouncing that Dortmund would go to the final via Gelsenkirchen. The atmosphere at the match was strange, with huge sections of the Parkstadion empty and the Schalke ultras setting fires within their own enclosures. After the game there was a physical altercation between

Frank Pagelsdorf and a journalist from the national newspaper *Bild*. According to Schulze-Marmeling, this ultimately stemmed from the bad relationship between Dortmund and paper at the time. *Bild* had been given the cold shoulder by the club while they tried to reinvent themselves, and they resented it. Their reaction was to provide more favourable coverage of Schalke. In time, things got personal and out of hand.

The semi-final also had its share of controversy. As the Dortmund players entered their dressing room after the final whistle the Stuttgart players were protesting the decisive goal. The match completed a Swabian Cup double: in the previous round Borussia had won 1-0 against Stuttgart's traditional local rivals, Karlsruhe, thanks to a goal by Michael Zorc. History repeated itself when Zorc put the home side ahead in the first half against Stuttgart. This was a keenly contested match against a strong team featuring a young Jürgen Klinsmann. Former BVB goalkeeper Eike Immel formed the base of the spine of the team that would win the Bundesliga title a few years later.

The cause of the rancour was the second goal, scored by Frankie Mill. By this stage of his career the veteran striker knew all the tricks of the trade. You don't get to be a successful player without having a bit of chicanery in your arsenal and Mill was a very successful player. Just before the hour mark the ball came into the box and was nodded home by Mill. As soon as he wheeled away to celebrate what was surely the winning goal the Stuttgart players were up in arms because one of their number –according to them, at least – was pushed in the back as the ball came in, taking the defender out of play and giving Mill a free header. It was a subtle nudge which the referee did not see but, according to the replay, it looked like the Stuttgart players had a case, to put it mildly.

And so to the final against a fine Werder Bremen team that finished the Bundesliga season in third position. Coached by former BVB boss Otto Rehhagel, this Werder squad included several names familiar to Dortmund fans. Manni Burgsmüller and Mirko Votava had been mainstays in the Dortmund team earlier in the decade. The former was at the veteran stage at the age of 33 and had scored six goals in the 1988/89 season. Joint top scorer for Werder that season was Karl-Heinz Riedle, a player who would become very well known to Dortmunders a few seasons hence. Borussia had had a fairly average league season, which was par for the course. After the financial issues of the 1970s and the nail biting narrow escapes of the mid-1980s it was a relief that nothing too traumatic was occurring. Of course, once the prospect of a major trophy was on the horizon, and the prospect of relegation was not really a consideration, the club could focus on the cup.

That being said, this was a game that Borussia were not expected to win. The Black & Yellows had colourful fans who were relishing their literal and metaphorical day in the sun, but against the pedigree of that Werder side it was not expected to be enough. Of course, that didn't prevent the understandable optimism and sense of hope that comes when any underdog makes it to a cup final. Hesse was pessimistic but it was not a pessimism shared by all:

"I went to the game with my older brother. He's 12 years older than I am. So for him Borussia Dortmund were a club that used to be really big and had sort of fallen on hard times and was now coming back. For me, I didn't have that background. Of course I knew about the championships and the European Cup win in 1966, but for me Dortmund had always been a club that tried to hang in there in the Bundesliga. The first thing that I think of the 1980s is a half-empty south stand, a steady drizzle and losing 1-0 to Waldhof Mannheim. (I don't know if this game ever happened but you get what I mean). And so ,when we went to the game, I just went there because it was a cup final and because my team was in it. And it wasn't until I actually was in Berlin and saw all the other Dortmund fans that I realised that some people actually thought that we could win this. It was very strange."

For the record, Dortmund did indeed lose 1-0 to Waldhof Mannheim in the 1980s. Twice, in fact – both in the 1987/88 season. Former Dortmund striker Bernd Klotz scored for Mannheim in both games. BVB also lost to the same opponents 4-1 in 1983, as mentioned in the previous chapter.

The Borussia Dortmund team sent out by coach Horst Köppel for the final was: Teddy de Beer (in goal), Thomas Kroth, Günter Kutowski, Thomas Helmer, Murdo MacLeod, Günter Breitzke, Michael Zorc, Andreas Möller, Michael Rummenigge, Nobby Dickel and Frank Mill. For some, this game would represent a pinnacle of their career. Others would enjoy greater success in black and yellow. However, for one player, this match would enshrine his name among the greats of Borussia Dortmund.

Norbert Dickel's career was already over before the DFB-Pokal Final and he probably knew it. The injury to his knee that had kept him out of so many games in the previous season was not going to get better. By his own admission he was, "… not fit but operational." He knew that he would have to retire soon and played in this final as though it were his last. "Even if I had not played, I think the course of the injury would have been exactly the same," he told *11Freunde*. "The knee was still in the bucket anyway," he said to *Westdeutsche Zeitung*. That being said, Köppel had originally planned on leaving their most instinctive goal scorer out of his starting eleven altogether.

"There were violent discussions around Norbert Dickel," said Andreas Möller, years after the game, to *Ruhrnachrichten*. "Köppel had a more defensive line-up in his head, then Nobby bursts into the team meeting and says, 'I will play!' He made everything possible, despite his broken knee, and sacrificed his health. That is why he completely deserved to be the hero of Berlin."

Berlin can be glorious in May. The sun is strong and it was under its gaze that the game kicked off. After 15 minutes it looked as though all the passion, fervour and inflatables were for naught. Thomas Schaaf played a through ball into the path of Riedle, who slotted the ball past De Beer at his far post with a first-time daisy-cutter.

"When the Bremen team shot the 1-0," recalled Dickel, "We thought, 'Oh shit!'" However, Nobby's moment of destiny was to follow seven minutes later. Mill picked up the ball on the left flank. After a short burst of pace he sent in an arching low cross that the Werder centre half could not cut out. There to meet the cross was Dickel, who didn't need a second touch. He rifled the ball past Oliver Reck and wheeled away in blissful celebration. "When we got the equaliser and went into the break with a 1-1 draw, we said, 'What's the matter? Now it's 45 minutes, and it's all right, now we can attack.' Maybe we just had more courage to hold on to it, and in the head the blockade was gone, that Bremen is the overpowering opponent. Suddenly we knew again that we could also play football. And that has finally turned out to be true."

After weathering the early storm Frankie Mill put Dortmund 2-1 up. Michael Zorc hooked in a cross for Mill to head home. The decisive goal was scored by Dickel. Dortmund cleared the ball from a Werder attack and Mill charged through the middle past the out of position Bremen defenders. His shot was saved by Reck but Mill was able to salvage the ball and recycled the attack. His assist was a lobbed pass that looped up and down to the oncoming Dickel, who hit it on the volley from the left just inside the box. Dickel, arms aloft, was mobbed by his team-mates.

Günter Breitzke made way for Michael Lusch after 72 minutes. Dickel followed Breitzke to the bench shortly thereafter. They both watched substitute Lusch pick up a long ball that was sent up the field by Thomas Helmer. The Werder players were by now absent, helping out up front, seeking a way back into the game. Lusch, on his own, picked his spot and chose Oliver Reck's far post. The score was 4-1 and Borussia Dortmund's long wait for silverware was over.

The victory was greeted with joy in Berlin and pandemonium back home in Dortmund. Who knows how many of the fans that greeted the team upon their return from Berlin foresaw that this trophy was to be the first of many throughout the following decade? Zorc, though, reflected on the Borussia Dortmund website that the DFB-Pokal win was, "like a sporting resurrection. It has returned to the whole club a self-confidence, which, with a little time lag, ultimately led to the German championships in the 90s."

Interestingly, Uli Hesse saw it a little differently: "I think the legacy of that cup final has more to do with the fans than the team, if you know what I mean. It just changed the atmosphere and you suddenly had this euphoria around the club and they carried on this party atmosphere in the regular league season. For the next couple of years the atmosphere was just amazing at the ground and it was not necessarily because the team was so good. That became the thing to do – to go to a football game and party."

There are echoes of this sentiment in something that Möller said, as reported by *Ruhr Nachrichten*: "I am thinking of the sea of inflatable bananas in the Olympiastadion, over 30,000 black-yellow BVB fans around the track, who carried us on a wave. There is, in my opinion, a new fan culture emerging."

For Dickel, the 1989 DFB-Pokal win was to be his defining moment in a short career blighted by injury: he retired the following season. His personal legacy lives on in the trophy cabinet and through the loudspeakers at the Westfalen, where he remains the stadium announcer. "But it was also very special for some of them to get a title after 24 years," he said. "There are many people who have been there and have absolutely positive memories. Thank God, they forgot all my bad games."

1993

Glorious Failure
Hitzfeld arrives and the good times are almost here

It has been unfairly and inaccurately reported that Horst Köppel oversaw the longest run of defeats in the history of Borussia Dortmund. "That was in the *Bild* newspaper and that's not true," he told *Scwarzgelb.de* in 2001. The story goes that Dortmund suffered 14 straight defeats. "If you look," said Köppel, "we lost only 10 games in the whole season. So you cannot lose 14 games in a row."

The run in fact refers to 14 games without a win in the 1990/91 season. Eight of those were actually draws, all of them score draws at that. It was, however, a traumatic spell which many fans could not explain. "The opponent's goal often has to be five times bigger," claimed a local Bratwurst salesman in *Kicker* magazine. The run lasted 167 days and, at times, defied explanation. It turned a team confident of challenging for the Bundesliga title into potential relegation candidates. It also accounted for the end of the first coach to bring silverware to Borussia in over two decades.

In modern day football it is likely that having an 11-1 defeat on your CV would permanently damage your reputation. However, the Arminia Bielefeld coach that oversaw (if that's the right word) his team's thrashing to Dortmund back in 1983 survived the experience and indeed prospered. That coach was Horst Köppel. Born in Stuttgart, Köppel enjoyed a distinguished career as a striker for his hometown team, VfB Stuttgart, and after that at Borussia Mönchengladbach. He also had a modest career as a German senior international and was on the international scene when West Germany won the European Championships in 1972, although he did not feature in the title win.

After a brief stint in Vancouver playing for the Whitecaps in NASL in 1976 and 1977, Köppel returned to Germany and FC Viersen, an amateur club from the Lower Rhine. His career as a coach began there and, in 1981, Köppel made the short trip to Cologne to join the legendary Dutch manager Rinus Michels at the Müngersdorf Stadium. His first head coach job was at Bielefeld in 1982. Despite that thrashing at the Westfalen his team finished the season in mid-table. Köppel left Bielefeld to become an assistant coach once again, this time for the West German national team. Franz Beckenbauer was given the job as head coach but did not have a licence. Köppel was brought in as nominal coach but was in fact assistant to the former Bayern Munich player.

Köppel returned to club football with Bayer Uerdingen in 1987 but did not stay long – just 18 league matches and two cup ties – before departing in December. The following summer he was announced as the new Borussia Dortmund coach. At the end of the 1990/91 Hinrunde, BVB were in sixth place in the Bundesliga. They rounded the year off with a 2-0 win against St. Pauli and were only 4 points behind table toppers Werder Bremen. Köppel wished his players a Merry Christmas and looked forward to a new year with the prospect, albeit an optimistic one, of another trophy for the cabinet. He ended the season out of the job.

The winless run began on the first day back. The Winterpause had been lengthy and the season did not start until 23rd February. Michael Zorc described it as a "cruel day" as the Borussia players returned to Dortmund from Stuttgart after a 7-0 defeat. They were 4-0 down before the half-hour mark and it got worse in the second half. The first home game was against Karlsruhe, a match that Dortmund would reasonably expect to win. They found themselves 2-0 down within the first quarter of an hour of the game. Michael Rummenigge scored twice to rescue a point.

After that came a succession of draws, beginning against Kaiserslautern, who would go on to be champions, and at home to Düsseldorf. BVB looked to have broken the run at Bochum but conceded a last-minute equaliser and had to settle for yet another single point. Then came the defeats: 2-1 at Mönchengladbach and again at Cologne, 4-0 at HSV, and 3-0 at home to Eintracht Frankfurt. Points were salvaged against Wattenscheid and Hertha but, by the time Christian Ziege had scored an 87th minute winner for Bayern to win 3-2 at the Westfalen, the Dortmund fans were at their wits' end, especially in view of the fact that their team had taken the lead twice in the match. According to *Schwarzgelb.de* club manager Michael Meier, in a desperate attempt to alter their fortunes, extended his lent period until Dortmund won a game. That year he'd forsaken alcohol, a decision he came to rue with each passing game without a win as he was unable to drown his sorrows.

Relief finally came in the third to last game of the season, at home to a Bayer Uerdingen side that had a young Stéphane Chapuisat up front. The streak had not only proved dispiriting for the fans but had left the club in twelfth place. Avoiding relegation was still well within their grasp but after such a horrible run it was difficult to know from where the next win was coming from. Also, Dortmund's goal difference of -16 was among the worst in the Bundesliga. After having bitten their nails down to the quick, the only goal of the game came in the 85th minute from none other than Jürgen Wegmann. The Cobra had returned to Borussia from Bayern in the summer and only contributed six goals all season, none more valuable than this one.

After that Dortmund were safe from the drop and the seal was broken. The season ended with another two wins, 2-1 against Leverkusen and a 5-2 home thumping of a compliant St Pauli. It was too late for Köppel, however. Shortly after the victory against Uerdingen, the club announced that the coach for the following season would be Ottmar Hitzfeld. In Switzerland they called him 'St Gottmar'. Elsewhere he was 'The General'. Hitzfeld is rightly regarded as one of the greatest managers of all time. When he retired from coaching in 2014 he had 24 trophies to his credit, earned as coach of Grasshoppers in Zürich, Bayern in Munich and, of course, Borussia in Dortmund.

Hitzfeld was born in 1948 in the city of Lörrach in south Germany, very close to the borders with France and Switzerland. His father was a dentist and a football fan. Ottmar's first name was given in homage to the Kaiserslautern striker and 1954 World Cup winner Ottmar Walter, brother of Fritz Walter. The young Hitzfeld proved to be a decent player and goalscorer and played for his local club, FV Lörrach. He made the short trip across the border to Switzerland to begin his senior career at FC Basel in 1971. The Swiss league was not fully professional and Hitzfeld retained his amateur status. As such, he was able to compete in the West Germany 1972 Olympic football tournament, in which he scored five goals in five appearances.

Football, then as now, was a perilous and insecure way to make a living and, while at Basel, Hitzfeld went to college. He finished with a qualification in mathematics teaching and football coaching. In fact, the young Hitzfeld was set to become a teacher but grew so frustrated with the entrance exam process that he decided to become a footballer instead. Despite this loss to the teaching profession he would take his academic skills and apply them to his coaching. Hitzfeld was said to apply his mathematical knowledge to his tactical approach in football management.

German football journalist Raphael Honigstein once characterised Hitzfeld as a tactical pragmatist, a coach who adapts his tactics according to the strengths and weaknesses of his players. Hitzfeld was never a tactical ideologue or a subscriber to a particular school of thought. What was consistent in his approach was the need for tactical discipline, something that he enforced vigorously on the training ground. "I'm the boss - and an authoritarian one," he once said. "If you want to have a winning attitude you have to be ready to win every match – even in training."

It is fair to say that Hitzfeld the player was not quite of the same calibre as Hitzfeld the coach, but he did have his moments. He only scored five goals in his short 1. Bundesliga career but he does have two Swiss championships and a Swiss Cup to his name from his four years in Basel. In 1975 Hitzfeld moved to VfB Stuttgart. The Swabian club had been relegated the season before and were looking for a goalscorer to get them back into the top flight. VfB did not go straight back up at the first time of asking but that was not down to Hitzfeld. He scored 11 goals in 21 games during his first season and Stuttgart finished in eleventh place. In his second season Hitzfeld played 13 more games and his goal tally increased accordingly. Stuttgart scored an impressive 100 goals in the 1976/77 season. Unsurprisingly the team finished top of the table. Hitzfeld weighed in with 22 goals in 34 matches. Six of them were in one game against Jahn Regensburg on the penultimate week of the season. Hitzfeld remained at Stuttgart for another, more modest, season – his only one as a player in the top flight – before returning to Switzerland in 1978.

After scoring 35 goals for Lugano and 30 for Lucerne, he turned to coaching. His first job was as a player-coach and then full time manager at SC Zug. The president of the club was self-made millionaire

Werner Hoffstetter. The construction magnate built his empire off the back of hard work and long hours, values that he believed should be transferred to any profession, including football. Hitzfeld disagreed and the two regularly clashed. The coach banned his boss from entering the players' dressing room on matchdays. On one occasion, after a last gasp defeat to Winterthur, Hoffstetter was so incensed that he tried to turn the shower temperatures up to the hottest setting while the players were cleaning up. Just before the press conference there was a physical altercation between the two. Hitzfeld claims he was grabbed by the throat. Hoffstetter recalls that he, "just grabbed him with both hands and shook him up."

Hitzfeld was in post at Zug for one year before being offered a new position at FC Aarau. In his four years there he won the first of what would be a large number of trophies, the Swiss Cup in 1985. In 1988 the Grasshoppers club from Zürich recruited Hitzfeld as their head coach. Four more trophies were to follow: two Swiss Cups and two Swiss championships. Grasshoppers won the double in 1990. Yet Hitzfeld's appointment at Borussia Dortmund raised a few eyebrows. It had been suggested that Otto Rehhagel would return but an arrangement could not be made to bring the more experienced coach back to the Westfalen. In Hitzfeld, they saw the mathematician "gentleman" coach who eschewed the traditional sportswear usually associated with Bundesliga trainers. Here was an unknown coach with experience unsuited to the rigours of the Bundesliga and the potentially revived ambitions of Borussia. These concerns were to be allayed very quickly. After one season at the helm, Michael Rummenigge proclaimed that, "He's the best coach I've ever had... He works absolutely professionally... He remains calm and matter-of-fact, even when we play very badly. He then confidently explains what to do and he is right."

With Hitzfeld in place, Borussia's jigsaw was complete and they were about to embark upon another golden age. There was just one more false start to go through before they could get out the silver polish.

The 1991/92 season was huge for Dortmund. The day after the final game at Duisburg a reported 30,000 fans flooded the streets to welcome the Borussia players home, congratulate them, and thank them for a fantastic campaign. You would think that such a reception is worthy of a championship or a cup win. In fact, Dortmund finished the season with no further additions to the trophy cabinet. In spite of this the Dortmund public came in their droves. It is not that surprising for a German football club to celebrate such a transformation while falling short of the ultimate prize of a Bundesliga championship; in a landscape dominated by Bayern Munich, many great German football stories are told from beneath the shadow cast by the Bavarians' mighty tree.

However, the second season of the new decade was not one dominated by Bayern – in fact, no single team emerged at the front of the pack and the Bundesliga title was won by a hair's breadth on the last day of the season. The race for the title was between three clubs, one of which was, totally unexpectedly, Borussia Dortmund. They ultimately had to settle for a podium finish but the significance of the season was greater than the final league position. It also saw the arrival of a player who would become a bona fide Borussia legend.

With Bayer Uerdingen suffering relegation the year before they were happy to sell the promising young 22-year-old striker Stéphane Chapuisat to Borussia Dortmund. Chapuisat was born in Lausanne, Switzerland. He is the son of Pierre-Albert Chapuisat, a former Swiss international who, like Stéphane, started his career at FC Lausanne. 'Chappi', as he became known, initially trained as a clerk before turning professional as a footballer. "In the eighties, professional football was still different and more difficult in Switzerland," he told *11Freunde* in 2013. "So I first finished an apprenticeship as a commercial clerk in a trust office and then came the football."

Between 1987 and 1990 Chappi played up front in the blue and white of Lausanne. He scored 36 goals in 104 games and caught the attention of the scouts at Uerdingen, moving in the following January. Sadly, Chapuisat's opportunities were limited at Uerdingen due to an injury in the following pre-season. He made just 10 appearances in the entire campaign, but one of those games was against Dortmund and one of his four goals came in a 2-2 draw against Bayern Munich.

The approach came from Dortmund and the deal was sealed when BVB confirmed Hitzfeld as coach. With his compatriot in post, Chapuisat had no hesitation in signing on the dotted line for Dortmund. Chappi and Hitzfeld would go on to enjoy a great friendship: "Sometimes you can not explain the connection between two people down to the last detail. We have experienced a lot of beautiful things together… the chemistry was right between us. Maybe because we're both from Switzerland. When we met in the early 1990s, we were both in the right place at the right time."

BVB started the season at Karlsruhe, in their below-capacity Wildparkstadion. The Swabian club was in the process of building a 6,400-capacity main stand. Despite the empty side of the stadium there was no shortage of atmosphere in what was an action-packed 2-2 draw. The home side included a young Oliver Kahn in goal and Mehmet Scholl scored the second goal, a smart lob over Dortmund goalkeeper Teddy de Beer, who had raced off his line. Substitute Gunter Breitzke came off the bench to grab a late equaliser for the visitors. Chapuisat scored the first goal for BVB.

Dortmund waited one more game for their first win of the season and it was their first match at the Westfalen, a 2-1 win against Werder Bremen. Frankie Mill took charge with a brace. Klaus Allofs made the final ten minutes more interesting but the Black and Yellows closed the game out. Then came a set-back in the unlikely shape of Hansa Rostock, though it wasn't much of a shock when you consider that Rostock's previous match had been a 2-1 win at Bayern Munich. Stefan Böger was nearly kissing the ground he had stooped so low to head the ball into the back of the net for the first goal. Czechoslovakian striker Roman Sedláček took a nice chance by collecting the ball from a poor defensive header to score Rostock's second and his first of two on the day. It just wasn't Dortmund's afternoon as the post denied them and they gave away two penalties. They could only muster one Chapuisat goal against Rostock's five. The Hanseatic club from the old GDR sat proudly atop the fledgling Bundesliga table and Dortmund were sent home on the end of a humping.

Borussia bounced back with a 2-0 win at Bielefeld in the DFB-Pokal and then again the following weekend at the Westfalen, with a tidy 3-1 win against Fortuna Düsseldorf, who were coached by the former Austrian national team coach Josef Hickersberger. This game was memorable for a sweet long-range effort by Knut Reinhardt who had signed for Dortmund from Bayer Leverkusen the previous summer, and for a delicate chip from Flemming Povlsen to make it 3-1. Thomas Helmer almost eclipsed them both with a glorious strike from the right side which clattered off the crossbar. Sadly, he later left the field with an injury and would be unable to play for weeks. He missed the 5-2 defeat at Schalke the next weekend, about which the less said the better, frankly.

The Dortmund players worked out their issues on a ten-man Dynamo Dresden team but a tough and physical opponent gave them a strong test. The first of BVB's four goals did not come until the 66th minute, Chapuisat once again on the mark; he scored twice in this 4-0 win. A 0-0 draw with Bochum followed and, after that, a 3-1 win against 1. FC Köln with Povlsen scoring the third goal against his former club. However, those results were separated by a 3-2 defeat at home to second division Hannover 96 in the DFB-Pokal.

After an injury, Thomas Helmer returned to the starting line-up for the game against reigning Bundesliga champions Kaiserslautern, but his presence did not help matters at the Betzenbergstadion. Jürgen Degen scored three goals for the Red Devils and Dortmund were thrashed 4-0. Degen's hat trick made up three of the five goals he scored in his 19-game career at Kaiserslautern. The 3-0 loss at Eintracht Frankfurt was especially painful as some of the players were unhappy with the referee. Moreover, the third goal was scored by Andreas Möller, once of the Dortmund Parish, who elected not to celebrate. The travelling Dortmund fans in the stadium did witness an attempt to win a penalty by Möller that was characteristic of the man. This proved to be the nadir of the season for Dortmund, however. A spirited 3-2 win against FC Nürnberg at the Westfalen started the unbeaten run. The following week they travelled to Bayern Munich and won 3-0.

It is fair to say that this was not a vintage Bayern team. Despite finishing second in the table the previous season they were to go on to finish tenth, only five points from relegation. The manager was Søren Lerby, a legend as a player for Ajax, PSV Eindhoven and Bayern, but as a coach he wasn't up to it. The home loss to Dortmund on a grey Saturday afternoon in October, in front of 27,000 spectators, was his first in a short spell as coach of the Bavarians. The match was spicy but the home team's heart was not in it. Michael Rummenigge opened the scoring after a defensive mistake and Flemming Povlsen slotted home the second on the break at the start of the second half. The final indignity came when Bayern goalkeeper Gerald Hillringhaus rushed out of his area to clear a through ball, only for it to cannon off substitute Markus Münch, going back the way it came and bypassing the hapless Hillringhaus en route to the net. As own goals go, it was a screamer from Münch. With that, a manager's career ended. Lerby did not coach another team, perhaps deciding that football management was not for everyone.

A 3-1 win against Stuttgarter Kickers yielded their last win before a series of draws; 0-0 against Stuttgart, 1-1 against Mönchengladbach and a disappointing 1-1 with lowly Wattenscheid followed. However, BVB hit the mid-point of the season on a high after two wins against Bayer Leverkusen and MSV Duisburg. Dortmund had risen to third in the table, behind Stuttgart and Eintracht Frankfurt, with the second half of fixtures still to play. Two games later they entered the Winterpause after 1-0 wins against Karlsruhe and Werder, finally saying farewell to 1991 with a 4-1 win against Rostock. This was a heart-warming return of the favour from earlier in the season against a Rostock team that had declined sharply and would not finish the season with their coach Uwe Reinders. Michael Rummenigge scored a brace in that match. A few weeks later he extended his contract until 1994. Additionally, Michael Zorc extended to 1995. The latter's signature was of no great surprise given the fact that Zorc had been at the club man and boy, not to mention the fact that he was still coming back from injury. But Rummenigge was a top player in demand. He committed to black and yellow because he felt the club could fulfil his ambitions. "I have not decided against Bayern, but for Dortmund," he said after signing the new deal.

The unbeaten streak continued but points were dropped. It is here, in the early stages, that the title was probably lost. A 2-0 Revierderby win was surrounded by draws with beatable opponents: 1-1 at Fortuna Dusseldorf, 0-0 at Dynamo Dresden, 1-1 at home in the mini-Revierderby against VfL Bochum. Six valuable points lost, with title rivals Eintracht Frankfurt and VfL Stuttgart to still play.

Once again Andreas Möller lined up for Eintracht Frankfurt against his old club. Relishing his second spell at his boyhood club, Möller was part of a powerful team who were worthy title contenders. Although obviously not known at the time, this Frankfurt side was one of the great nearly teams of the Bundesliga. Up front were the two strikers, Jørn Andersen and Tony Yeboah. Andersen was a powerful yet nimble Norwegian who made the best out of even the most unlikely pass.

Yeboah needs little introduction to anyone who followed English football in the 1990s. His 47-game sojourn in the Premier League for Leeds United had the local net-makers in tears, such was the power of his shot. Supporting the two frontline strikers was Axel Kruse, who would go on to kick the extra points for the Berlin Thunder gridiron team and became a broadcaster for the German sports network *Sport1*. Adopting coach Dragoslav Stepanović's ultra-progressive pressing style, dubbed "Football 2000", this turned out to be a very much a win or bust season for his squad. However, you can read more about that when someone writes an English language history of Eintracht Frankfurt.

The match finished 2-2, which was good news for Stuttgart, the other party in this title race. As impolitic as it might be to say it in a book about Dortmund, this Stuttgart side was as worthy a title-winning side as you'll find in any season. The squad boasted some fine professionals: Matthias Sammer who, at 24, was approaching his imperial phase; Maurizio Gaudino, whose legacy is tarnished somewhat by being rugby tackled by notorious English politician and eventual Prime Minister, Boris Johnson, in a charity soccer match; Italia '90 winner Guido Buchwald; Michael Frontzeck, who carved out a decent career as a head coach despite no one ever being entirely sure why; Uwe Schneider; and the experienced Serbian Slobodan Dubajić. In goal was former Dortmund regular, Eike Immel, and in Fritz Walter they had the eventual top scorer for the season. On the bench was head coach Christoph Daum, who was about to win his first title.

No one at Stuttgart was in any doubt as to the significance of the match at home to Borussia; you could tell by the drawn and pallor faces of manager Dieter Hoeness and coach Daum during the pre-match press conference. Match tickets were doing a roaring trade on the black market. There wasn't a spare seat or piece of terraced concrete available in the Neckarstadion. The Dortmund fans in attendance were raucous with their chanting, flags and pyrotechnics. Their passion was rewarded after 14 minutes when Povlsen rifled home a low shot from outside the area. It was a Dortmund player who scored the second, albeit at the wrong end. Thomas Helmer scored an own goal with an emphatic free header after 32 minutes. Povlsen thought he'd retaken the lead only for his goal to be disallowed. Then Fritz Walter struck. He met a through ball after a lovely diagonal run and gently lifted the ball over the onrushing Stefan Klos.

Not unexpectedly Dortmund came racing out of the blocks in the second half, missing some chances and making Eike Immel work to repel others. However, with national team coach Berti Vogts watching from the stands, it was Walter who extended the lead for the home side after 71 minutes. In fact, it was the knee of Walter that met Sammer's cross at close range. Irrespective of body part, Walter had done well to glide through the defence seemingly unnoticed to put the game beyond Dortmund's reach. Or so it seemed. 13 minutes later Helmer scored for the right team by placing his glorious mullet on the end of a Michael Zorc free kick. Helmer nearly scored again, with a header this time, but was denied at close range by Immel. Gaudino broke the tension in the 90th minute by taking the ball from inside his own half and barging past a now fragmented Dortmund back line to slot the ball past Klos. Pandemonium ensued on the bench as photographers swarmed around Hoeness and Daum. Their relief was almost tangible. The title race was by no means over but they, Stuttgart, were still in it. Frankfurt were top of the Bundesliga on 45 points and with only goal difference separating themselves from Stuttgart and Borussia Dortmund.

What Dortmund desperately needed next was to not drop points. However, and perhaps predictably, that's exactly what they did in the following game at home to Mönchengladbach. They needed a goal from Michael Zorc in the 89th minute to salvage even a point from a 2-2 draw. Nevertheless, a 1-0 win at Wattenscheid and a 3-1 victory over Leverkusen at the Westfalen took them into the final game of the season with a chance of winning the title.

After the penultimate round of fixtures Frankfurt were top of the Bundesliga table with Stuttgart second and Dortmund third. Crucially, all three teams were level on 50 points. Eintracht really should have clinched the title on that penultimate round by beating a Werder Bremen team that was still drunk from celebrating their UEFA Cup Winners' Cup final win against Monaco only three days earlier. Former Werder player Uli Borowka stated that he and his team-mates still had some alcohol in their blood during the game after the team had been out celebrating for three days straight. But somehow Die Adler contrived a draw and it was a result they were to rue. Their final game was at relegated Hansa Rostock. Despite dominating the game they could not find a winner. In fact, Eintracht's Ralf Weber had to be restrained from confronting the referee after the official did not give what, in Weber's mind, was a clear penalty. With the score at 1-1, Rostock's Stefan Böger scored a winner in the 89th minute. At the final whistle an outraged Weber ran amok and, in his fury, kicked a TV camera.

Eintracht had snatched defeat from the jaws of victory and the triumph went to Stuttgart, who beat Bayer Leverkusen 2-1 at the Ulrich Haberland Stadion (now known as the BayArena) to clinch the title. Dortmund matched the Stuttgart result at MSV Duisburg but not their goal difference. Stuttgart's winner came late in the game so for a while Dortmund were top of the league. Sadly for Dortmund and Eintracht, Guido Buchwald popped up to score the winner four minutes before the end of that game.

Dortmund finished a more than creditable second. Uli Hesse was in the stadium at Duisberg for the game. "The coach and the players were really downtrodden," he told me. "They hadn't expected to win the league but when you're top of the league with only four minutes left in the season that's pretty tough to lose." However, the reaction from the fans in the stadium was almost a polar opposite, as Hesse explained. "But the fans were totally enthusiastic. There was a pitch invasion and they carried the players around on their shoulders."

"Losing that title," said Hesse, "proved to be a blessing in disguise because Dortmund qualified for the UEFA Cup." To modern eyes that statement may seem peculiar. After all, UEFA's second tier competition is often regarded as a consolation for ambitious clubs and is portrayed – certainly in the English language media – as an unwelcome distraction. However, this is not universally the case and in the early 1990s the competition enjoyed more prestige because of the allocation of TV rights in Germany at the time. "It was the first season of the Champions League," said Hesse, "and the system in Germany was that all the money from the television stations went into a pool and it was distributed round by round amongst the teams that were still in the competition."

The following season ushered in the Champions League. Bundesliga champions Stuttgart were knocked out at the qualification stage by Leeds United after having had to play a controversial third match in the Camp Nou in Barcelona. This was because Stuttgart coach Christoph

Daum fielded an ineligible fourth foreign player in the second leg of the play-off. VfB won the tie but in contravention of the rules, hence the third game which they subsequently lost. "So Stuttgart go out," continues Hesse, "and all the other German clubs go out as well and suddenly Dortmund have this huge amount of money because they got to the UEFA Cup Final. And that's where it really started."

Dortmund's participation in the UEFA Cup proved to be quite the money-spinner and set the club up financially to go on to sign the players they needed to achieve real success, to win actual trophies. But first, it was necessary to do a bit more losing…

"There were some processes inside a team that act like a virus," Michael Schulz told Nobby Dickel during an interview for *BVB World* in December 2017. The context of that remark was the poor performance of the Borussia team at the time under Peter Bosz. Schulz was speaking ahead of the home game against his hometown club, Werder Bremen. That game was to be Bozs's last after BVB lost 2-1 against the struggling northerners. However, Schulz was not just talking about the 2017 team. He was drawing upon his experience of the 1990/91 season. He said it was a miserable campaign in which the team dropped into the relegation zone, "…and you don't know why."

"I think it was in the year we played well in the UEFA Cup but had a horrible series here…you just don't get it out of your mind and it was not the coach's fault. Ottmar Hitzfeld was our coach back then, it couldn't have been his fault."

It's possible that Schulz was conflating the 1992/93 season under Hitzfeld with the 1990/91 season in which Horst Köppel was the coach. Domestically, Dortmund had a slow start to the former but remained a top six side from Matchday 6 onwards. In 1990/91, they flirted with relegation in Köppel's final season and their UEFA Cup journey ended with defeat to Anderlecht before Christmas. However, they very nearly emulated the heroes of 1966 by reaching the final of the UEFA Cup in 1993.

Schulz joined BVB in the summer following the 1989 cup win and slotted into the Dortmund team straight away as a defender or defensive midfielder. Some reports of his playing style suggest a penchant for a cross. His real signature, however, was his tackling. He was, it's fair to say, a determined challenger for the ball and a proponent of football's darker arts. In his 166 competitive games for Borussia, Schulz received an impressive 30 yellow cards (but, as he points out only three reds). There is some glorious footage of Schulz making mischief in a defensive wall, grabbing the buttock of an opposition player. "Sometimes you need to do forbidden things," as he once said

Schulz was a youth player at TuS Nettlingen, TuS Sulingen and TuS Syke. His senior career began at Oldenburg. In 1987, at the age of 26, he made the move from the Oberliga Nord to the Bundesliga and 1. FC Kaiserslautern. After just over half a century with the Red Devils he moved to the Ruhr. He would move on at the end of the 1993/94 season to Werder Bremen but by his own admission, he was a card-carrying Borussen. "I have a black and yellow heart. Even if the time in Bremen was very nice," he told *Der Western* in 2017. "The five years in Dortmund have been the best in my career. The club just lives, the city is football crazy, the people are just awesome – it was all a lot of fun."

While it may have been fun it was fruitless, in terms of silverware at least, with one moderately notable exception. Dortmund were definitely on their way back as a force in German football and Schulz was very much a part of that journey, but he would fall short by a season in terms of meaningful trophies. This was, it turns out, characteristic of his career. In his eventful time at Dortmund he saw the team gradually shift from plucky cup winners to title challengers, albeit punctuated by the terrible slump that did for Horst Köppel and paved the way for Hitzfeld. Schulz's first competitive appearance was in July 1989 in the German Supercup against league champions FC Bayern Munich.

The DFB/DFL Supercup had only been founded two years earlier. As you would expect it acted as a showpiece curtain-raiser to each football season and was played between the previous season's Bundesliga champions and the DFB-Pokal winners. In modern times the Supercup is held at the home stadium of one of the competing teams but at the time was held at a neutral venue and in 1989 the match took place at Michael Schulz's former home ground, the Fritz Walter Stadion, home of 1. FC Kaiserslautern. Making his second debut for Dortmund was Jürgen Wegmann, who had been transferred back to BVB from their opponents, Bayern Munich. Sadly, the game did not generate much interest and the stadium was far from full, which was a shame because Dortmund emerged victorious after a cracking 4-3 win. Andreas Möller scored the winner in the 88th minute. It was an encouraging start to the season and a great way for Schulz to start his career at Dortmund.

Schulz scored seven goals for Borussia Dortmund. The most memorable strikes were an equaliser against Schalke in a 5-2 Revierderby loss for Borussia in 1991 and a long-range shot against AS Roma in the quarter-final second leg of the 1992/93 UEFA Cup. Dortmund were a Siniša Mihajlović goal down from the first leg in the Olympic Stadium in Rome. Schulz equalised the tie and laid the foundation for a dramatic 2-1 aggregate win over Vujadin Boškov's talented but underachieving side.

Domestically the 1992/93 season was a decent one for Dortmund. They finished fourth without ever challenging for the Bundesliga title, an honour that went to Werder Bremen. In the cup BVB reached the quarter-final, beating Bayern on penalties on the way to a 2-0 loss to Werder Bremen. Their top goalscorer was Stéphane Chapuisat on 15, with Michael Zorc not far behind on 10 along with new signing Matthias Sammer, of whom there will be more later.

However, the real excitement for Borussia that season was in their European exertions in the UEFA Cup. By the time the quarter-finals came around Dortmund were the last German team standing. This meant that should BVB play all six possible remaining games in the UEFA Cup, all the money for appearing on domestic German television would be due to them. This cannot be overstated because German football rights were subject to great interest from private broadcasters anxious to cash in on the high ratings that the Bundesliga and other football generated. The increased competition in the market was such that there was considerable money being spent on TV rights, the kind of money that could and would strengthen their squad and allow the Borussens the resources to make a concerted challenge for the title.

The price war among German broadcasters played right into Borussia Dortmund's hands. The coffers were swelled further by the sale of Thomas Helmer – eventually – to Bayern Munich in the previous summer. In April of 1993, *Kicker* reported that Helmer had put in for a transfer. Later, Helmer would tell the same magazine that he had requested either a move to Bayern or to a club outside Germany. Initially Bayern had hoped to orchestrate a move for Helmer to Auxerre in order to facilitate a transfer from the French club at a substantially reduced price. Michael Meier was determined not to sell such a vital part of the team to a direct rival and, despite attempts to improve his terms, the dispute became public in the ensuing weeks, with both Meier and Helmer explaining their own positions. Essentially, under the terms of his contract, Thomas could move abroad but not to another German club. Amid much acrimony (which bled into the German national team's preparations for Euro '92) the deal was eventually done and Helmer became a Bayern player, with Dortmund DM 7.5 million the richer for it. Part of the money was used to pay for the signing of Australian international Ned Zelic from Eintracht Frankfurt, Stefan Reuter to replace Helmer from Juventus and, of course, a little later, Matthias Sammer.

Hitzfeld's team took full advantage of the opportunity presented by the windfall. His players faced the relatively straightforward challenge of the Maltese club Floriana before meeting considerably harder opposition in Glasgow Celtic (whom they beat 3-1 on aggregate), Real Zaragoza (4-3), Roma (2-1) and Auxerre of France before making it to the final and a meeting with the Italian superclub Juventus.

The semi-final was a nail-biter that ended in a 2-2 draw and had to be decided by penalties. Auxerre were and indeed still are a small club, but rose to prominence in the 1980s and 1990s thanks in large part to their coach, one Guy Roux. The first leg in April 1993 was a convincing 2-0 win at the Westfalen. Manchester City fans who were around in the 1990s may recall Steffen Karl's six appearances in 1994. Karl joined from Dortmund, where he played 87 games and scored just five goals, one of which was a sweet long-range strike in the 58th minute of this game. Zorc missed a penalty in the second half but made amends by scoring the second goal with a bullet header from a corner to give his team a two-goal advantage in the second leg.

Auxerre's Stade Abbe-Deschamps is a small and compact stadium and was jumping that night. German TV covered the game from a fanzone in Dortmund. Nobby Dickel, by now retired, was interviewed about his club's chances but he could barely speak, such was his nervousness. On a giant screen, both he and thousands of Dortmunders unable to make the trip to France watched in anticipation of a return to a European final for the first time since Glasgow in 1966. After seven minutes Corentin Martins put the home side ahead. Roared on by the crowd, Auxerre squared the tie after half an hour. Michael Schulz played a significant role in the second leg, although not in the way he would have wanted. He was beaten in the air by Frank Verlaat in the 26th minute for Auxerre's equaliser and, to add insult to injury, was booked in the 71st minute.

After a period of extra time which saw Dortmund go down to ten men when Günter Kutowski was sent off for a second yellow card, the tie went to penalties. Michael Schulz stepped up to take his and did not disappoint. Michael Zorc was on the mark too. In fact, all the Borussia players lived up to the emerging cliché of Germans in penalty shoot-outs. No one missed. It was Auxerre's Stephane Mahe who shot straight at Borussia goalkeeper Stefan Klos to lose the tie. The tiny stadium went silent, save for a pocket of delirious Dortmunders screaming, cheering and igniting flares. Borussia were in another European final, the first of a number of great European clashes with the Old Lady of Serie A.

If this was the dawning of a new era for Borussia Dortmund then the same could be said of Juventus, to an extent. The mid- to late-eighties was the era of Diego Maradona at Napoli and Arrigo Sacchi's great AC Milan team, who were dominating the trophies and headlines. Between their title win in 1986 and 1993, the Turin club won just the Coppa Italia and UEFA Cup in 1990; I say "just" to illustrate the extraordinarily high standards that this club and its fans expect. This was to be the final season for their manager Giovanni Trapattoni in his second spell for the club. Marcello Lippi took over the following season and oversaw their ascension to the status of European and domestic giants once more. They would certainly meet Borussia Dortmund again as the clubs were on a similar trajectory.

Roberto Baggio, Dino Baggio, Gianluca Vialli and Antonio Conte would become household names, at least in households that follow a lot of football. But Júlio César, Jürgen Kohler and of course Andreas Möller would not be long for this team. In due course they would travel to (or, in Möller's case, back to) Germany and Borussia Dortmund.

Despite the first leg at the Westfalen starting in the best of circumstances with a sublime finish from Michael Rummenigge after two minutes, it all went south from there. Dino Baggio equalised after 26 minutes, with Roberto Baggio netting four minutes later and then again on 74 minutes, effectively killing the tie before the second leg. After that it was a party. The Dortmund fans that populated the small section of the Stadio delle Alpi for the second leg were happy to join in with the Mexican wave before kick off. During the game the fans distinguished themselves with noise and pyrotechnics. They watched their team lose 3-0, with two goals from Dino Baggio and one from their former player Möller, who had the good grace to celebrate his goal as befitted the occasion.

Borussia Dortmund had failed to win their first European trophy since 1966. However, while they lost in silverware they didn't miss out on coin. A cool DM 25 million was earned thanks to that UEFA Cup run and the generosity of the other Bundesliga teams that retired early. In the summer, more players would arrive and the next golden age would begin. Sadly, Michael Schulz was not to be a part of that melting pot of talent about to bloom. Schulz never won a proper trophy at Dortmund. In fact, he never won anything anywhere, arriving at a club just before or just after they had tasted genuine success. Schulz joined BVB from Kaiserslautern two seasons before they won an unlikely Bundesliga title in 1991. His departure from Dortmund was in the summer of 1995 so he missed Borussia's first Bundesliga title in 30 years the following season. Schulz's destination was Werder Bremen, who had won the Bundesliga as recently as 1993. Sadly, the Green and Whites would not win another league title until 2004, by which time Schulz had hung up his boots. "I always really managed to change the club at the exact wrong time," he told *11Freunde* in 2013. "If you like, I'm the Michael Ballack of my generation. At least as far as the missed titles are concerned."

For Schulz, a personal highlight of the 1993/94 season was scoring an 86th minute winner for Dortmund in a 2-1 win against his former club, Kaiserslautern. "I would have loved to stay there and for the fans I was certainly not the least popular player." This was certainly true if the frequent chants of "Scuuuuuuulz!" from the Südtribune were anything to go by. "But then began the time when BVB suddenly took a lot of money into their hands and all the Italian legionaries were brought into the Westfalenstadion. There was suddenly no room for me, at 32."

After he retired, Schulz pursued a career in journalism. His sharp tongue and penchant for an anecdote make him a popular choice as a pundit and columnist. Now he can be found in television studios, still with the shock of blond hair (albeit a little greyer than in his pomp) dispensing blistering takes with the gusto and sincerity which are key to being a good pundit. However, if you think all that time sat on sofas being interviewed has softened him up, think again. He recently and quite literally built his own house.

1994-95

The Italian Job
Bundesliga Glory, 1994/95

One night in the city of Dortmund a young man decided to spend the evening at a disco. The young man was from Brazil and was new to Germany. He had engaged the services of a translator rather than attempt to get by on his Italian and Brazilian Portuguese. When he tried to enter the disco he was prevented from doing so by the doorman. They stopped him because of the colour of his skin. He was one of the many black people that make up Brazil's massively diverse culture. So furious was he that he threatened to quit his job and leave Dortmund.

His name was Júlio César da Silva and he was a centre back-cum-libero, once of Juventus and now of Borussia Dortmund. The incident made the local news and was a matter of great scandal. Dortmund, like many cities in Europe, is fantastically diverse, with people of many backgrounds and shades of skin living and working there. Like other cities most people don't see this is an issue and get on with life. Also like other cities there is a small percentage of people who cannot and simply will not. Racists and racism exist in almost all aspects of civil and social life and it's naive to say any different. Black and Turkish men who have played for Dortmund have been racially abused by their own fans and it's likely that all but a handful of clubs have a similar history that they would sooner not reflect upon. Dortmund are not unique in this matter.

However, it is also a fact that like other clubs and institutions in our civil society, the majority are not racist and a great number, when sufficiently roused, can make a stand against racism. Once the news broke there was a picket of the disco that barred Júlio César. Messages of solidarity and support for him were issued by numerous fan groups in the Westfalenstadion. Decent people rallied and Júlio César stayed.

His decision was rewarded with the greatest successes a club footballer can achieve.

Júlio César had signed for Borussia Dortmund in the summer of 1994 from Juventus and was one of five Bianconeri to switch colours to Schwartzgelb. Already at the Westfalen was Stefan Reuter, who joined in 1992, and joining them was Andreas Möller, who returned to Borussia for his second stint. A year later another player from the Juventus team that beat Dortmund in the UEFA Cup final joined, in the not inconsiderable shape of Jürgen Kohler. In 1997 Paulo Sousa would also relocate to the Ruhr from Turin. A year earlier two more players had arrived from Italy. You already know about Matthias Sammer, but the BVB frontline was strengthened by Karl-Heinz Riedle's arrival from Lazio, completing Borussia's Italian Job.

The role of the *libero* is an important one in German football, not just in terms of raw tactics but in the culture of football tactics. The spare man was a feature in the German game for decades. Júlio César da Silva was technically not a libero but a centre back who played like one. A native of Sao Paulo, Júlio César started his career at Guarini before moving to Europe, where he signed for Brest in the French league in 1986. The following year he was transferred to Montpellier, where he won the Coupe de France.

It would be easy to look at the tall Brazilian and assume him to be a burly defender, short on guile and technique, but Júlio César was rangy and covered a lot of ground very quickly. His aerial ability, technique with the ball and goalscoring from set pieces added up to a decent list of reasons to love watching him play football. There was also flamboyance to his game and a sense that he did not take it too seriously. This was a misunderstanding. The number of trophies he collected in his career is evidence that Júlio César was an ambitious professional.

In 1990 he joined a Juventus team that was in the doldrums, relatively speaking. While his 91 appearances only yielded that UEFA Cup win, Júlio César's *joie de vivre* on the pitch made him a fan favourite and it was a loss to the Bianconeri faithful when he departed to the recently monied Borussia Dortmund. While Juve went onto great success in his absence, he did not miss out on silverware at his new club. Under Ottmar Hitzfeld Dortmund were assembling the best squad for the most money. In 1994, even Bayern Munich were not spending the same kind of money on transfers as BVB. Andreas Möller had left Germany to pursue success in Serie A with what was without question the strongest team in the league at the time. Once that star waned, Möller made the obvious choice to follow the trophies back to Germany and Dortmund. It paid off.

In some quarters Möller is unkindly regarded, largely because of his subsequent decision to leave Dortmund in 2000. Dietrich Schulze-Marmeling contends that he, "was not a leading player, not a doer, not a fighter." He quotes the German newspaper *Die Zeit*, which described Möller thus: "Only ten others have in more than a hundred years played more often in the national team than Andreas Möller, but Möller never became a German star. Measured by achievements he has become a star but not a hero to the masses." From where I sit on this island I find this an extraordinary position to take. As an Englishman haunted by those high profile defeats to Germany, Möller was respected and feared. Moreover, I'm of the view that had he elected to move to the Premier League, even towards the end of his career, after an initial period of pantomime villain boos and jeers he would have been adored. Perhaps some insight into why Möller is not celebrated comes from the man himself.

"For me the team's success was important. My personal appearance was never important. Success was more important," he told *Schwarzgelb.de* upon leaving for Schalke. "I wanted to finish my career maybe abroad, but Schalke gave me the opportunity once again to make a difference and to roll up my sleeves. Once again I wanted to show that I can lead a team, you can't have success without me. It's not a simple situation, most fans don't understand that but I was without a contract and accepted a new challenge."

You would think that someone who identified himself as a team player would win the hearts of many fans. However, 'the team' is not the same as 'the club' and I suspect that Möller was a player who was more excited by playing for teams than any particular football club.

Had Stefan Reuter stayed at Juventus for another season he could have won that UEFA Cup in 1993. Reuter moved to Juventus after a successful spell at Bayern Munich. Before that he played for a Nürnberg side that won promotion from the 2. Bundesliga. A rapid, industrious, hard-working flank player, Reuter could be regarded as a forgotten man or an unsung hero. His medal haul for club and country, and his continued career in first class football in Germany – at the time of writing he is the Sporting Director at Bundesliga club FC Augsburg – suggest otherwise. The Franconian-born utility player has five Bundesliga titles to his name along with a Champions League medal, and was a World Cup and European Championships winner in 1990 and 1996 respectively.

In Dortmund they awarded Karl-Heinz Riedle the moniker of 'Air Riedle'. As the nickname suggests, he liked a header. He was a goalscorer with the ability to arrive late in the box, that is to say he arrived too late for the opposition defenders. Riedle joined Dortmund in 1993 from Lazio. He began his career in Augsburg but was snapped up by Blau-Weiss Berlin in 1986 for the capital city club's one and only season in the 1. Bundesliga. The overmatched minnow from the Mariendorf district of Berlin only managed 36 goals in their solitary season in the top flight. Riedle scored 10 of them. That goal tally proved sufficient for Werder Bremen to sign him. The northerners were looking for a replacement for the Italy-bound Rudi Völler. Riedle scored 38 goals in green and white during a productive three years. There, he picked up a Bundesliga title in 1988 and, of course, a DFB-Pokal runner-up medal in 1989, as well as another in 1990. In 1988, Riedle made the first of 42 appearances for the German international side, for which he scored 16 goals. He was in the 1990 World Cup squad as back-up to Völler and Jürgen Klinsmann.

His time at Lazio was not as glorious, although there can be few complaints about his personal performance. 30 goals in 84 games is a decent enough haul, but when Borussia Dortmund were looking to strengthen their attack still further, Riedle was called upon for a transfer fee of DM 9.5 million. By comparison his goal per game ratio was not as good as at Lazio. However, the goals that he did score in the 112 games he played in black and yellow would shape the history of the club.

You would think that there would be an entire chapter of this book devoted to Matthias Sammer, given his achievements. A former striker for Dynamo Dresden and Stuttgart, Sammer was the focal point of Hitzfeld's plan for a championship-winning team and it paid off. Hitzfeld identified Sammer as better suited to a sweeper role, playing behind the defence. The results were spectacular. Sammer played through the middle of the team causing chaos wherever he went. Sammer won three Bundesliga titles and a Champions League as player and coach of Borussia Dortmund. By rights there should be statues and streets named after him. However, despite his great achievements Sammer, is not a celebrated figure.

These days there is a big ceremony and anticipation about winning a Ballon d'Or. We live in the age of Lionel Messi and Cristiano Ronaldo, who have in their own right become institutions with powerful corporate interests that demand pomp and circumstance behind this most prestigious individual award. In 1996 the recipient was Sammer, and he found out while shopping with his wife. He took a call from his agent who gave him the good news. His reaction was to continue shopping. "Actually I'm against individual awards," he told *World Soccer* in 1996. "Football is a team game, without your mates you've no chance."

If you wanted to over-analyse him, you could say that his background growing up in Communist East Germany instilled a collective spirit in him, meaning he eschewed individual achievements. This is possible, but prioritising the needs of the team over the individual is hardly unique among those who play a game in which it is impossible to succeed on your own. Matthias is the son of Klaus Sammer, a noted midfielder for Dynamo Dresden, who played for the East German national team and went on to be a coach. His boy joined the Dynamo youth team and was promoted to the senior squad in 1986. Sammer won both league and cup in the black and yellow of Dresden, a club that was one of the strongest in East Germany.

Dresden were given a spot in the Bundesliga after German reunification but Sammer did not stick around. He joined VfB Stuttgart in 1990 and was also called up to the combined German national team. In the first Bundesliga season after reunification Sammer, then a striker, won the title in that nail-biting championship for Stuttgart, pipping Eintracht Frankfurt and Borussia Dortmund on the last day of the season. He later joined BVB from the Serie A club Internazionale in Milan, where he wasn't happy. He scored four goals in eleven matches for the Nerazzurri but the Italian life wasn't for him and he accepted the move to Borussia in 1993. Initially, the striker was concerned about his new position in defence and this soured his relationship with Hitzfeld. In time he came around to the coach's thinking and extended his contract to finish his career as he started it: in black and yellow.

"I see myself as a midfielder but I have no problems playing at the back," he said. "Either behind the lines of defenders or among them or in front, makes no difference to me... There were some irritating disagreement between us but the mutual trust is improving... I expect to finish my career here."

Not everyone sees artistry and beauty in the work of a central defender. Marco van Basten bemoaned the so-called dark art of defending as denying supporters what they want to see. "People like... Jürgen Kohler would often obstruct me ten to fifteen times a game; fifteen times the ref would give a foul, but it also meant that my action was stopped fifteen times and the fans were robbed of fifteen chances of an exciting moment." No wonder Jürgen Köhler was also described by *Gazzetta* as "Van Basten's nightmare".

Köhler is rightly held up as one of the best defenders of his era and possibly among the best of all time. On the one hand he was a clean shorts centre half whose positional awareness resolved defensive problems before they occurred. On the other he was a tough bastard who could rip the soul out of a football match. His highlights reel is full of meaty challenges, towering headers, last-ditch clearances and crucial interceptions, including one off the tips of his studs to deny Eric Cantona in the Champions League in 1997.

The great American college football coach Bear Bryant once said that, "Offense sells tickets. Defence wins championships." This is most certainly true about proper football. According to Chris Anderson and David Sally's book *The Numbers Game*, soccer teams earn more points from clean sheets than through goals. Few players exemplify that axiom more than Jürgen Köhler. Nobody ever thanks players like him for doing what they do but everyone is grateful that he is on their team.

Paolo Sousa's stint was brief but glorious. The defensive midfielder was a member of the great 1990s Portuguese 'Golden Generation' along with such greats as Lúis Figo, Fernando Couto, Deco, Rui Costa and more. This was the team that entered every international competition among the favourites to win, but would end up disappointed. What Sousa missed in international trophies he made up for in club honours, winning a Portuguese cup and league title with Benfica, and a Scudetto, Coppa Italia and the Champions League with Juventus. Sousa knew the taste of champagne before arriving at Dortmund in 1996.

The 1994/95 season is remembered for the title win but it can't be forgotten that there was another worthy run in the UEFA Cup. In fact, it could have derailed their title chase just as the European Cup Winners' Cup victory did in 1966. Only Eintracht Frankfurt in September beat Borussia in the Bundesliga before March, when Kaiserslautern won 1-0 straight after Borussia returned from a Wednesday night trip to Rome for the UEFA Cup quarter-final first leg against Lazio. They lost 3-0 to Bayer Leverkusen in the game after the second leg at the Westfalen. Between the Lazio game and the semi-final Dortmund played three Bundesliga games and only picked up two points. To compound the pressure, the UEFA Cup quarter-final win came at a cost. Stéphane Chapuisat suffered a knee injury and was to be out for at least the rest of the season, and indeed a good deal longer than that. All of this was adding to what *Kicker* magazine called "The drama around Dortmund".

Between the two legs of the semi-final there were only two league games. The first was an unsatisfying Revierderby against Schalke, which ended 0-0. The second was a win, but it was a win which came at some cost to the reputation of the club and one player in particular. It was against a decent Karlsruhe team with a number of quality players, among them Thomas Häßler, Slaven Bilić and Sergej Kirjakov. KSC have rarely enjoyed great success domestically but were seventh in the table at the time and were gunning for a UEFA Cup spot. Fatigued, Dortmund were struggling against this determined side and 1-0 down through a goal from Gunther Metz in the first half. BVB laboured in the second half but their hard work bore no fruit until Andreas Möller won a penalty in the most extraordinary manner. Möller went down in the box under what can only very loosely be described as a challenge from Karlsruhe defender Dirk Schuster. However, that term presupposes that there was some form of contact; in truth, Schuster was nowhere near Möller when he went down. Arguably, Schuster could not have got close to Möller even if he tried.

"Between him and me [you] could have parked a small car," recalled Schuster in 2010. "I was absolutely stunned when referee Günther Habermann actually whistled for a penalty."

It is regarded as one of the worst "swallow dives" in the history of German football and, on reflection, it was one of those refereeing calls where everyone in the stadium except those who mattered could probably see it for what it was. Not that the partisan home crowd cared. Their team had been thrown a lifeline, one that Michael Zorc was not about the throw aside from the penalty spot. Ten minutes later, Matthias Sammer scored the winner.

Needless to say there were recriminations after the game. According to Schuster, Möller privately admitted to him that he'd dived while stating publicly that he thought that Schuster was going to clean him out and he acted to protect himself. In post-match interviews Möller is quoted as saying that he would have come clean about the incident at the time were Karlsruhe not coached by Winfried Schäfer, a man with whom there had been some prior bad blood: "I would have told the referee that it wasn't a foul if it had been any other coach."

Ever the one-eyed Dortmunder, Zorc spoke of "compensatory justice", having had clear penalties not given during the games against Stuttgart, Leverkusen and Kaiserslautern. The media whipped up a storm and Möller was persona non grata at the German FA. The German international was fined DM 10,000 by the DFB and given a two-match ban. National team coach Berti Vogts dropped him for one game. That said, Dortmund's title challenge was back on track. Karlsruhe failed to qualify for the UEFA Cup.

According to Schuster, Möller has subsequently apologised for the dive. However, to what extent he should is a matter of perspective. Part of the reason why players like Möller are so good is their competitive streak and willingness to do what is necessary to win. There is no question that Dortmund were up against it. A defeat to Karlsruhe would not have ended their title hopes but would have been precisely the sort of loss you look back on and say, "This is the game where we blew it." Möller's dive was unedifying and in the weeks that followed the match he suffered abuse from opposition fans. In fact, it is still remembered to this day. If you allow yourself to succumb to the narrative, though, Möller's act put Borussia back on the path to their first national championship since 1965 and all it cost was the reputation of a player easily thick-skinned enough to suffer the slings and arrows, and who was destined to sod off to Schalke anyway.

Dortmund's UEFA Cup journey was ended, not for the first time, by Juventus. It seems that even relieving the Turin giants of some of their players couldn't deny them a place in the final. BVB would have another chance to deny them again later in the decade, on a much bigger stage and with the ultimate club prize at stake.

While the players brought in from Italy played a significant role in a few glorious years for Borussia Dortmund, they were not the only ones to do so. Martin Kree was a barnstorming defender in the classic nineties football mould, aggressive and tough-tackling but also, it's been said, blessed with one of the hardest shots in the game. A native of Wickede, which is about 30 kilometres from Dortmund, Kree was and is a lifelong Dortmund fan. Both he and his father watched BVB from the terraces at the Westfalen when they were a second division side. His career started at VfL Bochum before he moved to Bayer Leverkusen (where he won a DFB-Pokal medal). He finally arrived at Borussia and he couldn't have timed it better.

"I was signed by Borussia at what turned out to be exactly the right time," he said in an interview with Ben McFadyean in 2017. "In hindsight, when I think about it, that move came at exactly the right time. I get goosebumps just thinking about that part of my career with Borussia."

Despite being a dyed in the wool Dortmund fan, the majority of Kree's career was spent elsewhere. His 81 appearances for BVB were beaten both at Leverkusen and at Bochum. In fact, Kree returned to Bochum after his playing days were over and joined the management team at the Ruhrstadion. However, those 81 matches were productive: he won two Bundesliga titles, one Champions League and an Intercontinental World Cup. Not bad for a sub-centurion.

Knut Reinhardt's parents insisted that he complete his education before turning professional, a decision that proved to be wise in his future. Like Kree, Reinhardt is another son of North Rhine Westphalia and, like Kree, he played for Bayer Leverkusen before joining Dortmund in 1991. Born in Hilden, Reinhardt was a no-frills left winger by trade. The Südtribune loved him and would frequently call out "Knuuuut!" as he ran down the touchline. Reinhardt played 27 matches in the 1994/95 championship-winning season and 20 in the following season. Injuries took their toll and he played fewer and fewer times for Dortmund. He was not picked for the Champions League final in 1997 and lost more than his place in the side before leaving for Nürnberg. His wife, Conny, left him for one of his team-mates, none other then Jens Lehmann. After retiring in 2000, Reinhardt left the professional game to become a primary school teacher in north Dortmund. He remarried and, at last reports, is happy. In 2017 he wrote a book about his professional and personal experiences at in football. He states that he harbours no ill will to Lehmann and Conny.

At DM 100 000 Bodo Schmidt was a steal. The centre half was originally from Niebüll, which is all the way up in Schleswig-Holstein in north Germany on the Danish border. Schmidt earned a place in the TSB Flensburg youth team and then moved to Rot Weiß Niebüll. That was before getting a call from his former coach, Fritz Bischoff who had become coach of the Bayern Munich second team. There are very few professional clubs in Schleswig-Holstein and it's not easy to get noticed. Had Bischoff not made the move south then it's entirely possible that Schmidt would not have had the career he did. At Säbener Srtaße he played alongside Lothar Matthäus, Klaus Augenthaler and Michael Rummenigge, and was coached by a certain Jupp Heynckes. Schmidt never made the move up to the first team and he was moved onto Unterhaching, a club to the south of Munich, then in the second division. From there he was signed by Dortmund as a supplemental player. At least that was the plan. In fact, Schmidt played in 30 games in the 1994/95 season and thoroughly merited his title winner's medal. He played fewer matches the following season, albeit enough to claim another championship medal, but with Jürgen Kohler now in situ, it was time for Schmidt to move on. From Dortmund he moved to 1. FC Köln but was laid off when the Billy Goats were relegated. It's hard to imagine that a double Bundesliga champion would be unemployed, even for a few months, but it's true. He was rescued once again by his former coach, Bischoff, who introduced him to Hans-Dieter Schmidt, coach of Magdeburg. There he became captain and is celebrated by the fans for a spell of 111 games in the regionalised third and fourth tiers, plus the odd appearance in the DFB-Pokal, one of which was a shock penalty shoot-out win over his old club Bayern Munich in 2000.

Described by *Süddeutsche Zeitung* as "probably the greatest football talent of the last 20 years" and by *Corriere dello Sport* as "Germany's Del Piero", Lars Ricken has had a lot to live up to. Indeed, in many respects the Dortmund-born attacking midfielder has fulfilled his potential, especially when you consider his medal haul. However, his career was blighted by injuries which ultimately denied him so many other possibilities.

Ricken was a youth player at TuS Eving-Lindenhorst. He had

predecessors at that club in the shape of Stefan Klos and Michael Zorc. From there he moved to Eintracht Dortmund and finally Borussia Dortmund. By the age of 17 he was a senior player, making his Bundesliga debut in March 1994 against Stuttgart. That appearance made him the youngest ever Bundesliga player at that time. He scored his first goal for the club in his following league game against MSV Duisburg. However, it became clear just what a special player he was destined to become when he rifled home a shot from outside the area at the San Siro in the second leg of the UEFA Cup quarter-final, still within the month of March. Dortmund won that leg 2-1 but it was not enough to overcome Internazionale after a 3-1 loss at the Westfalen in the first leg.

Ricken was an attacking midfielder with a penchant for moving between the lines unnoticed. His slick style, technique and movement made the comparisons with Alessandro del Piero understandable. He could receive the ball at pace and this made him a valuable player in a Dortmund side that liked to moved the ball forward with gusto. His unrehearsed and gangly goal celebrations were symptomatic of a player who did not score enough to create a trademark, combined with the joy of scoring for his local team.

Between the Borussia Dortmund first and second teams Ricken played 340 games, scoring 57 goals. In the 1994/95 season, and at the age of 18, he played in 21 matches and netted twice. The first was as a second-half substitute against Bayern Munich, Dortmund's consolation in a 2-1 loss in the 84th minute. The second was a landmark goal on the final day of the season against Hamburg. "We had to win the game 2-0 to be crowned German champions," he told *FIFA.com* in 2014. "I scored to give us the 2-0 lead and finally seal the Bundesliga title after a 30-year wait. The atmosphere inside the stadium was so incredible that I even shed a few tears."

And who can blame him? Ricken would have grown up knowing a very different Dortmund. In the previous decade the Westfalenstadion was a solemn, poorly-attended place with huge gaps in the seating and terraces, home to a cash-strapped club with little future beyond mid-table mediocrity at best and financial collapse at worst. In May 1995, as Ricken wheeled away in front of a vibrant, energised, packed-out home crowd, the transformation of the club was sealed with a championship. Outside the stadium, in the city centre, thousands more assembled in front of a giant screen to watch a live feed of the match. As Ricken scored BVB's second, the crowd erupted. If you haven't experienced the feeling of seeing the club you love winning a title after having never thought you would then it will be difficult to imagine, much less articulate. However, watching a sea of black and yellow humanity instantaneously expressing mass euphoria serves as a good illustration.

Borussia registered some handsome wins in the opening few weeks of the season against 1860 Munich (4-0), Köln (6-1) and Stuttgart (5-0). Dortmund did not drop out of the top two for the entire campaign. In fact they were top for all but eight rounds. Their primary challengers for the title were Werder Bremen, with Kaiserslautern and Freiburg (yes, really!) waiting in the wings. BVB beat Werder and lost to the club from the Weser, which meant that they were unable to establish a psychological edge or additional points advantage. By the final game of the season they were level with Werder but ahead by a nose on goal difference. Borussia needed a 2-0 win, or rather needed to better Werder's result. As it happened, the Bremen club had to travel to Bayern Munich. The Bavarians were both comfortable and uncomfortably in sixth place. It had not been a great campaign for this proud and usually dominant club, so they were not inclined to see a visiting team win the championship on their turf. The record champions won 3-1 and the title was decided in Dortmund's favour.

Dortmund's other goal against Hamburg on that day was scored by Andreas Möller. The universally unpopular player scored 14 times that season, which was eclipsed only by the captain – and by now living legend – Michael Zorc, who scored 15. Additional highlights in what was a season of great moments came in the form of a 3-2 win against Schalke and a 1-0 victory against Bayern. It had been close and they needed to keep their nerve, but Hitzfeld had done it. After 30 years you would not expect an easy ride to the title and so it proved. However, to use an unsavoury metaphor, it seemed that Borussia Dortmund had broken the seal. Or, to put it another way, like London buses, you wait ages for one and then two come along at once.

1995-96

"God Must Be a Borussia Fan"

Heiko Herrlich must be a pretty stubborn man, a trait that set him in good stead in a career and life of tremendous obstacles, one of which almost took his life. Herrlich confessed to stubbornness when recounting the circumstances of his move to Borussia Dortmund from Borussia Mönchengladbach in the summer of 1995. The German striker was the Bundesliga top scorer in the 1994/95 season with 20 goals. He also scored in Gladbach's 3-0 win against VfL Wolfsburg in the DFB-Pokal final at the end of that season. After such a fantastic campaign it was little surprise that other – and dare I say bigger – clubs wanted to sign the 23-year-old, who made his German international debut in March 1995.

Sure enough, a bid came in from Borussia Dortmund. "There was a verbal commitment from Borussia Mönchengladbach that I may go for DM 4.5 million," he recalled to *mitgedacht-block.de* in 2017. "This agreement was already made before anyone would dream that I would be top scorer or an international. Eventually the day came and there was an offer from Borussia Dortmund. The club no longer remembered the deal."

Herrlich dug his heels in and wanted the move, much to the chagrin of the Gladbach fans and club. "I was very stubborn," he said. "Today I would react differently." In the end the deal went through after some horse trading and the intervention of the DFB as mediator. In the summer Herrlich was finally unveiled as a Dortmund player. However, there were consequences that went beyond invoking the ire of the fans of Mönchengladbach. The deal soured the relationship between the two Borussia clubs and he was criticised by the German print media as being greedy. "In my first year with BVB I was insulted in every stadium. Although, in my opinion, I acted absolutely correctly."

Herrlich hails from Mannheim and began his senior career at Bayer

Leverkusen, having previously played for the SC Freiburg youth team. Between 1989 and 1993 Herrlich scored a modest six goals in 75 games. His goal ratio at Gladbach was a much more impressive 28 in 55 games, hence the disgruntlement at his departure. In the 1995/96 season Herrlich played 26 times and scored nine goals between the Bundesliga, Champions League and DFB Pokal. In his entire spell at Dortmund he would play 183 games in all competitions and score 56 goals.

Herrlich played at the Westfalenstadion for a total of eight years but there is a huge punctuation mark in the form of a malignant brain tumour of which he was diagnosed in the year 2000. At Bayer Leverkusen Herrlich befriended his teammate Jorginho, who won the World Cup in 1994. The Brazilian full back was a devout and proselytising Christian. "When I saw how this man treated everyone with the same kindness and goodness," Herrlich recalled to *11Freunde* in 2014, "I was intrigued. I accompanied him to his Bible studies and discovered what a wealth of unshakable faith brought me in any situation. It benefited me during my cancer."

Mercifully for Herrlich and his wife, who was carrying their first child at the time, the tumour was treatable and in less than a year he was back on the pitch for Dortmund, making his return in the Revierderby on 15th September 2001. He was given a rousing welcome by the crowd, including the Schalke contingent. Alas, Herrlich was unable to recapture his form and that, plus a number of injuries, meant that he only played a handful of matches before hanging up his boots in 2004. He stayed on at Borussia as a youth team coach and then moved on to the Germany Under-17s and Under-19s, and then as head coach with Bochum, Unterhaching, Bayern Munich Under-17s and Jahn Regensburg, followed by a return to Bayer Leverkusen as head coach.

In a recent interview Herrlich said that trophies do not interest him: "It is the community, the coexistence, the Christian values which are required in team sport that is fascinating." No doubt his religious beliefs provide him with the sincerity of his words. It also helps to have actually won some silverware in order to form such an opinion. By virtue of joining Dortmund when he did, Heiko Herrlich's spiritual and physical trophy cabinet is full.

His first season was relatively modest in terms of goalscoring compared to his previous season at Gladbach. This was because he needed surgery on one of his ankles in March 1996 and he only managed to play in 16 Bundesliga matches. However, Herrlich did score some valuable goals in what was a difficult start to the season for his new club, including a strike on his Bundesliga debut for Dortmund, a 1-1 draw against Kaiserslautern. He also scored a brace in his new club's first away league win at St Pauli. Both Karl-Heinz Riedle and Stéphane Chapuisat were injured for the early part of the season, which placed extra pressure on Herrlich. It also prompted Borussia to bring in another back-up striker, Rubén Sosa, who joined from Internazionale for DM 2.8 million on the eve of the Champions League transfer deadline. Ottmar Hitzfeld described the Uruguayan as, "a key player, he can hold the ball and play crucial passes." Before arriving, Sosa was already a serial winner with three domestic Uruguayan championships as a Club Nacional player. He also won a Copa del Rey medal with Real Zaragoza and a UEFA Cup with Inter.

Sosa had played with Riedle at Lazio. The German stated that he set up "two thirds of my goals" in the eternal city. In the Ruhr, however, his role was peripheral after Chapuisat and Riedle returned and Sosa started a lot of games on the bench. Nevertheless, his contribution is noteworthy for more than the three goals he scored. His all-action style and enthusiasm for the game made him a popular figure at the Westfalen, as did his understanding of his role in the squad. "I'm not the type to complain," he told *Welt* in 1995. "I do not need to prove anything, because I scored 84 goals in Italy and have 12 professional years behind me." Perhaps his finest intervention was in assisting Lars Ricken for an equaliser in the Revierderby in October 1995. Youri Mulder put the Gelsenkirchen club a goal up at the Parkstadion but Ricken equalised before Zorc scored the winner in the 90th minute. These seemingly small moments can go a long way.

In spite of Hitzfeld's warning that they did not "oversleep" at the start of the season, Dortmund took a few weeks to hit their stride in the Bundesliga. Injury problems and their impending debut in the Champions League took their toll. This was Borussia's first foray into the revamped European Cup, based on the group system. There were four groups of four, made up of actual domestic champions rather than the additions of runners-up and third- or fourth-placed teams that we see today. The 1995/96 season was the first in which three points were awarded for a win. After the completion of the group stages the restriction of a maximum number of three foreign players per team was lifted following the Bosman Ruling in December 1995. Borussia were in Group C with the Romanians, Steaua Bucharest, and two clubs with echoes of Dortmund's European heritage both recent and distant. The Rangers club from Glasgow, the city where Dortmund won the Cup Winners' Cup in 1966, and, of course, Juventus. Presumably UEFA did not want to live in a world where BVB and Juve did not meet wherever the situation presented itself.

Borussia finished a poor second in the group, four points behind the Old Lady, who would go on and beat Ajax in the final in Rome. The Amsterdam club knocked BVB out in the second round. There was a high point, though, against Juventus. The Italian champions had won at the Westfalen in the opening match of the group but Borussia were able to reverse that result in the penultimate round, with a 2-1 win at a half-empty Stadio delle Alpi. It was Lars Ricken who scored an absolute traumtor to win the game. The Juve back line failed to clear a looping cross. The ball fell to Ricken just on the edge of the area and he lifted the ball over the head of Angelo Peruzzi in the Juventus goal. It was strangely reminiscent of another goal that Ricken would score about a year and a half later from about the same distance and against the same opposition.

Borussia's main rivals for the Bundesliga title in this season was a resurgent FC Bayern Munich, who had overcome their problems from earlier in the decade. The Bavarians had upset the hierarchy and Dortmund by trying to turn the heads of some of their players with transfer bids. Consequently, there was some bad blood between the two clubs and a sort of cold war existed between them. This added an extra edge to the matches between the two sides. They met at the Westfalen in October 1995. Bayern were top of the table by seven points, ahead of Borussia. The home side took the lead when Markus Babbel fouled Heiko Herrlich in the box. Steffen Reuter converted the penalty on 41 minutes. On the other side of half time Christian Nerlinger turned in a cross to equalise. Hitzfeld made some replacements: Michael Zorc replaced Jürgen Kohler, Ruben Sosa replaced Lars Ricken, and Ibrahim Tanko was replaced by Patrik Berger. The latter was a surprise choice to partner Herrlich up front but the intervention proved profitable. Sosa had only been on the pitch for two minutes before hammering home Dortmund's second goal. The Bayern players had lined up a wall for a free kick, expecting it to be an attempt on goal from Andreas Möller. Instead, the German made a short sideways pass to the Uruguayan who smacked the ball from outside the area and past the despairing Oliver Kahn in the Bayern goal. In the 82nd minute, Zorc wrapped up the 3-1 victory for the Black and Yellows.

The return fixture against in March was a bad-tempered affair at the Olympiastadion, where Borussia lost 1-0. There was an altercation involving Uli Hoeness and Julio César with Gerd Müller on the touchline, which added a frisson of controversy to proceedings. By this point Dortmund were just a point clear of Bayern and feeling the pressure. There was open disagreement between Hitzfeld and Matthias Sammer about the tactics in general and Sammer's role in the team in particular. After a frustrating 2-2 draw six matchdays later against Hamburg, then coached by Felix Magath, Sammer criticised Hitzfeld's approach to the game. Dortmund entered the changing rooms at half time with a 2-0 lead thanks to goals from Zörc and Möller, but the young HSV manager altered his tactics for the second half. He forced his players further up the pitch and pressured Dortmund into turning the ball over. Knut Reinhardt described it as "Hara-kiri football." The great HSV goalscorer of yore, Uwe Seeler, watched the game and described it as a "tactical master performance". *Kicker* reported that when Sammer was asked immediately after the game why his team did not react better to Magath's tactics, he replied, "You must ask the coach. HSV played man-to-man only we didn't realise it."

Sammer's uncertain relations with the coach were exacerbated by continuing speculation about whether or not the Dresden-born midfielder would extend his contract and a controversy regarding his sponsorship arrangement with a boot supplier. Dubbed 'Schuh Krieg' (boot-gate) in the media, the row stemmed from the fact that Sammer was sponsored, like so many other German players, by adidas. However, the official boot supplier for his club was the American company, Nike. Sammer's frankly less than diplomatic way around this was to apply three stripes, synonymous with the adidas brand, onto his Nike boots. This enraged the US firm to the point where they threatened to impose a contract penalty which, *Kicker* reported at the time, was up to DM 1.5 Million. Borussia's Sporting Director, Michael Meier, felt that the best way to resolve the matter was for Sammer to switch from adidas to Nike, but that only opened up the thorny question of who bought him out of his existing deal.

Mercifully the whole tawdry affair was settled by Nike who, perhaps seeing it as a good marketing opportunity or perhaps out of the goodness of their hearts, took the higher ground. In an open letter to Matthias Sammer, published as a full-page advert in *Kicker*, Nike said that Sammer can wear whatever boots he feels will help him perform at his best. "Nike will not burden its six-year partnership either by a lawsuit or instigate a boot war," it declared magnanimously. Nike also pointed out that it hoped that the Nike-sponsored players, including Andreas Möller, Lars Ricken and Heiko Herrlich, be allowed to wear their boots when playing for the national team, rather than the "other" manufacturer's boots. "Equal rights for all!" they exhorted with barely appropriate haughtiness.

Meanwhile, in the Dortmund treatment room, Stéphane Chapuisat was hard at it, getting fit after a knee injury sustained against Lazio in the UEFA Cup the previous season. His return was marked by 3000 Borussia fans who had 'Chappi is Back!' t-shirts made up especially for the occasion. This was just as well, as the following month Herrlich injured his ankle and did not return for the rest of the season. By then the Swiss maestro was up to speed and finally announced his return to form with two goals in BVB's 5-0 win at Stuttgart. He scored again the following week in a 6-0 trouncing of Eintracht Frankfurt. After that followed a four-game winless streak, including the aforementioned 1-0 loss to Bayern and an unsatisfactory 0-0 draw at home to Schalke. There may have been an element of karmic restoration for their Hinrunde match earlier in the season between these two sides.

"Berger's Bitterest Defeat", screamed the *Kicker* headline after that first game. Jörg Berger, the Schalke coach, was recovering from groin surgery but received a mighty kick in the balls with this result. By common consent this was a match utterly dominated by Schalke. The Dortmund players played "like the Easter bunny" according to Michael Zorc, and he admitted that they could easily have conceded four goals before the half time. However, as I'm sure I've said before, the football gods punish teams that don't take their chances. Zorc's 90th minute winner had left Berger furiously throwing his jacket onto the running track surrounding the pitch at the Parkstadion. "They had three chances and scored two goals," said the Schalke goalscorer, Youri Mulder, after the game. "We had eight and scored one. Who was good and who was bad?" he asked pointlessly.

It was Dortmund's first derby win at the home of Schalke since 1983. However, in the context of the league title challenge, it meant a good deal more. "We must wake up," said Sammer after the game. "This game…has done a lot." Dietrich Schulze-Marmeling wrote that Gerhard Niebaum allowed himself to be a tad more spiritual in his reflections: "God must be a Borussia fan."

All told, it was a punishing back end of the season for Dortmund with four "English weeks" (so called after the English tradition of midweek fixtures that are relatively uncommon in the Bundesliga) to contend with from March all the way through to a rearranged game in May at home to Leverkusen. However, with the exception of a pretty horrific 5-0 loss at Karlsruhe, still managed by Winfried Schäfer, Dortmund held their nerve. In the penultimate game of the season BVB needed to better Bayern Munich's result at Schalke. Despite the implications involving their hated rivals, the Gelsenkircheners obliged Dortmund with a 2-1 win over Bayern. Borussia managed a 2-2 draw at 1860 Munich, so the same club that had denied them a title 30 years previously were present as they claimed their second title in succession and fifth national title altogether.

Since its foundation, only three teams had successfully defended the Bundesliga title up to that point: Bayern Munich (obviously), Borussia Mönchengladbach and Hamburg. In 1996, Borussia Dortmund became the fourth. At the time of writing the count remains at this number, which underlines both the grip that Bayern have on the league and the difficulty of the task for challengers to reach and stay on their level. That burning ambition to reach genuine parity and take their place as an alpha in the Bundesliga pride would prove to be Dortmund's undoing. Indeed, the signs of their future folly were evident in the wake of this Bundesliga championship win. In an interview with *Kicker*, the Sporting Director, Michael Meier, spoke of stadium acquisition and investments in the club's merchandising.

"With the fan products we can close the gap on Bayern in three years," he boldly claimed. He pointed out that Dortmund shirts were outselling Bayern's in Hamburg, outside the local area of either club. "Thirty people were in Marienplatz [when Bayern last won their title], half a million were in Dortmund," he said. "…Departure is our motto and that is why we had the courage to invest DM 60 million without any subsidies… We cannot stop now. We cannot lay the trowel after the topping." He confidently predicted that by 1999 the club would be turning over DM 50 million.

In the shorter term, Hitzfeld called for a hat-trick of title wins and more players to strengthen the squad and overcome key injuries that affected the club in the second title-winning season. "We must put an end to the constant ups and downs," declared Jürgen Kohler. Dr. Gerd Niebaum (who became president ten years earlier in 1986 and must have been flushed with success) echoed Meier's confidence. "In 1986 we were light years away from FC Bayern," he said. "Today… we are almost in the same breath." His intention was to put Borussia on the top table of European football along with Juventus, Barcelona and Real Madrid. Niebaum anticipated that, "at least ten years' hard work would be required."

These words turned out to be hubristic. Ten years later Borussia would be emerging from a financial crisis that almost proved ruinous. However, back then life could not be much better if you were a Borrusen. Actually, that's not quite true. The following season, BVB would reach the summit of club football. To make the achievement even sweeter, it would happen in Munich.

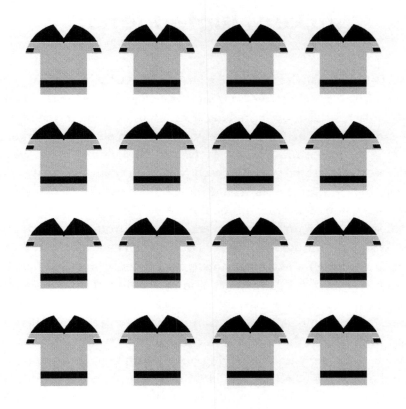

1997

"Ricken, lupfen jetzt!"

It was Paulo Sousa who looked like he could have had a crack at goal. He beat Eric Cantona to the ball but it travelled out of his reach and René Tretschok leapt on it, making it his own. Looking at the replay you can see Sousa half turning away, perhaps in slight exasperation at seeing the opportunity go by. Tretschok, on the other hand, was a goalscorer. At least, he was supposed to be. His chances to play were limited and, in fairness, he would have been nowhere near the first team for a game of this magnitude if it weren't for all the injuries.

The journeyman turned and unleashed a shot from 20 yards. It was headed straight for the Manchester United goalkeeper, Raimond van der Gouw, himself a late replacement after Peter Schmeichel failed a last-minute fitness test. The Dutchman had plenty of time to see the shot, which wouldn't have demanded much more of him than to raise a hand to stop the ball. Alas, for him it wasn't to be. Gary Pallister's raised boot altered the shot's vector and it flew to his right and hit the back of the net with a satisfying bulge. With that, Dortmund had taken the lead in the first leg of the 1997 Champions League semi-final, an even and intense contest with the English champions, and René Tretschok had earned a place in the Borussia Dortmund history books, specifically this one.

Believe it or not, five years later Tretschok was unemployed. Into his early thirties and with a number of injuries on his body, the forward player, born in Wolfen in the Saxony-Anhalt region, could not get a gig at a professional club. "To rely on young players is alright, but on the other hand you cannot do without experience," he told *Der Spiegel* at the time. "Clubs today rather look at age as the quality of a player. I'm now at a disadvantage. It is frustrating when you sit in the stands and think, 'I'm not worse than the one that plays down there, just older.'"

Tretschok joined Dortmund as a prospect in 1992, from Hallescher

FC. He spent one season in Berlin playing for Tennis Borussia and became not much more than a makeweight. After Dortmund he would return to the capital and Hertha BSC. He scored just eight goals in his 85 appearances wearing the Dortmund shirt, not the greatest of records given that he was meant to be a goalscorer. However, one of those eight was of such importance that it helped shape the destiny of this great football club.

Stéphane Chapuisat, Jürgen Kohler and Ibrahim Tanko were injured for the semi-final. To add to coach Ottmar Hitzfeld's burden, Matthias Sammer was suspended. So, in addition to Tretschok, Wolfgang Feiersinger was drafted into the BVB defence despite nursing a back injury himself. The Austrian defender was another back-up player who played 83 times for Borussia in his four years at the club. Perhaps understandably, Feiersinger didn't have the dynamism of Sammer. Kohler, who played behind him, described him as "rather conservative and significantly less risky" than the player to whom he was understudy.

Not that Kohler was complaining. The centre back had personal issues of his own going into the match. His wife lost their unborn child only a few days before the game, a tragedy that is difficult to imagine and one to which no one can say what is the right way to react. Kohler and his wife agreed that the show must go on. "My wife agreed, so I flew," he told *Kicker*, remembering the match 20 years later. "At that time as well as today I am characterised by the fact that I remain calm in stressful situations…that was and is one of my greatest strengths." Kohler was a colossus in the match and much of his reputation is based on this performance and helping to nullify the great Eric Cantona. At the airport on the way home from the match, English journalists were asking Kohler when he was coming to Old Trafford.

Sadly, neither Tretschok nor Feiersinger would make the first eleven for the final in Munich, although the former would be given a place on the substitutes' bench. However, without these players stepping out of the shadows, there would have in all likelihood been no showdown with a by now old enemy: Juventus of Turin.

In England this was seen as an excellent chance for Manchester United. Dortmund's profile was still pretty low despite having players like Sammer and Andreas Möller in their side, players well known to England fans the season after Euro '96. With the notable absences the stage was set for Alex Ferguson to take his superb Manchester United team to the European Cup final, the first for an English club since the formation of the Premier League and, more pertinently, since the return of English clubs from a five-year ban following the Heysel Stadium Disaster. The result was a bitter disappointment to Ferguson, who would have to wait until 1999 before lifting the Champions League trophy. The semi-final also marked the final European game for their captain Eric Cantona, who announced his retirement at the end of the season. However, for Borussia Dortmund, the 1-0 win set up a redemption story of their own: a showdown with a familiar competitor in their European exploits of the nineties. The goalscorer was Lars Ricken and served as another step on his journey to football immortality.

The 1996/97 Champions League was the final season before its expansion from four to six groups of four clubs. Dortmund had been drawn in Group B with Atlético Madrid, Widzew Lodz and Steaua Bucharest. They had no difficulty qualifying for the quarter-final, losing only once in the group stage, 2-1 against the Madrid club at the Westfalen. On paper, and with the filter of hindsight, Borussia drew the long straw when Auxerre were pulled out of the hat for the quarter-finals. This small club from Burgundy consistently punched above its weight thanks almost entirely to their legendary coach Guy Roux. A player from 1952 and player-manager from 1961, Colmar-born Roux steered AJA from the humble regional leagues to the national top flight, Ligue 1, in 1980. Under Roux and with careful development of home-grown or wayward talents they remained a force in French football, lifting four French Cups and an historic league and cup double in 1996, which took them into the Champions League when it was still a league of champions.

Five years earlier these two teams had met in the UEFA Cup. It took a nail-biting penalty shoot-out to settle the tie in favour of BVB. This time no spot kicks were required. Just another moment of quality from Lars Ricken. Karl-Heinz Riedle turned in a diving header from a spectacular overhead cross by Chapuisat, who was the first to react when the ball ballooned into the air after a challenge.

Substitute defender René Schneider scored with another header from a free kick. A long-range shot from Sabri Lamouchi was deflected in by Stefan Klos to put Auxerre back in the tie at 2-1. However,

Borussia furthered their advantage when Möller put away the third goal after receiving a beautifully weighted pass, which was stroked into his path by the ever graceful Tanko.

In the second leg at Auxerre, Borussia prepared for an onslaught. "The Dortmund defensive line was positioned in front of the penalty area," reported *Kicker* magazine, "and was secured by Sousa and Ricken." The striker was working hard, tracking back to help out in the defence. "Even Möller and Riedle had to help out." However, Ricken was on the mark once again with a "millionaire goal". Riedle picked up Heinrich's cross with his back to goal. He laid it off for Ricken, whose long-range shot took a deflection. Ricken waved his hands aloft as the small number of Borussens in the stadium celebrated. Job done. Dortmund were going to Manchester.

Interestingly, as much as this season is remembered rightly for its Champions League success, the priorities of the club, at least as far as its president was concerned, were elsewhere. Before the season began Hitzfeld declared that, "The goal is the title defence and in the Champions League, something more." After the Auxerre quarter-final Gerd Niebaum warned that, "As we progress we have bigger problems defending our title." The hat-trick of Bundesliga titles was very much on his mind, characterising the Champions League as a "Sunday trip". Jürgen Kohler also said as much at the time after announcing he'd renewed his contract, which effectively meant that he would stay at the club until the end of his career. He said that losing the quarter-final would not have been a disaster as Dortmund were still very much in the hunt for the title: "I'm convinced we can make the hat-trick."

The Champions League final was the first one-off major final for Borussia Dortmund since the DFB-Pokal in 1989. The 1993 UEFA Cup final was a two-legged affair, you will recall. There was a Scottish connection between these two finals. In 1989 Murdo MacLeod turned out in black and yellow in Berlin. In Munich another proud Scotsman lined up for the Westfalen club: Paul Lambert. It is a tragedy of the modern game that coaches can be judged by their current profile rather than what they achieved in the past. As a coach, Lambert's reputation is somewhat patchy. He did a fine job at Colchester United and Norwich City, but joined Aston Villa and Stoke City at the wrong times in their stories. Yet, Paul Lambert the player was a colossus in the central midfield.

Today he would probably be characterised as a defensive midfielder. Back then he was simply a plain old central midfielder. His brief time in Dortmund saw him produce some epic performances, particularly against Manchester United and in the final itself, where the dubious task of keeping the prodigious Zinedine Zidane quiet fell upon Lambert's shoulders. "It wasn't really an instruction. I kinda knew my role in the team," he told *Deutsche Welle* in 2016. "We played against a lot of superb number tens at that time: Gheorghe Hagi, Paulo Sergio, Olaf Thon and so many others. So this was nothing different."

Lambert is from the great city of Glasgow and started his footballing career at St Mirren, which is located close to Paisley, near the airport just outside the city. Before joining Dortmund he had 330 appearances under his belt for the Buddies and then Motherwell, winning a Scottish Cup for the former. One of those matches was as a Motherwell player in the UEFA Cup against Borussia in 1994. Lambert, by then a full Scotland international, impressed Ottmar Hitzfeld to the extent that enquiries were made about his availability: "I always wanted to try to play abroad and the agent arranged something with Dortmund. I had nothing to lose at the time and never knew how things were going to pan out."

In a short time the tigerish Scot became an essential part of the team. "From the moment I signed for Dortmund I became one of them," he told the *Daily Record* in 2017. "I wrote everything down. I wrote down what we did at training, what I ate, everything I did. I completely immersed myself in German football culture. I forced my way into the Borussia Dortmund team on the opening day of the Bundesliga season and I was never out of the side." Lambert's willingness to learn and desire to embrace the club made him a popular figure in the squad. His daily games of head tennis with Andreas Möller became legend. "Before we trained, we would both go down to the basement below the training ground and set up. It was our ritual. Before long all the lads were playing and it was unbelievable. We were all sweating before first team training had even started."

However, while Lambert was very happy in Dortmund it was reported that his wife, Monica, was less so and wanted to return to Scotland. Michael Meier was keen to discuss Monica's issues and try to resolve them as they were very keen for him to stay. Whether those issues were addressed or not is a moot point. By November 1997 Lambert was on his way back to Scotland and Celtic, where he went on to captain the club and collected four league titles, two Scottish Cups, and two League Cups. He also led Celtic's heroic run to the 2003 UEFA Cup final in Seville, cut short by Porto under that perennial party pooper, Jose Mourinho. Before leaving Borussia, Lambert thanked the fans by unveiling a flag thanking them for their support.

In March 2015 Juventus and Borussia met for the eighth time in European competitions. This time it was a second round game in the Champions League. To inspire the players the Borussens on the Südtribune unveiled an enormous choreography of Lars Ricken, flanked by Karl-Heinz Riedle and Ottmar Hitzfeld, holding the Champions League Trophy aloft in triumph. Underneath the enormous choreo was a banner with the words spoken by the German football commentator Marcel Reif mere seconds before Lars Ricken scored probably the most famous goal in Borussia Dortmund's history and arguably one of the most famous in the history of European Cup finals. Reif has not always been considered a friend of Borussia fans. In fact, fans from numerous clubs have had beef with the controversial and decorated commentator. He suffered verbal abuse from fans of both Dortmund and Schalke for his opinions expressed during various commentaries. He had a beer mug thrown at him by an angry BVB fan, and had his car jostled by fans after a Revierderby game in 2015, the same year in which the choreo was unfurled. It is one of life's little ironies that such a contentious commentator's words should be so well remembered and celebrated years later.

The goal itself is well known to anyone with even a passing interest in Borussia Dortmund or the Champions League. It is, by any objective measure, one of the best goals ever to be scored in a European Cup and, by any subjective measure, *the* best. But it wasn't the only goal of the game.

There was understandably a great deal of extra interest in Germany leading up to the 1997 Champions League final; it was staged in the Olympic Stadium in Munich. The desire to see a German finalist was strong and, as we know, there was only one participant from Germany and that was Borussia. In addition to the glory of representing the nation in a home final there was also a rare opportunity to paint the city of Munich – home of longstanding rivals Bayern and 1860 Munich

– black and yellow. On the day of the final the Bavarian capital's Englischer Garten and Marienplatz were awash with travelling Borussens who made the trip from the Ruhr. In the stadium itself, the Yellow Wall had moved from the Westfalen to the Olympiastadion in Munich. Unsurprisingly, the travelling support from Turin was somewhat diminished in the face of those from Dortmund. Stephan Uersfeld, now a journalist for *ESPN* and *11Freunde* was 18 at the time. He described the scene to me as like a Dortmund home game. Stephan had just come out of surgery and was walking with crutches. He queued for 19 hours for a ticket to the game and travelled there by minibus with a group of friends.

For those BVB fans that didn't make the trip the Friedensplatz in Dortmund was converted into an enormous fanzone with a giant screen transmitting the match in front of thousands of fans. Juventus, managed by the great Italian coach Marcello Lippi, were of course the Champions League holders having unseated the previous holders, Ajax, the year before. Like Dortmund they had the benefit of playing the final in their homeland, in their case in Rome. Despite the disadvantage of playing a final in the nation of their opponents, Juve were clear favourites to win the match. Their line-up oozed with European pedigree against the relative upstarts from the Ruhr. In the Old Lady's starting eleven in the 1997 final were such names as Peruzzi, Ferrara, Di Livio, Jugovic, Deschamps and, from the bench, a young Del Piero. Also included in the Italian giant's line-up were Alen Boksic, Christian Vieri and, of course, the great Zinedine Zidane. For Paulo Sousa this was a second consecutive final, having played in the black and white in 1996 and switched to black and yellow the following season.

I remember watching this game on the TV in the UK. I'd like to say it was a transformative moment for me in terms of my love for Borussia but that would be untrue. That would come seven years later. At the time I remember that Dortmund had in their favour that they were a German team that weren't Bayern. They were also the side that knocked out Manchester United, so they couldn't be all bad. The match was commentated upon by the legendary Brian Moore and the somewhat less than legendary Ron Atkinson. The latter's knowledge of Dortmund was perfunctory to say the least. Moore had done his homework on the Dortmund side, however, and relished the task of calling a game that was clearly not going according to the script.

Dortmund lined up with Stefan Klos in goal behind Martin Kree, Jürgen Kohler, Matthias Sammer, Stefan Reuter, Paul Lambert, Paulo Sousa, Jörg Heinrich, Andreas Möller, Stéphane Chapuisat and Karl-Heinz Riedle.

"Nothing was really said to be honest before the game," Lambert told *Deutsche Welle* in 2016. "Most of the guys had experienced big games before and I wasn't too nervous."

It was a relief to Hitzfeld that he could pick from a full complement of attackers and leave room on his bench for Lars Ricken and Heiko Herrlich. Both of these players were to join the fray later in the match along with Michael Zorc. Before the match he reassured Ricken that he would be called upon at some point, despite not starting. "Of course I did not think it was great to sit on the bench," Ricken told *Der Westen*. "But Ottmar Hitzfeld told me the night before that my time would come." And, of course he was right. Sadly, however, there was no place for René Tretschok, the hero of the semi-final.

Well, you all know what happened. Juve were the stronger side, on paper at least, but Hitzfeld – anticipating an onslaught from the favourites – set up his team to defend. However, the first goal came from Borussia in the 29th minute. Riedle took the ball on his chest at the far post and just outside the six-yard box. He slotted the ball home and pandemonium ensued. Five minutes later Riedle struck again, this time with a header from a corner. Unbelievably, Dortmund were 2-0 up and at that point the match needs to be won by attrition and by nullifying Boksic and Vieri, a task assigned to Sammer, Kohler and Kree. Meanwhile, the dubious honour of keeping Zidane caged in the midfield was left to Sousa and, of course, Lambert.

They couldn't keep everyone at bay, though, and Lippi changed things up by bringing on Alessandro Del Piero, who scored with a splendid backheel that suddenly illustrated the axiom that 2-0 is a dangerous scoreline. Hitzfeld made a change of his own. Chapuisat, disappointed to not make a bigger impact on this game, departed in favour of Ricken in the 70th minute. Within seconds of his joining the action the fate of the final was sealed, as was Ricken's name in Borussia folklore. The through ball from Möller came from deep. It found itself in the stride of Ricken who had literally just stepped onto the field. With the aplomb of a confident striker accustomed to scoring decisive goals, Ricken lobbed the ball over the head of Peruzzi and into the net.

"Ricken, lupfen jetzt, Jaaaaa!" exclaimed Reif into his microphone. It was a goal for the ages, celebrated wildly by a city that now knew that feeling of winning a European trophy, a sensation recalled, only in the distant memory of those who were there in 1966. "Five seconds on the pitch," Reif continued. "Five seconds!"

"Peruzzi was always too far out of his goal," Ricken said on one of the countless times he has been asked about that strike, this time to *Der Westen*. "And during the first half I said to Heiko Herrlich, 'The first ball I get, I'm shooting directly for goal.'" Ricken had practised for precisely this sort of long-range shot and it paid off big time. While he admits that perhaps eight or nine times out of ten the shot would not have gone in, he was a player with the technique and the brass balls to pull it off. It is for this reason that it must take its place in the pantheon of great European Cup final goals.

Martin Beckner, a fan who rented a car and drove with his friends from Dortmund to Munich, recalls the moment Ricken's goal was scored in Uli Hesse and Gregor Schnittke's oral history of the club's supporters, *Unser Ganzes Leben*. "There was no stopping it. It was just screaming and smouldering. We hugged each other for several minutes, one above the other, one after the other."

Ricken himself has heard stories of fans who met during the celebrations and went on to forge relationships and start families after that night. He also spoke with a fan who at the time called him an idiot for taking the shot on, only to leap in the air in jubilation mere seconds later.

The 1997 Champions League final is one of those moments when all Dortmund fans knew where they were, what they were doing and – in some cases – who they were doing it with. After his marathon queue for tickets, journey to Munich and celebration as the players lifted the trophy, Stephan Uersfeld hobbled on his crutches out of the stadium looking for his wheels. He spotted Júlio César, injured for the match, chatting with the fans by one of the gates. He set off to the minibus only to encounter him again at the same place sometime later, and again later still. At this point he knew he'd been going round in circles. Eventually he made it to his ride and after the long journey home joined the celebrations in the town square. From there it was onto a birthday party where he continued his celebrations with friends, some of whom were Schalke fans still in the afterglow of their UEFA Cup final win over Roy Hodgson's Inter the previous Wednesday. His odyssey ended with him waking at a bus stop up the next morning.

After the game the accolades poured in for the victorious Borussia, Rainer Holzschuh, the editor-in-chief of *Kicker* magazine, praised them for, "an outstanding tactical defensive performance with first class counter-attack." German national team striker Oliver Bierhoff said, "Ricken's shot was simply sensational." Werder Bremen's Andi Herzog described Ricken's strike as "insane" and the Schalke goalkeeper Jens Lehmann, in a moment of magnanimity, said it was "unbelievable".

There was, however, another story running alongside this historic and glorious journey to Munich and ultimate success. The club's inability to challenge for the domestic title drew a great deal of criticism from the media and indeed from within the club itself. Shortly before the final, Dortmund could only manage an unsatisfactory 1-1 draw at Karlsruhe. This was immediately after a 2-0 loss at Bielefeld and a disappointing performance, despite the 1-0 win, against Schalke. The performance against KSC frustrated Dr Niebaum to the extent that he went public with his criticism. "The team did not have the firm will to win," he said. "Another team should represent us at the final in Munich."

Michael Meier, in an attempt to contextualise Niebaum's anger, said the president was concerned that the team had essentially given up on the league campaign in order to focus on the Champion League. It is worth reminding ourselves that the premier European club tournament was expanding for the following season and finishing second was enough to qualify. So, whilst winning the title was beyond them, a runner-up spot was not. After the Karlsruhe game, Dortmund were in fourth position in the Bundesliga, six points behind Leverkusen. Given the DM 63.9 million Niebaum had spent on behalf of the club and the potential earnings that could be lost by not qualifying for the Champions League it is easy to understand why the league campaign was of great importance. Of course, BVB would qualify if they won, but given the ability and pedigree of their opponents the safer and less risky route back into the Champions League was through the league. Moreover, Niebaum's criticism of the players was that they played as though they were one of the top European clubs in Italy or Spain.

Dortmund, though ambitious, was a working class club not yet eating at that top table. Their bread and butter was the Bundesliga and the players would do well to remember that.

Similarly, it is as easy to understand why the players are focused on the glory of being a European champion. When your career is only likely to last until you are into your thirties you have a few years to collect as many trophies as you can. When presented with the opportunity of ultimate glory, it is understandable that you may take your eye off the ball when it comes to Bielefeld or Karlsruhe. One of the many skills in successfully running a top-flight football club is managing the short-term ambitions of players should they conflict with the club's long-term goals.

In fairness, there were more obvious factors behind Borussia's disappointing league campaign. Matthias Sammer, such a pivotal figure in front of defence, only played 16 games due to injury problems. Steffen Freund played only two games for the same reason, as did Júlio César, who managed just ten. After a hard-fought 2-1 win at Freiberg in March, Hitzfeld was missing seven first team players.

There were also disagreements from within the squad, specifically Sammer and Zorc, although the latter was coming to the end of his career. In this dispute Niebaum fell on the side of the players and took the decision to "promote" Hitzfeld to the position of sporting director, a relatively new role in German Football at the time. Hitzfeld would take overall control of club matters, chiefly recruitment. The role of the sporting director is essential in modern professional clubs but in the late nineties it was not really that big a deal. I asked Uersfeld if Hitzfeld was, to coin a phrase used in British politics, being kicked upstairs? He agreed, using a German phrase to describe Hitzfeld's elevation as being made a *Frühstücksdirektor* or breakfast director, that being a job of apparent importance and prestige, but without genuine power or influence.

Dietrich Schulze-Marmeling wrote that Niebaum's decision was, in part, due to a desire to not repeat the mistakes of 1966, when the club did not regenerate itself and its squad and consequently went into decline. As in the late sixties, this nineties Dortmund had an aging squad which needed a refresh. Moreover, in the view of Niebaum the club needed to modernise and part of that modernisation was a restructure. Hitzfeld's move upstairs was partly due to disagreements with Niebaum and some of the players, most prominently Sammer, about the direction the club should be taking. Also, after six years enduring the sort of pressure that is hard to imagine for us mere mortals, Hitzfeld may well have welcomed the opportunity to spend time out of the hot seat. This spell in the new role as sporting director would prove to be a hiatus. Hitzfeld left Dortmund in 1998 for Bayern Munich and enjoyed a glittering career in Bavaria.

Hitzfeld's successor was Nevio Scala. The Italian enjoyed a distinguished career at both Milan clubs, Roma, Fiorentina, and others. He won a Serie A title, a European Cup and Cup Winners' Cup as a player with AC Milan. If you know your 1990s Italian football then you'll remember with great fondness that Parma team with the likes of Tomas Brolin, Faustino Asprilla, Gianfranco Zola and Alessandro Melli. They played scintillating football and won European honours but were never able to manage a Scudetto. Scala was the coach of that team.

At Dortmund, Scala added to his list of honours in the form of the Intercontinental Cup the following season in Tokyo. As European champions Dortmund played Cruzeiro, who were the South American equivalent, or in other words the winner of the 1997 Copa Libertadores. Not many Dortmunders could make it to Japan and once again Dortmund city centre was packed with Borussens eager to watch their players in this most unusual of fixtures. The level of importance of the Intercontinental Cup, or the Club World Cup as it is now known, is very much in the eye of the beholder. Traditionally it is thought to be of greater importance in South America, where fans and clubs see it as an opportunity to get one over the Europeans. Conversely, clubs in the UEFA confederation tend to regard it as prestigious but a nuisance. Judging by the reaction of the Dortmund public there was no such attitude. Dortmund won the game 2-0 with goals from Zorc and Herrlich. The Borussen fans needed no excuse to celebrate being crowned World Champions.

The Intercontinental Cup was not the only example of impressive international exploits from Borussia Dortmund. The club made a real fist of defending their Champions League title, making it as far as the semi-final and beating Bayern Munich on the way, only to be thwarted by Real Madrid at the second-to-last hurdle. These adventures, while great for the international profile of the club and prestige of the players, could do little more than paper over the cracks of what was an aging squad that had, by their high standards, a very poor domestic season.

The squad was also shorn of one of its key players. In the summer of 1997, Karl-Heinz Riedle was sold to Liverpool. Joining to bolster the Dortmund ranks was the Scottish striker Scott Booth, who left Aberdeen on a Bosman in the hopes of making a similar impact as Paul Lambert. Sadly it wasn't to be and he made only a handful of appearances. With no further signings of significance coming in and with a battle on two fronts, Dortmund struggled to tenth place in the Bundesliga. The season ended with a 4-0 thumping at the Munich Olympiastadion at the hands of Bayern. This was a form of revenge for the Champions League defeat but also some small form of consolation for the Bavarians missing out on the league title. That honour went to Kaiserslautern.

All the talk was that changes would have to be made for the following season and both Niebaum and the coach put on a brave face, claiming that Borussia would challenge again for the title. However, Scala did not stay. He left the club in the summer. Perhaps the signs of an impending crisis were looming even then. Borussia would go on to win another title in 2002 but despite that success it looked very much like BVB's attempt to reach the top table of European football had backfired. Like Icarus, Dortmund had flown too close to the sun.

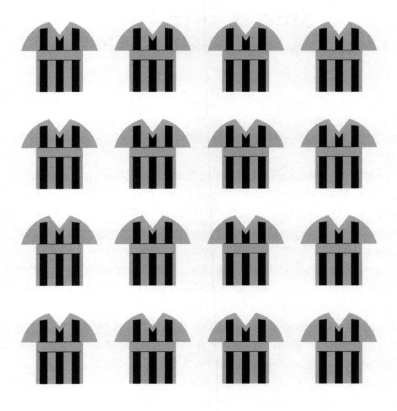

2012-13

Stones and Legs
The birth and near death of modern Borussia

The BBC's chief sports correspondent, Phil McNulty, called it, "the final that confirmed Germany as the new power base of European Football." This sentiment was echoed by *Kicker* magazine which, on the strength of the semi-final first leg result, led with the headline "Wembley: Wir Kommen". A year later the German national team would cement German football supremacy at international level by winning the World Cup. In May 2013, the hallowed turf of Wembley Stadium played host to the two best teams in Europe in the Champions League final, and both of those teams were German. Wembley Way was for one afternoon converted into a mixed promenade of Bavaria and the Ruhr as Bayern Munich and Borussia Dortmund competed for European club football's ultimate prize.

Of course, you know the result of the game. A heart-breaking late winner from Arjen Robben won it for Jupp Heynckes' all-conquering Bayern team. This victory sealed an historic treble for the Bavarians and exorcised a few demons for the club itself after its devastating defeat to Chelsea, on penalties, in the 2012 final in their own stadium. It was also a personal victory for Robben, who had ghosts of his own to lay to rest after some high profile errors that proved pivotal in recent confrontations with Dortmund. The trophy served as an exclamation point on a season that Bayern dominated, but as is often the case that does not tell the whole story. Few will argue that between their European and domestic achievement Bayern were the best team in Europe, but had Borussia taken advantage of their opportunities then Bayern fans would have had cause to look back on the great 2012/13 season with some mixed emotions.

"It was a weirdly open game for a final," Archie Rhind-Tutt recalls from his memory of sitting with the Dortmund fans at Wembley during the match. American Bundesliga viewers will be familiar with Rhind-Tutt as the touchline reporter for *Fox Sports'* TV coverage of the league. "I just remember how many chances that Borussia Dortmund spurned during the first half. There was a save that Neuer made... it was just one of those games when you're thinking the more and more chances that Dortmund spurn the more likely Bayern are going to end up winning it. It is one of those things with Jürgen Klopp sides that they always have that moment in a game where they're dominating but that if they don't score when they're at that peak then you worry for them and I think that's kind of what happened."

This was a position with which McNulty agreed from his view in the press box: "They paid a heavy price for failing to capitalise on a first half-hour in which they dominated Bayern and were only kept at bay by the brilliance of Germany keeper Manuel Neuer... he made five important saves in the first 35 minutes."

Sadly the football gods struck again and punished Dortmund for their profligacy and Bayern took the lead. Franck Ribery and Arjen Robben combined to give Mario Mandžukić a tap-in. Dortmund responded seven minutes later after the Brazilian centre back Dante kicked Marco Reus in the box; İlkay Gündoğan converted the spot kick. As the clock drew our attention to the prospect of extra time, the chances of that extra half an hour were extinguished by Robben.

"I'll never forget the ball just trickling into the net from Arjen Robben," Rhind-Tutt told me. "It was just so tantalising. And with that goal being so close to the end you knew that as the ball was rolling over the line so too the Champions League was rolling away from Borussia Dortmund. There was a lot of talk from Dortmund fans afterwards as to whether Dante should have been sent off for that tackle but at the time they didn't really care. They just saw it as a route back into the game."

If you've reached this far in the book you'll know that such moments as a Champions League final are rare experiences for Borussia Dortmund fans. Other books about other clubs will be a procession from one trophy to the next. However this club, with its huge stadium and multitude of passionate supporters, finds the mantle of champions a difficult fit. Defeat at Wembley for Borussia was not greeted with a shrug of the shoulders, confident that there will be another final along soon, at least not by most Borussens. Granted, there are some younger fans who had been converted by the swashbuckling heavy metal football of Jürgen Klopp and his super-talented cut-priced phenoms such as Robert Lewandowski, Shinji Kagawa, Mario Götze and the rest, but most supporters were and are long enough in the tooth to know that silver is not a natural colour in Dortmund. Of course there have been successes, plenty of them. But there have also been failures both dismal and, in their way, glorious. Sometimes they have been both.

In 2003 Borussia Dortmund were on the rack. Superficially you would not have known, but if you look under the bonnet it was a different matter. Between them Gerd Niebaum and Michael Meier had greenlit heavy spending on building Borussia into a club that could compete not just against the best of the Bundesliga, but in Europe. The problem was that the results were not keeping up with the rate of expenditure.

With the new millennium came a change in the ownership rules that would be far-reaching and, in Dortmund's case, result in the club's almost complete collapse. German football is well known for their 50+1 rule, which means that the club's supporters must own just over half of a football club. This is seen to be beneficial as it prevents unnecessary commercialisation of clubs and stops a single investor from taking overall control. It also discourages a club from spending significantly more money than their competitors. There are arguments and examples that dispute that which can be explored in a different book, but it is fair to say that it is a source of tension between supporter groups and some owners who seek to exploit commercial partnerships and raise ticket prices. Anyway, in the year 2000 the DFB allowed professional football clubs the opportunity to incorporate themselves as businesses. The clubs would remain as such but the professional parts within would be run commercially. This was music to the ears of Niebaum. While other clubs took a more measured approach, Borussia floated itself on the stock market and raised €130 million.

Flush with their recent successes on the pitch, Niebaum began a programme of investment in "Steine und Beine", or stones and legs. The stones came in the form of a huge redevelopment of the training facilities and expansion of the Westfalenstadion which would eventually bring the stadium up to the 80,000-capacity cathedral that exists today. The legs came in the shape of players; lots of them and of high quality. Matthias Sammer took over as coach in 2000 and his already impressive squad was enhanced over the next couple of seasons with the mercurial talents of Tomáš Rosický from Sparta Prague, Sunday Oliseh from Juventus, Ewerton from Corinthians in Brazil, and Rosický's countryman, Jan Koller, an archetypal big target man with the presence, technique and tactical understanding of his role to create space in the most constricting of circumstances.

After the Champions League win the recruitment of top players continued. Most notable was the import of former Schalke goalkeeper Jens Lehmann, who joined from AC Milan, and Christian Wörns from PSG. Wörns was an experienced Bundesliga operator who began his career at Waldorf Mannheim. His name was made with a seven-year stint at Bayer Leverkusen where, contrary to that club's nickname of 'Neverkusen', he won the DFB-Pokal in 1992. He was also part of the 1997 team that missed out on the Bundesliga title. His time in Paris for PSG was short and in 1999 he crossed back over the border to Germany and Dortmund. From there the Mannheim defender occupied a crucial role as centre back or sweeper in the BVB defence until his departure in 2008. The role of the sweeper in the German game was for decades as institutionalised as the long ball was in England, and Wörns was one of the greatest proponents of that art. It is likely that were he born 10 or 15 years later he would have sat as comfortably in a modern defensive set-up as either of his long-term successors, Neven Subotić or Mats Hummels.

Sebastian Kehl comes from Fulda, in Hessen. A graduate of the Hannover 96 youth system, he moved to Freiburg and played with distinction under coach Volke Finke in 2000. The Black Forest club qualified for the UEFA Cup with Kehl as their sweeper. The following January he was gone. Initially the plan had been for Kehl to move to Bayern Munich; in fact, he accepted an advance on his contract. The money was returned, of course, but so outraged were the Munich club that they threatened legal action against him when he transferred to Borussia in the winter of 2002. Nothing came of it, however, and the transfer was allowed to stand. Now there's a sliding doors/tackles moment to think about. The notion of Kehl playing for years in the red of Bayern is truly bizarre. However, this was the measure of his reputation at the time and it was well earned. Kehl settled into the Borussia team as a defensive midfielder and very quickly became a leading member. He made 15 appearances in the second half of the 2001/02 season and celebrated his first season by lifting the Meisterschale. When Christian Wörns left the club in 2008, Jürgen Klopp had little hesitation in selecting Kehl as the next captain. "Whenever one thinks of Dortmund, Sebastian is the player who first springs to mind," he explained at the time.

Kehl's career was interrupted by knee injuries. At times it looked like he would have to retire. He only played three games in Klopp's first title-winning season but he bounced back and led the team to a domestic double the following season. Kehl played in the black and white of the German national team from the Under-18s to the seniors, for whom he earned 31 caps. Fans of the beautiful game may recall that he was in the starting line-up for the 2006 World Cup semi-final in his home stadium – one of the best football matches in the history of the tournament, at least in my opinion.

However, of all the great players of this team Leonardo de Deus Santos is perhaps the most popular. Signing from Atlético Mineiro in 1998 at the tender age of 20, Dede – as he came to be known – played as a left wing back in black and yellow for 13 years. In the seasons that followed the Brazilian would become known as 'The German' among his compatriots. He would also see the club reach two peaks and one almighty trough, but through it all he would be keeping that left side of the Dortmund defence in good order. After he left, a testimonial was held for Dede in front of a packed Westfalenstadion. Truly he remains one of the club's most beloved players and added consistency in the Dortmund defence and midfield over so many years. Full backs and wing backs don't always get the same recognition for their work as players in other positions who have more exciting numbers. But as anyone who regularly watches the same team knows, the value of an ever-present player cannot be understated and it is gratifying that he was given such a send-off. On the other side of the BVB defence was another Brazilian by the name of Evanílson. The right wing back would play 170 games before returning to Brazil and Atlético Mineiro.

Stephan Uersfeld told me that the 2002 team was the "forgotten championship" and it's easy to see why. For one, it was a title win that was built on a foundation of sand. The club was never likely to make back the money that it was spending and, despite the many criticisms of UEFA's Financial Fair Play rule, it is possible that the club would not have been able under its watch to have spent the money that they did, at least not on the players. Yet, this squad oozed quality and, particularly in Kehl and Dede, created club legends. The former's legacy continues as Sebastian Kehl, after finally returning in 2015, has joined the club staff as head of player licensing. Every day he works with the current players, mentoring the youngsters and reinforcing to them what it is to be a Dortmund player.

It should also be said that Borussia Dortmund's spending could be described as irresponsible and injurious but it was not at the same levels as the big state-owned clubs of today, who use all manner of chicanery to get round the already pretty liberal financial fair play laws laid down by UEFA. That said, given the traumatic events and the painstaking rebuilding that were to follow, no one should be blamed for placing an asterisk next to the 2001/02 title-winning team. Equally, I know Borussia fans who came to the club because of this team and hold this crop of players very close to their hearts. If the title win is "forgotten" then so too is the tremendous UEFA Cup run of the same season. Dortmund's run, which was marked by an excellent 4-0 win over AC Milan in the first leg of the semi-final, was halted in the final by a 3-2 defeat to Feyenoord. The defeat was doubly sorrowful as it marked an undistinguished end to the distinguished Dortmund career of Jürgen Kohler, who was sent off for fouling Jon Dahl Tomasson in the penalty area after 31 minutes of his final game for the club.

Perhaps it is more appropriate to say that the successes of the early part of the decade were overshadowed by what was to follow. As the expenditure piled on, the results on the pitch were unable to keep pace. Football finance expert Kieron O'Connor summed it up on his *Swiss Ramble* blog in 2010: "The club's difficulties first became apparent in 2002, when poor financial management resulted in an unmanageable debt load that meant the club had to sell its famous Westfalenstadion to a real estate trust. All the funds raised from their flotation on the German stock exchange two years before (the first and to date only listing of a German football club) had effectively been squandered."

The season after the title win saw Borussia finish third. This was perfectly credible but meant a play-off for the Champions League. As the Dortmund players went into the two-legged match against FC Brugge it was generally understood that failure to beat the Belgian team and qualify for the group stage would have dire consequences financially. It was another Brazilian, this time Márcio Amoroso who managed to snatch an away goal in a 2-1 first-leg defeat in Belgium. It was hoped that the striker's contribution would prove to be a lifeline and help to pay back some of the DM 51 million fee that Dortmund had committed for his transfer from Parma. The deal to bring Amoroso to the Ruhr was eye-watering at the time although mitigated by the exchange of transfer rights for the Italian club over Evanílson should the wing back ever have been put up for sale. Nevertheless, the Amoroso transfer is still among the biggest ever deals in the Bundesliga, even all these years later, and is a fine example of just how much money was being spent and exactly what was at stake.

In a febrile atmosphere at the Westfalen, Dortmund rolled the dice and lost the second leg after penalties. Amoroso put BVB ahead after just three minutes only for Andrés Mendoza to equalise. Four minutes from full time Ewerton snatched a second for the home team to win the match but square the tie. Extra time yielded nothing but a nerve-shredding penalty shoot-out in which Dortmund came up short. Messrs Niebaum and Meier sat helplessly in the stand and watched their chickens coming home to roost. Without the additional revenue from the Champions League the club would not be able to meet its commitments.

The club's share value dropped dramatically and the players' wages grew in proportion to the club's income. So began the spiral of debt that resulted in three managerial changes and an alarming decline. It was a classic example of the truth behind the fable of Icarus. Not so much "Steine und Beine" as "Feather and Wax". As O'Connor put it, "In a scenario horribly reminiscent of Leeds United's misguided strategy, Borussia effectively gambled on competing regularly in the Champions League to fund their spending. Although they managed to avoid relegation, the club's record losses and massive debts put them in a 'life-threatening situation'."

Bert van Marwijk replaced Matthias Sammer in the summer of 2004. The Dutchman's spell was unsatisfactory but on reflection could have been worse. It ended in December 2006 when Jürgen Röber took over. However, the former Partizan Belgrade coach from the old East Germany only lasted in Dortmund until the following March. He was replaced by the former German international Thomas Doll. By this point Borussia Dortmund were on their way back, although you wouldn't have believed it by watching the team on the pitch. In fact, without the new coach bounce in the 2006/07 season all the good work rebuilding the club's finances and restructuring of their debts would have been in jeopardy had the team not managed to just about haul itself out of the bottom two by the end.

The financial turnaround began on 14th March 2005 in what Uli Hesse described in The Blizzard in 2011 as a "cheap, ugly building made of corrugated steel" in the Düsseldorf airport compound. In that building a meeting was called with the club's creditors. There, the club's new CEO set about the onerous task of convincing the 444 people in the meeting that it would be a good idea to defer repayments of that €120 million and allow them to implement their recovery plan. It is no exaggeration to say that the club's existence was in the balance – had the creditors voted down the plan there would have been no way back. Borussia's assets would have been liquidated and spread thinly among its creditors. The meeting took hours but eventually and mercifully the creditors were satisfied and agreed. In fairness, despite the club's considerable investment in Steine, its physical assets may not have been sufficiently valuable to cover what was owed. Assuming they could stomach the financial impairment, it made sense to wait until the club was ready to pay back the money. Some of the 444 would have been emotionally attached to the club and would not want to be the people that oversaw its demise, even though that would have been an unfair accusation to level. Borussia and Borussia alone were responsible for their own situation. In any event, given the speed with which BVB were able to bounce back the creditors must have been pretty confident that they would get their money back.

American investment bank Morgan Stanley, put up a €75 million loan which was used to buy back the Westfalenstadion. As O'Connor explains, "The remaining €22 million was used to reduce and refinance existing liabilities, which enabled the creditors' agreement of March 2005 to be annulled in June 2006." International sports rights agency Sportfive signed a 12-year marketing agreement that was so lucrative that the loan from Morgan Stanley was paid back years ahead of its due date. Local insurance firm Signal Iduna took on the naming rights to the stadium. From 2005 onwards the Westfalenstadion was called

Signal Iduna Park, an arrangement that may have upset traditionalists but was a necessary compromise for a club that was doing whatever it took to get back to a solid financial footing. In short, beggars can't be choosers.

By this time the almost continual redevelopment of the stadium since its construction in 1974 continued and by 2003 the corners had been filled in to bring the capacity to approximately 81,000 spectators for domestic league games where standing is permitted. Despite the heavy cost, this asset and the club's top class training facility are key components in its revival and prosperity. The seething mass of humanity that is the Südtribune, the colour, the noise, the passion that is conveyed on the matchdays, is so powerful that it can be felt thousands of miles away across television signals and the internet. The experience in person is so visceral that it is difficult to stay focussed on the match. This raw emotion not only provides a tremendous advantage to the home side but contributes to the identity of the club, an identity that is highly marketable. All of this febricity is bottled down into the marketing slogan of "Echte Liebe" or "Real Love".

Despite the errors in judgement made by Gerd Niebaum, the decision to invest in the Steine of the Westfalenstadion was probably enough to persuade those 444 creditors sitting in an ugly building outside Düsseldorf that they had the wherewithal to survive. It was a close call and looking back could have resulted in the demise of a great football club. However, the investment eventually paid off. "Steine und Beine" worked, after a fashion, but it would not be a strategy to recommend for the future. To illustrate this further, life after Borussia Dortmund took a turn for the worse for Niebaum. A series of unwise property investments led to his disbarment as an attorney and notary. This was followed by the Dortmund public prosecutor filing a suit against Niebaum on suspicion of fraud. In 2015 he was convicted and given a 20-month sentence for which he was paroled and given community service.

It has probably never been said that there is a corner of south London that is forever German. However, were some bleeding-heart quinoa-quaffing remoaner ever to make such a bold claim then they would, without question, be referring to the Zeitgeist on Black Prince Road on the cusp of Kennington and Vauxhall. The establishment was and

I suspect still is actually called The Three Jolly Gardeners, and there are plenty of traces of the livery from that bygone era. It is located on a road that runs through what was a Le Corbusier-inspired brutalist council estate. As a young man in the late 1980s I used to stomp there. It was a difficult place, having been neglected by the local authority. Its inhabitants were at best ignored by the Thatcher government. Around 20 years later the place has been largely gentrified. Many of the flats were sold off and now it is populated by energetic young professional couples. Those that don't have children are preparing for that eventuality with pre-conceptual rituals such as street basketball, cycling and jogging. I say the area has been largely gentrified because there was and still is a prominent working class population in the area. Not far from the Zeitgeist a young Jadon Sancho was playing in the cages of Kennington Park.

Amid this feverish environment sits the Zeitgeist, a pub for Germans living or visiting London. I discovered this place in 2010 when I met a fellow Bundesliga enthusiast for a drink. Entering the bar was like entering Germany. There were only German beers on tap and in the fridges, only German food on the menu, and the first language was German. The décor is not in the style of your typical Bierhaus. The staff do not wear ridiculous Oktoberfest-style Dirndls. This was not a place for tourists. This was a staging post for Germans to gather, catch up, watch Fußball, and network. I watched a Champions League match there on *SKY Deutschland* and hatched a plan with my new friend to launch an English language Bundesliga podcast.

While not exactly a second home, I still retain many happy recollections of entering this place. I have vivid memories of squeezing in to watch a Bayern Munich Champions League game. Of standing next to a giant (and I mean he was a giant) Borussia Dortmund fan during the DFB-Pokal final in 2012. Of slowly backing away from a very earnest new arrival from the Fatherland bemoaning the fact that everyone in England kept reminding him about the war and that he didn't understand because, "Hitler was a fucking Austrian anyway." In subsequent years the place is a little less busy, perhaps because of the emergence of Bavarian-style beer halls north of the river or perhaps because the "locals" grew weary of having to put up with dreadful English hipsters looking for authenticity. Nevertheless, the Zeitgeist remains an essential location for strong German beer and Saturday afternoon Bundesliga Konferenz (the SKY Deutschland equivalent of Soccer Saturday only where they actually show the football).

One of the most memorable nights was Friday 14th January 2011. It was the opening game of the Rückrunde between Bayer Leverkusen and Borussia Dortmund. The Black and Yellows sat proudly atop the table. Over the winter break there had been a concern about the restart. Japanese genius Shinji Kagawa was injured and absent from the squad. Bayern Munich were having, by their exalted standards, a shocker under head coach Louis van Gaal and were in fifth place, 14 points behind Borussia. The second-placed team in the Bundesliga going into the Rückrunde were Mainz 05, coached by a certain Thomas Tuchel. Despite the handsome lead, these were nervous times. A rare and historic title win was on the cards but such is the length of Bayern's shadow, everyone knew that this was still a title that Dortmund could lose. Moreover, despite BVB's superb Hinrunde, Leverkusen were a top team who had won the reverse fixture, 2-0 at the Westfalen, on the opening day of the 2010/11 season.

Such was the narrative ahead of the game. This was a stiff test of Borussia's credentials and it was a test that they passed with flying colours. In a crowded Zeitgeist myself and a couple of mates watched Dortmund win 3-1. Mario Götze scored the third but the first two came from a relatively unlikely source. A burly 5'11" midfielder scored a brace in a four-minute spell four minutes into the second half. Two minutes later Götze had made it 3-0 and, in spite of a late consolation, the result was settled and Dortmund were on their way to their first Bundesliga title since 2002 and the start of a golden phase of black and yellow was underway.

Coverage continued after the match and into the *SKY Deutschland* studio emerged the goalscoring midfielder, still in his kit but also wearing an overcoat. With an irrepressible toothy grin, he was happy to share his joy with the *SKY Sport* team. The sound was down so we had no idea what he was saying. My mate leaned over to me and said, "Look at him, he's loving it. He looks like a bloke who's just walked into the pub straight from the park." I laughed. It was true. This player didn't look like a polished modern professional footballer. He didn't behave like one either. Not for him the Important To Get The Three Points or I'm Just Happy For The Team. No. This guy had scored two goals in a pivotal moment in the season and was absolutely loving it.

"What's his name again?" asked my mate.

"Kevin Grosekoitz" I replied in my slightly drunk Croydon accent.

"Who?" he replied above the chatter of slightly drunk Germans.

"KEVIN GROSEKROITZ" I responded.

"Kev!" he cried out with the elation of someone who thought he's just happened upon a meme. "His name's Kev. That is brilliant. He's just scored two goals and his name's Kev. Big Kev." And so it stuck. From that point on Kevin Grosskroitz... (or Großkreutz, to use his actual name) became Big Kev.

The district of Eving in Dortmund was predominantly a mining town for many years before the pit closures. After the Second World War it became a centre for displaced persons who were brought to Germany during the war from foreign countries but were unable to return. Hessische Straße was the main settlement for these people who significantly boosted the population of the district. It is very much a working class neighbourhood which suffers from a high proportion of unemployment. This is the place where Kevin Großkreutz was born. Like many in the district, Big Kev is a devoted Borussia fan. "Dortmund was and still is my life," he told *Deutsche Welle* in 2011. "My dad and I went all over for the matches, to Milan, Rotterdam... Dortmund is equally important to my whole family. I was four the first time I went to the stadium." His participation in one of the club's golden eras is a personal triumph for him, particularly in view of the fact that there were significantly better players than he.

Großkreutz played most of his 236 games for Borussia Dortmund on the left wing. However, you could say that some of his most important work was in the 2013/14 season when he was converted to right back during one of the squad's not entirely uncommon injury crises. Łukasz Piszczek, the longstanding and popular Polish international right back, injured his hip in the summer and would not return until June. Dortmund coach Jürgen Klopp had identified Großkreutz as a replacement and had been playing him as right back in pre-season. He was already established as a flexible player, willing to do what it took to keep his place. The previous May he stood in as goalkeeper for the final 10 minutes of the 2-1 defeat against Hoffenheim at the Westfalen after Roman Weidenfeller was sent off. His first act was to pick the ball out of the net after Sejad Salihović scored the resultant penalty.

The following season Kevin played as right back for all but three games in the first 19 fixtures of the season. When Piszczek returned, Großkreutz was deployed in his more familiar position on the left side of the attack. He also plugged gaps where required in the centre and on the right wing. In fact, the only positions he didn't play in were centre half and striker. In that season Big Kev made 18 appearances as right back, 10 as left winger, two as right back, another two as a central midfielder and one on the right wing. He also played in three different positions in Dortmund's ten-game run that took them to the quarter-final of the Champions League. Included in that run was the crucial winning goal in the final game of the group stage at Marseille.

In the early days under Jürgen Klopp's management, recruiting top class talent to the club was something of a challenge. The modern Borussia can attract the best, brightest and youngest. It has the money and enjoys the trust of the top young players, their families and their agents. In 2009 the situation was a little different, although the Borussia squad was coming together nicely. Nuri Şahin was now well established in the midfield. Mats Hummels' defensive partnership with Neven Subotić was to be the foundation of what was to come. Lucas Barrios, a Buenos Aires native, joined from Colo-Colo in Chile. The young *regista* Sven Bender joined from 1860 Munich. These transfers proved significant and the players made important contributions to the future success of Borussia, as did the signing of Großkreutz, a former Dortmund youth team player who didn't make it and in 2006 had been moved on to Rot Weiss Ahlen, where he made a name for himself as a hard working attacking right winger. Großkreutz was part of the 2007/08 team that won promotion from the Regionalliga Nord, the regionalised third tier at the time, to the 2. Bundesliga. He played alongside another Dortmund lad by the name of Marco Reus.

Großkreutz was not the best ever player to wear black and yellow. His appearance and gait may have been something of a throwback by comparison to the modern player, an off-the-shelf suit in amongst the bespoke athletes, their bodies tailored for the specific demands of a by now ultra-professionalised sport. That being said he was more than just a cheerleader or a voice of the fans in the changing room. Großkreutz was a classic barrel-chested player containing a mighty pair of lungs and a heart to match. What Kevin Großkreutz could do was run. Perhaps not as fast as others but his stamina was incredible. He could also pass, cross and score the odd goal. He was also very good at subsuming his interests on the field to the team. In short, he played like a man who knew his place and was prepared to do what it took to win. Just the sort of hard-working utility player that Klopp needed in order to plug the gaps.

The season before had been more than decent for Dortmund, finally revitalised after the painful, ruinous years that brought the club to the edge of bankruptcy. Klopp's first season in charge had had an almost instant effect. Gone were the moribund days of Thomas Doll, whose unspectacular time in charge had the peculiar effect of almost relegating the club while in the same season entering them to the UEFA Cup and taking them within a hair's breadth of a glorious cup final win against Bayern Munich in the DFB-Pokal. Despite a dismal season BVB negotiated their way past Bremen, Hoffenheim (who were an up and coming second division club at the time) and Carl Zeiss Jena to arrive at the Olympiastadion in April for the final of the DFB-Pokal.

Their opponents were Bayern Munich under former BVB coach Ottmar Hitzfeld. Needless to say Bayern were the heavy favourites against struggling opponents who were missing first choice goalkeeper Roman Weidenfeller through injury. Marc Ziegler deputised. A goal after 11 minutes from the brilliant Luca Toni looked to set the tone for the evening but Dortmund showed the sort of character that frankly they had not displayed for much of the season. They kept going until the 90th minute, when Mladen Petrić equalised. Sadly for Dortmund it all fell apart. Toni scored the winner in extra time and Jakub Błaszczykowski was sent off. The defeat was hard to take and also gave the inbound coach, Klopp, the added wrinkle of UEFA Cup football as the spot that is awarded to the winner for the cup was not required by Champions League-bound Bayern.

The following season saw a change of personnel on and off the pitch. Klopp's arrival coincided with the departures of some Dortmund stalwarts: Christian Wörns, Diego Klimowicz and Petrić all moved on. In came Neven Subotić; Nuri Şahin back from a loan at Feyenoord; Mohamed Zidan and Patrick Owomoyela from Werder Bremen; the Brazilian defender Felipe Santana; the Hungarian international Tamás Hajnal; and Kevin-Prince Boateng from Tottenham Hotspur, among others. Also joining from the second team was a 20-year-old full back by the name of Marcel Schmelzer. The season was a marked improvement under Klopp with the team finishing strongly in sixth.

Indeed they could have gone one better and qualified for the UEFA Cup. Dortmund were in fifth place going into the final matchday but could only manage a point at Mönchengladbach. That would have been enough were it not for Piotr Trochowski, whose last minute winner for HSV in their 3-2 win at Eintracht Frankfurt lifted the Hamburg club into that final European spot.

The Dortmund players and coaching staff took to the field after the final whistle with one foot in Europe but when the news came in about the Trochowski goal the mood changed. After having spent years in the doldrums BVB had returned to prominence in the space of a year under their new coach. Earning a spot in the Europa League through the league rather than as a lucky loser in the DFB-Pokal would have been quite the cherry on the top. The long face on Jürgen Klopp as he saluted the away fans on the field of Borussia Park illustrated what it meant. However, they were to go one better the following season.

Klopp's refreshed Dortmund team that started the 2009/10 season did not come straight out of the blocks. The campaign started well enough with a 1-0 win against 1. FC Köln but that was followed by a heavy defeat to HSV, points against Stuttgart and Frankfurt, and then by a 5-1 trouncing at home to Bayern. Worse was to come when they lost 1-0 to Schalke, again at the Westfalen. However, the tide began to turn after a 2-0 win against Bochum. That began an 11-match unbeaten run that was only interrupted by a cup defeat to Osnabrück. Notable performances included a decent point against an equally decent Bremen side, a 4-0 win against an admittedly less than decent Nürnberg, and a 3-1 win at the reigning champions, Wolfsburg. The run continued after the winter break and was finally halted by a 4-1 defeat to Stuttgart followed by more losses to Frankfurt and again Bayern Munich. BVB recovered to beat Hannover 4-1 but then lost the derby again, this time 2-1 in Gelsenkirchen.

In mitigation this was an excellent if prosaic Schalke team, coached by the notorious disciplinarian Felix Magath, who only the season before had guided Wolfsburg to their first Bundesliga title. Nuri Şahin had put the Dortmunders a goal up just before half time but S04 stormed back through Benedikt Höwedes and Ivan Rakitic. "The Blues did not do shit," Kevin Großkreutz wrote in his column for *Schwarzgelb.de* the following March, "but they converted a set piece and got another lucky shot at our goal." Prior to the game Großkreutz, being something of a hate figure for Schalke fans, discovered that his mobile phone number had made its way into the wrong hands. "The day before the match I had 200 calls on my cell. Some Blues must have gotten hold of my number and called me – not to chat, I can tell you. I did not care. Let them have their fun. Still, threatening my life was a bit over the top."

Dortmund rallied to an extent and registered impressive wins against Leverkusen and Werder, who would finish above them in the table. However, they managed only one win on their last five and ended the season with a very disappointing 3-1 defeat against a decent but beatable Freiburg side coached by Robin Dutt. Borussia finished the season in fifth place and that earned them a play-off the following season in the recently rebranded UEFA Europa League, previously the UEFA Cup. However, they only finished four points off a third-place finish and a chance to qualify for the Champions League.

Easily the most eye-catching contribution to the season was that of Lucas Barrios. At just over €4 million the former Argentine represented a significant outlay for a club that just a few years ago had nearly gone to the wall. Barrios's time at Dortmund was brief but his contribution was telling. The Buenos Aires-born striker scored an astonishing 49 goals in 53 games for the Chilean club Colo-Colo. While some players that travel long distances to very different countries can take time to settle, Barrios only needed seven games. "I went as a scorer of the world and I had a lot of responsibility. The first few months were difficult for adaptation," he said to *Goal.com* in 2017. "Two, three months. Then came the goals." His first was in the 1-0 win at Borussia Mönchengladbach. He scored braces against Bochum, Leverkusen and Wolfsburg. In the 3-2 win at Nürnberg he scored a hat-trick. Barrios could score from both outside and inside the penalty area. He could work with his back to goal and could turn and shoot. He was also adept at closing down the goalkeeper and picking up goals from rebounds.

Barrios finished that season with a mammoth 19 goals. Other top performers were Mo Zidan, who played a full season, with six goals. However, the campaign also saw the emergence of Nuri Şahin, who scored four goals and also eight assists from midfield. Big Kev weighed in with five goals and three assists in 32 games and played mostly on the left. Not a bad haul for a player who was not necessarily the best in the Dortmund attack. His enthusiasm, zest and ability had more to give in subsequent seasons.

Borussia Dortmund's unbeaten run of twelve matches was an indication of the squad's potential. In the following season it would be realised in spectacular fashion.

In an interview with *11Freunde* in February 2018, Jakub Błaszczykowski was asked for the definition of luck. His response?

"Malaga."

They say that you make your own luck. If so then in the case of Malaga, Borussia Dortmund must have had a veritable sweatshop full of the stuff out the back. Dortmund were drawn against the Spanish team at the quarter-final stage. Malaga were enjoying a period of unprecedented success thanks to the patronage of their owner Abdullah Al Thani, who invested in the club located on the Mediterranean coast as part of a broader property development plan. The idea was that by giving the community a football club of which they could be proud, it would gratefully allow him the planning permission he needed. It didn't, and while the club spent plenty of money on Beine there was very little in the way of Steine. Malaga eventually fell foul of UEFA's Financial Fair Play laws and went into decline. However, the 2012/13 season was peak Malaga and the club went on a dreamlike run to the latter stages of the Champions League, just like their quarter-final opponents, Borussia Dortmund.

Malaga's dream came crashing to an end in controversial and acrimonious manner with a last-ditch goal from Marco Reus and the winner by Felipe Santana, the Brazilian centre back signed as a backup for Mats Hummels and Neven Subotić. The replay of the winning goal did not reflect well on the officials. There was, to use a cliché, more than a hint of offside when the ball came into the six-yard box from a hopeful cross by Robert Lewandowski. Julian Schieber's close-range mis-hit shot was characteristic of the striker's time at Dortmund but Santana was on hand to stab the ball over the line. Since Klopp's arrival at Borussia we had seen Dortmund play some glorious football and put away some sensational goals but this was a scramble more worthy of a Sunday morning park game. Kuba called it luck. Abdullah Al Thani called it racism. Nobby Dickel's commentary from within the stadium for Borussia's own radio station reflected the pandemonium at the time. When the game clock struck 90, the away side were 2-1 up and going through to the semi-final. The first leg finished 0-0 so even if Dortmund did equalise Malaga would still carry the day on away goals. But in such moments there is no accounting for mistakes made in the heat of the moment and, even with my official Borussia Dortmund patch firmly installed over one of my eyes, it is hard not to concede that Santana's goal was very much offside.

After the game Klopp was in bits. His interview with *Sky Sports* in the UK, in a language that he was not used to, was almost incoherent. The polished, guarded Klopp of Liverpool FC did not exist yet and the over-excited Dortmund coach who had helped drag a club from the depths of mediocrity to this moment just stood there with his glasses all steamed up and wonky, a goofy grin on his face like he'd won first prize in a Star Trek-themed pub quiz.

Błaszczykowski acknowledged that the linesman could easily have flagged for offside when Lewandowski crossed the ball. "It was an important victory," he said in 2018, "but you also have to enjoy this success with humility." This sentiment illustrates why the player overcame considerable obstacles and almost devastating heartbreak to rise to the position of captain of his national team and was a top-flight professional footballer for over a decade.

Jakub Błaszczykowski did not come cheap to Borussia, at least not relative to Dortmund's spending in the winter of 2007. At the time Michael Zorc wanted to bring the right winger in for €2.5 million but the 21-year-old's club, Wisła Kraków, wanted over €3 million. By the time the transfer happened in the summer the undisclosed amount was closer to the Polish club's valuation. Much like his compatriot Robert Lewandowski, Błaszczykowski – or "Kuba" for short –was a highly rated Ekstraklasa player, a "little Figo" according to Polish football great Zbigniew Boniek. Polish football broadcaster Roman Kołtoń called him, "one of the most interesting players of his age in Europe."

"BVB seemed to me like a smaller club, because the team did not play internationally," Kuba recalled. "However, my uncle said during the negotiations: 'Kuba, Dortmund is a top club. Fantastic stadium, great fans, great history.' And that's exactly what I would have said after a few weeks in Dortmund."

If you were to be objective about Jakub Błaszczykowski looking back at his career you would probably say he is a solid seven out of ten player. But this sort of analysis ignores the emotion and humanity that is vital when assessing the impact a player had on your club and on the game in general. In the great 2012/13 season that climaxed at Wembley Stadium, Kuba was perhaps Dortmund's best player. More than that, Kuba is loved not just for his goals and his assists, but because of his humanity. The Pole is a man who has lived a life and these experiences seem to have produced a human being that can love football with great passion and understand why so many of us have chosen to incorporate football into our identities, while at the same time put it in its proper perspective.

Kuba was born in a village called Truskolasy in southern Poland. He and his brother were raised from the age of 10 by his grandmother. Jakub, by then a promising footballer, nearly gave up the sport after witnessing his mother's murder. She was stabbed by Jakub's father. The journey to and from football training was arduous enough but after suffering such unimaginable trauma, he could hardly be blamed for reassessing his priorities. "Every day I drove from our village, Truskolasy, to football training in the city of Częstochowa. Six hours a week, two hours to get there and two back. In the evening I did not get to bed until ten or eleven. After my mother's death, I did not go to training for two or three months at all."

Six-year-old Jakub watched the Polish national team reach the final in the 1992 Summer Olympics in Barcelona, the first tournament to adopt the Under-23 format. Poland's star had waned in the late 1980s and 1990s but this group of youngsters made it as far as the final in Camp Nou. They lost 3-2 to hosts Spain with the winner coming in the last minute. Young Jakub was too young to catch Poland's fantastic wins over Italy and Australia live but had them taped so he could watch them over and over again. The captain of the team was Jerzy Brzęczek, who would receive 42 caps for the senior team and, in 2018, become its coach. To Jakub he was Uncle Jurek.

Brzęczek was the person who persuaded Jakub to return to football after his mother (Brzęczek's sister) was killed. He convinced his nephew to compete in a screening tournament and Jakub showed what he was made of when he was voted the best player. "Have you seen what you can do? And how good you could be if you trained regularly?" he asked Jakub. Those words were enough for him to start playing again.

"When he was younger he was an amazingly skilful player," Polish football writer Ryan Hubbard told me. "He would dance around the edge of the box. When he played at Wisła he was the standout player. The creative one in the middle of the park." Unfortunately injuries had taken some of the zip from his play and when he arrived at Dortmund it was as a winger rather than central midfielder.

In a Dortmund team that could be stodgy and pedestrian he was a breath of fresh air. His pace and technique added some real exuberance to the side. He was probably the first Klopp signing, albeit arriving before the Mainz coach had made the move north. Kuba would become that solid and reliable wing man who rarely lets you down and never dwells on his mistakes. "He's not the type of player to go missing in games. Part of me thinks that harks back to his upbringing. That sort of attitude that if something bad happens that you just forget about it and move on. He's the type of player that you could always rely on especially during his peak years," says Hubbard. "He captained the Poland team when it was at his lowest possibly since the 1990s."

Błaszczykowski was just the sort of player Klopp needed. The pair enjoyed a close connection, with Klopp declaring him to be the best player in the 2011/12 season. "I got along great with Jürgen. Like everyone in the team. At the time BVB was like a family – and Jürgen was the father. I have not only improved athletically at BVB, but also the time has brought me forward humanly," he said. He was the only Pole at the club when he arrived but was the first of a trio of Polish internationals that made such an impact on the side at such a crucial time in the club's history. In 2010 he was joined by childhood friend Łukasz Piszczek and a gifted but slightly unpolished striker, Robert Lewandowski.

As a youth player Piszczek was a goalscorer. He played up front for Gwarek Zabrze and it was his ability to find the back of the net that attracted the attention of Hertha BSC. The Berlin club loaned Piszczek out to Zagłębie Lubin, where he won the 2006/07 Ekstraklasa title. Such were his exploits that he earned a place in leading Polish football magazine *Piłka nożna*'s All-Star Team. A hip injury took its toll during the 2008/09 season and hampered his prospects in the Hertha first team. However, an opportunity came in the unfortunate form of an injury to Arne Friedrich which created a gap in the defence. Piszczek was converted to right back and it was as a right back that he was sold to Borussia Dortmund.

Lewandowski was and at the time of writing still is a cut above. Already a promising goalscorer at Lech Poznań, the 22-year-old made the move to Germany as a somewhat raw successor to Barrios. The move had an element of serendipity in that the young forward had appointments at Premier League clubs West Bromwich Albion and Blackburn Rovers but was unable to travel due to the enormous dust cloud created by the Eyjafjallajökull volcano eruption in Iceland, which shut down the air traffic in Europe for five days. Instead, Lewandowski took the somewhat lower road to Dortmund. It is worth reflecting for a short while how the path of one of Europe's greatest ever strikers could have led him had he ended up wearing the blue and white of Blackburn or the Black Country club.

What is there to say about this man that hasn't already been said? Were it not for the existence of the Ronaldo-Messi axis, Lewandowski would easily have won a Ballon d'Or. A rangy ball-playing centre forward with the ability to create goalscoring chances in the tightest of spaces, he had the positional awareness to make for an excellent target man in the event that Hummels or Subotić would send long balls his way, which they did time and again. That long stride of his gave him pace. He could drop deep, sit up top, whatever a coach wanted him to do. Lewandowski is possibly the best ever at his trade. Lionel Messi and Cristiano Ronaldo are a different hue of forward player but as a number 9 there are few to rival Lewandowski.

I will never forget the look of Jose Mourinho's face after Dortmund beat Real Madrid in the Champions league semi-final and Lewandowski scored all of BVB's goals in a 4-1 first leg win. "We know everything about Lewandowski. We studied him from every detail possible," the Madrid boss told *Sky Sports UK* after the game, but despite their preparation the Polish striker could not be contained. That semi-final represents one of the high water marks of Lewandowski's career at Borussia Dortmund. The other must be the hat-trick against Bayern Munich in the 2012 DFB-Pokal final in Berlin. For me this is the high point of the club's history under Klopp. Yes, beating Real Madrid is very impressive. But defeating the record champions to win a piece of silverware is a greater achievement.

I watched the game in the Zeitgeist which was full of Dortmund fans, most of whom were Germans. I think only my friend and I were native English speakers. The game was particularly memorable for the fact that I was standing in front of the tallest man I'd ever seen. He was easily 6' 10" and I had to stretch to high five his hand after the fourth goal. Watching from a somewhat better vantage point was then Manchester United boss Sir Alex Ferguson, who had made the trip to Berlin despite having a crucial Premier League match against Sunderland the following day. When the TV cameras found him there was a brief moment of extra excitement among the fans in the club. Who could the legendary Scottish coach be scouting? The fact that those fans reacted like they did tells you something about the club they support. History will remember Klopp's Dortmund as one of the best German club sides ever, but many Dortmund fans are still informed more by their failures than successes. The idea that the great Sir Alex should be taking an interest in the 'little' club (which regularly sells out its 80,000 capacity stadium) was a surprise.

While Fergie was treated to a virtuoso display by Lewandowski, he was actually there to see Shinji Kagawa. The Japanese central playmaker who played with a straight back and a high chin signed for Borussia from Cerezo Osaka for the paltry sum of €350,000. Used sparingly at first, Kobe-born Kagawa became a vital pivot in the team and that night in Berlin he was majestic. Nothing good that happened in that Dortmund attack happened without Shinji's say so. His only goal of the game came after just three minutes and it set the tone for the rest of the evening. It's possible that Kagawa was aware that the illustrious manager of Manchester United was studying in the stadium and waiting to be entertained. If he was then he rose to the occasion and was wearing the red of that club the following season. Lewandowski, meanwhile, was linked with a move to Old Trafford but would stay for another two seasons and help score the goals that took Borussia to the Champions League final at Wembley. In his final campaign he ran down his contract and played all the way to the DFB-Pokal final of 2014 against his next club, Bayern Munich. By this point the old order had been restored and Bayern, under at the reins of Pep Guardiola, won the match 2-0 after extra time, a scoreline that looks comfortable in the end but hinged on a goal earlier in the match that should have been given but was not, despite the ball crossing the line from a Mats Hummels header.

The Polish trio of Lewandowski, Piszczek and Błaszczykowski would help to define one of the most successful and, to my mind, most enjoyable Borussia Dortmund teams to watch. They were also a key component for the Polish national team as they co-hosted the 2012 European Championships, a team of which Kuba was the proud captain. Sadly for Poland it was not a vintage tournament despite acting as co-hosts. Błaszczykowski's goal against Russia was a personal highlight in what must have been an emotional time for him: 2012 was the year that his father died, shortly after having been released from prison.

"I wonder if Lewandowski would have been as good a player for the national team as he has been without Błaszczykowski," speculates Hubbard. "With Piszczek as well, the three of them had an almost telepathic link down Poland's right hand side. Obviously Lewandowski is a cut above the rest of the Poland team. But especially between 2012 and 2014 they were the three big players in Poland. They were the three who played for Dortmund, they all played together. They were the key men in the national team. It's a package: the three of them."

While the Polish threesome had a great understanding wearing both the black and yellow of Dortmund and the white and red of Poland, their personal relationships were and are not quite so harmonious. Piszczek and Kuba are old friends who were not on the greatest of terms with Lewandowski. Like the Manchester United pairing of Andrew Cole and Teddy Sheringham this did not stop them from playing some of the best football of their respective careers. Neither has dwelt publicly about their relationship. "We are different," said Błaszczykowski. "You don't need to drink coffee with another player just because he is a compatriot." Lewandowski did take Kuba's national team captaincy in 2014 but the poor relations pre-date that happening. In view of the persistent injury problems that have hampered Kuba's career, it is not surprising that the armband was passed to the national team's best player. No one should be surprised if this was simply a personality clash, the type that happens in any workplace. Both deserve credit for getting past it and helping Borussia Dortmund to two Bundesliga titles, a DFB-Pokal win and a Champions League final.

The aforementioned injuries cost Błaszczykowski dearly. The early stages of his time at Borussia were punctuated by thigh and muscular problems. Even before, at Wisła, he missed the 2006 World Cup and the 2008 European Championships. A cruciate ligament rupture cost him the 2014 World Cup and most of that year. By that time Dortmund under Klopp were coming down from the high. The effect of injuries and departing players were starting to bite and the prolonged absence of one of Klopp's most trusted lieutenants could not have made things any easier. It is sadly fitting that Kuba's final appearance should end with an injury. It came in a 1-1 draw at Hoffenheim just four games before the end of the 2014/15 campaign, also Klopp's final season. He pulled a hamstring and was substituted for Kevin Kampl. He did not return for the new season and, by the time he was actually fit again, Thomas Tuchel was the new coach and Jakub Błaszczykowski was not a part of the many great plans he had for Dortmund. Kuba spent a season in the beautiful city of Florence at the Serie A club Fiorentina. In the summer of 2016 he was transferred to Wolfsburg for €5 million. Not only did the club have his best years through another golden era, he also turned a modest profit for them when he left.

But the fans did not forget Kuba. Upon his return to the Westfalen as a Wolfsburg player in the 2016/17 season they chanted his name and gave him a rapturous applause when he took to the field after 75 minutes. Despite numerous injuries Jakub Błaszczykowski made 253 appearances for the club. If the testimony in this book contributes to his joining the pantheon of Borussia legends then it has been worth the writing.

It ends in an exhibition hall in Berlin on the night of the 2015 DFB-Pokal final defeat to Wolfsburg. I'm standing behind the tall and wiry frame of Neven Subotić. Peering over his shoulder I can see a stage and on that stage is a crestfallen Jürgen Klopp. He is saying goodbye. His final wish to parade the German Cup trophy in Borsigplatz has been denied by a combination of an emotionally drained Dortmund side that had endured a wretched season and a Wolfsburg team led by Kevin De Bruyne, probably one of the best players on the planet. The room is packed with the great and the good of Borussia Dortmund plus a number of assorted functionaries, employees of the club and one hanger-on who got in thanks to the good fortune of being a friend of those employees.

My memory of the event is sketchy. I had spent the day and evening drinking beer with a group of fans in the city and at the stadium before, during and after the match. It must have been the small hours of the morning by the time Klopp took to the stage. I didn't understand what he said. That is, I didn't understand the words, but the emotion was utterly comprehensible. Here was a man who had taken Borussia Dortmund to the top but was leaving them, superficially at least, not far away from where he picked up: mid-table and defeated in a cup final. His final public appearance as Dortmund coach, amid the opulence and roped-off VIP areas, was in stark contrast to his beginnings at the club.

The earlier stages of Klopp's career at Borussia were spent holding court in the pubs of Dortmund. In that first season in charge the former Mainz coach had a lot to prove and a lot of persuading to do. He would regularly hold meetings with fan groups in pubs in the city, drinking beer, smoking cigarettes and explaining what he was trying to achieve, how he was going about it and why it was vital that the fans on the Südtribune engaged with the project and kept supporting the team on the pitch, no matter how many bumps in the road there might be.

"This is the most emotional region in Germany," Jürgen Klopp once told Uli Hesse. "And even though there are some people 30km from here, in Schalke, who will vehemently deny it, I would say Borussia is the most emotional club."

Compared to some of the centre backs that have graced the pages of this and other books, Klopp falls very much into the journeyman class. From birth, he was encouraged to play sport by his father, who was an enthusiastic footballer and later in life a tennis player too. Despite never making it to one of the top clubs Norbert Klopp became a coach and something of a community leader. He loved sport and upon the birth of a son he encouraged his boy to take it up. Originally a striker, Jürgen converted to centre back and was a permanent fixture in the defence for FSV Mainz for 11 years, rising to the position of captain.

His coaching background also, unsurprisingly, stems from Mainz, and specifically from Wolfgang Frank. "When I became a manager years later I used a lot of the stuff I learned from him," Klopp said of his former boss to *Sky Sports* in 2016. "He was the perfect role model and a lot of his players are now managers or coaches around the world." Until recently Frank was a forgotten man of German coaching history. He counts 34 appearances for Borussia Dortmund in the late seventies in a playing career that took him to Stuttgart, Alkmaar, Nürnberg and Braunschweig. However, it is as a coach that he deserves recognition. Mainz's sporting director, Christian Heidel, recruited Frank from Rot-Weiss Essen in September 1995 with the team already struggling near the foot of the table. With no money for transfers, Heidel needed a coach that would be able to shake things up a bit and the team under Frank spent most of the season in the bottom two only to climb out with seven weeks remaining. The reason for the dramatic upsurge? He switched the playing style to 4-4-2. "It was new in Germany to play in a back four and play this way," says Klopp. "Mainz was the first to do it and the success was unbelievable. Frank was a very important person for all of us when he came to Mainz."

For decades German football was all about the libero. Dortmund can look to Wolfgang Paul, Matthias Sammer and Christian Wörns among the many proponents of this position. Frank's big change for Mainz was to abandon the sweeper and play with a flat back four. But that was not all; Frank's strategy was to employ a method of defending that was close to what modern tacticians would call pressing and the blocking of passing lanes. The playing style known as *gegenpressing*, utilised so effectively by Klopp's Dortmund, was born in Mainz under Wolfgang Frank and with Klopp leading the team on the pitch.

Frank's two spells at Mainz reshaped the club and the rest of German football as they embraced the back four. Today the libero is a redundant position, replaced with the deep-lying midfielder in the Sebastian Kehl or perhaps Julian Weigl mould. There is an argument that Frank is among the most influential figures in the modern development of Borussia, a former player who – without actually coaching the club – influenced one of its greatest.

Frank departed FSV in 1997 to join Austria Vienna but things didn't work out. In the meantime Mainz went through two permanent coaches, including former Dortmund coach Reinhard Saftig. However, neither coach could get his head around the kind of football that the players and Christian Heidel wanted to play, and after a year Frank was asked to return, which he did. He left again in 2000 and, when Eckhard Krautzun didn't work out, Heidel turned to his recently retired captain, Jürgen Klopp.

It is probably worth emphasizing that at this time FSV Mainz 05 were not a natural top-flight club. Indeed, in all their history (which goes back to 1905 as the name suggests) they had never spent as much as a season in the first Bundesliga. Certainly, the arrival of Heidel and then Frank signified a new ambition but achieving the feat of elevation to Germany's top flight was a challenge both operationally and narratively. Perhaps then it is no surprise that there were some desperately near misses in the years under Frank and Klopp before promotion was finally achieved in 2004. Klopp kept his team up for a season and even claimed a UEFA Fair Play award that gave them a UEFA Cup spot. The following season did not go so well and the 05ers were relegated. Klopp remained at the club for one more season but after failing, albeit narrowly, to regain top-flight status, he left. Despite these recent setbacks, Klopp was a highly regarded coach and rightly so. Anyone who could take this friendly but unambitious club from a carnival city and get them into Europe as well as the first division deserves huge credit. Klopp was and is a deeply emotional and demonstrative man. Always ready with a hug for one of his players or a bollocking for the fourth official, he exudes passion and his teams reflect that passion. What he needed for his next challenge was a sleeping giant of a club that was experiencing hard times but had a plan for a recovery and needed a young, hungry and innovative coach to overhaul the team and bring some punch back on the pitch. He was quite frankly the ideal coach for Borussia Dortmund. So it's just as well that Borussia Dortmund happened to be in precisely this state at the time.

Mainz were eventually promoted under Jørn Andersen but survived and thrived under Thomas Tuchel who, of course, went on to replace Klopp at Dortmund. Tuchel's legacy has yet to be measured fully. Not enough time has passed. But what we can say is that between the influence of Wolfgang Frank, Jürgen Klopp and Thomas Tuchel, FSV Mainz have played a significant role in the modern Borussia Dortmund, and they probably have much to thank them for, not least the €4.5 million signing of their centre back, Neven Subotić, who would become one half of probably the best defensive pairing in the history of the club.

When he arrived, fresh-faced and excited to be joining a great club, Jürgen Klopp was not aware of how close BVB had come to extinction. However, he was aware of the scale of the task at hand on the pitch. Borussia were a spent force with players on high salaries, some of whom were in need of a fresh challenge. In the preceding years some of these players had moved on – the mercurial but injury prone Tomáš Rosický headed to London and Arsenal; his Czech compatriot (and one of my favourite players of all time) Jan Koller departed for Monaco. The excellent German international centre back Christoph Metzelder was Real Madrid-bound. The eye-catching speedster David Odonkor, who made a name for himself in Germany's surprisingly decent 2006 World Cup team, left for Real Betis. Looking back on these names and more, it is disappointing that Borussia could not make more with these players, but by the time Klopp arrived the die was cast and they were gone, with more to follow. In his first season in charge Klopp said farewell to Diego Klimowicz, Mladen Petrić, Steven Pienaar, Giovanni Federico and – of course – Christian Wörns, who retired. This is perhaps just as well, since Klopp had no need of sweepers. The injury prone but free-scoring Alexander Frei also did not stay long after Klopp's arrival.

However, the new Dortmund coach had good reason to thank the Swiss international. He deployed Frei as a substitute in his first Revierderby, which was only Klopp's fourth game as coach. Schalke had taken a 3-0 lead in a fractious match that had seen Subotić handle the ball to give away a penalty and the ever classy Rafinha dry-hump one of the corner flags in front of the Südtribune after scoring his second. Schalke was a welcome opponent for Frei, who scored the first in the 2-0 win in 2007 to deny them what would have been their first ever Bundesliga title and provide Borussia fans with a rare moment of joy, albeit in the way that a child deliberately knocks over another child's ice cream. If there were a word in German for taking pleasure in the misfortune of others then it would have been ideal for that game. Two seasons later Schalke were in a position to exact a modicum of revenge against their vulnerable rivals but Frei denied them their fun. His corner proved to be an assist for Subotić's redemptive far post header to make the score 3-1. Frei then scored himself with a cut inside and shot from outside the area past Ralf Fährmann in the Schalke goal. The Gelsenkirchen team lost their heads completely and had Christian Pander and Fabian Ernst sent off for two agricultural tackles on Kuba. Finally, in the 89th minute, Frei converted a penalty to square the match. The handball decision that led to it does not bear close scrutiny but who cares? It's Schalke.

It is also worth pointing out that Lars Ricken also lost his place in the first team although this was due to premature retirement through injuries rather than any symbolic gesture. Replacing these big names was a mixture of the young and the cheap. The 2009/10 squad was an interesting combination of players who were interim solutions and those who would form the basis of the Bundesliga-winning squad in 2011. In goal was Roman Weidenfeller who, at 29, was an established custodian well on his way to taking his place among the great Borussia goalkeepers. Only Michael Zorc has played more games than Weidenfeller. The defence was almost complete with the two 21-year-olds, Subotić and Hummels, at the centre. Marcel Schmelzer played on the left and Patrick Owomoyela on the right. 'Schmelle' would go on to captain the club and was part of the quintet of defenders and goalkeeper that provided the foundations for the club's success in the ensuing years. Owomoyela made 84 appearances but was replaced as first choice right back by Łukasz Piszczek. Supporting the back four were Felipe Santana and, of course, Dede.

The midfield had the aforementioned Jakub Błaszczykowski and Sebastian Kehl (whose appearances were limited by injury) along with former 1860 Munich youngster Sven Bender, who made 19 appearances. Alongside them was 29-year-old Tamas Hajnal, a Hungarian attacking midfielder who was at Schalke as a youngster but arrived in Dortmund from Karlsruhe. While not a prolific goalscorer, Hajnal was one of my favourite players at that time and an important one as he brought much needed creativity into the midfield. I have fond memories of his performance in Dortmund's 3-0 home win over Stuttgart the season before, an example of his effectiveness. He scored the opening goal and set the tone for the rest of the match.

Up front was Barrios, supported by Kevin Großkreutz, Nelson Valdez, Mohamed Zidan and Dimitar Rangelow. Looking at this team you can see the makings of a decent side but what you could not predict is that two seasons later many of these players would be parading the Bundesliga title around the pitch at the Westfalenstadion. This is probably because very few people would have predicted the impact Lewandowski would have on the side and fewer still could have known for certain that Nuri Şahin would return from his loan spell at Feyenoord and be ready to take a senior role in the squad. There was also the emergence of the 18-year-old youth prospect Mario

Götze, who played in five games in the 2009/10 season and while there were high expectations for the lad it was way too soon to say if he would ever come good.

One of the best Borussia Dortmund goals I never saw was scored by Nuri Şahin. I was in the stadium for the home game against a Wolfsburg team that was coached by ex-England manager Steve McClaren, but was still waiting at the bar to get the half time beers in. It was still very early in the title-winning 2010/11 season and there was no feeling that Dortmund would be winning the title come May the following year. The score was 0-0 at half time and two of our party (me being one) decided it was beer o'clock. The queue was long and slow. My friend who had never been to the Westfalen before was getting politely anxious that the game had restarted and he was still in the queue. Ever the considerate veteran, I absolved him of his responsibilities and waved away the dust from the trail he left in his wake. The guy in front of me was having trouble paying. I bit my lip and waited patiently. As I did so Şahin played a loose one-two with Kehl, performed a neat pirouette and struck the ball from about 30 yards out, just over the fingertips of Diego Benaglio in the Wolfsburg goal. The strike had the virtue of being both clean and filthy in equal measure and I missed it. There was consternation in the bar when we heard the stadium erupt and the guy in front me, perhaps mindful in his role in so many of us missing it, suddenly found the requisite cash and was on his way. "You just missed the most amazing goal!" one of my friends helpfully shouted above the noise as I handed him his beer. I don't recall what I said in reply but still remember nursing a hangover the following morning and seeing the graphic in *Bild am Sonntag* outlining in precise detail just what a fantastic goal I didn't see. I've seen it plenty of times on YouTube and it is a smashing goal. I wish I'd been there.

Nuri Şahin is from Lüdenscheid which, as most Schalke fans will tell you, is not far south of Dortmund. A local lad who came through the club's youth teams and a proud Turkish international, the central midfielder emerged from the youth ranks to take his place in the centre of the midfield with the number 8 on his back. Şahin held the record as the youngest ever Bundesliga player at 16 years and 334 days old. That record stood from August 2005 to November 2020 when another Borussia Dortmund player, Youssoufa Moukoko, surpassed it. In November 2005 Şahin also became the youngest ever Bundesliga goalscorer, a record that stood until the super-talented Florian Wirtz of Bayer Leverkusen broke it in June 2020. The record now belongs to Moukoko too.

That goal against Wolfsburg was the first of four along with eight assists for the season. In my book this was Şahin at his peak. A deep-lying midfield playmaker who could pick a pass over long distances either to feet or into space, he was an ideal player for Klopp's rapid transition football that depended on moving the ball up the field as quickly and as efficiently as possible. The goals and assists were a tremendous asset but almost a bonus. Şahin would still have been an amazing player without them and his award of Bundesliga Player of the Season was thoroughly merited. Even before he lifted the Meisterschale in May there was talk that Real Madrid wanted to sign him and sure enough it was to the Santiago Bernabeu that he departed. His replacement was the young İlkay Gündoğan, who needed a bit of time to settle in but proved a more than able successor. Sadly for Şahin he never really fulfilled his potential in Spain. Injuries blighted his time there and he made just four appearances in white, which was fewer even than seven in the red of Liverpool when he was loaned out to regain his fitness. Eventually, in 2012, he returned to Dortmund, where he endured a sporadic and injury-blighted second spell at his hometown club before leaving for Werder Bremen in 2018.

But Şahin wasn't the only Dortmund youngster who came good in that season. Mario Götze is also something of a prodigal son. The Swabian-born versatile attacking midfielder – a household name thanks to his decisive goal for Germany that won the World Cup in 2014 – was a baby-faced assassin with a perpetual motion machine inside him. Like Shinji Kagawa he played with a high chin and could see what was going on around him. Most of the time during this season he was seeing opposition players falling in his wake as he proceeded to either score a goal or set one up for a grateful teammate. In the 2010/11 season Götze scored six and created 15 more. In the following season he was less productive, only playing 17 games but still scoring six and assisting five goals in that double winning season. Those three seasons were absolute gold for Götze and Dortmund: a league title, a league and cup double, and an emotional ride to the Champions League final. By the time Borussia reached Wembley, however, the milk had been soured. Bayern Munich had reacted to the resurgence of Dortmund by signing the former Barcelona coach Pep Guardiola. Also – and, in a fashion, characteristic of the Bavarian giants when they have lost ground – they signed their most dangerous opponent's best player. The announcement happened in April, instigated by Bayern only a day before Borussia's semi-final second leg with Real Madrid. They had triggered Mario Götze's release clause and he would be transferring to Bayern Munich in July 2013. As it happened, the new Bayern player was injured for the Wembley final and watched his new team beat his old team, no doubt with mixed feelings.

Upon his return to the Westfalen the following season Götze was forced to warm up in the tunnel, such was the anger aimed at him from the crowd – not just for leaving, but for his destination and because of the timing of the announcement. It could be argued that Bayern's deliberate intention was to undermine Dortmund prior to such an important game, which they lost 2-0 despite winning the tie. To make matters worse Götze came on as a substitute and scored the opening goal in a 3-0 win for the away side. "Today, three years later and at 24, I look at that decision in a different light," he said on his Facebook page shortly after it was confirmed that he would be returning to Dortmund. On paper Götze's spell in Bavaria was a productive one, with 36 goals and 24 assists in 144 games. There is also the small matter of the three Bundesliga titles and two German Cups he won in red. It was as a Bayern Munich player that Götze scored in the Maracanã in the World Cup final. Yet, there is a lingering feeling that he didn't fulfil his potential with the Rekordmeister, perhaps exacerbated by injuries and myopathy, a muscular disorder that went undiagnosed until 2017. Mario Götze was supposed to be the "German Messi" but somehow, despite the size of his trophy cabinet, that has yet to come to pass.

Even after beating Bayern 2-0 in the Westfalen in October 2010 it was still not entirely apparent that Dortmund might win the title. Barrios and Şahin – with a lovely free kick – carried the day, but while this was a strong Bayern team that had reached the Champions League final the previous season, Louis van Gaal's team were not regarded as all-conquering like the great teams that would follow under Jupp Heynckes and Guardiola. After the game the players and the coach were enthusiastic but downbeat. When it came to the return fixture in February 2011 at the Allianz Arena, there was a little more on the line.

Dortmund were by this point comfortably top of the Bundesliga table and by any objective measure running away with it – 10 points ahead of second-placed Bayer Leverkusen and 13 in front of Bayern Munich. Subjectively though, it was still hard to imagine that the collection of youth team graduates and relatively speaking cut-price signings could end the season as champions. However, if Borussia could go to the Allianz and win then this would give the club and its fans permission to believe that it was possible. There was a late setback in the form of an injury to Weidenfeller, who could not take his customary place between the posts. In his stead was a very young and nervous-looking Mitch Langerak, a 22-year-old from Melbourne who had joined as a back-up in the previous summer and was making his first team debut very much in the lion's den. If the Australian was as nervous as he looked then it didn't matter. Dortmund were the better team on the day, as they were all season, and won the match 3-1 with goals from Barrios, Şahin and Hummels, who was returning to his hometown club. Şahin's glorious curling shot from outside the area was one for the ages and leaves a legacy in the Borusseum, which proudly displays the pair of Jürgen Klopp's glasses that Şahin broke when celebrating the result with Klopp immediately after the final whistle.

The match was a watershed in more ways than one. Primarily, it was the result that confirmed that all Borussia needed to do now was, to quote the great darts commentator Dave Lanning, pin their ears back and head for the finish. But it also showcased this hitherto unknown team to the football world outside Germany. The match was televised live around the globe on a Saturday evening and benefitted from the fact that there was no Premier League fixture up against it. Usually there is a corresponding game from England that competes for international TV eyeballs with the Bundesliga Topspiel at the same time. With the field clear, football fans looking for an alternative turned over to the Bayern v Dortmund game and were treated to an unexpected tour de force. Possibly for the first time ever outside Germany, Borussia Dortmund were "trending".

Amid a delirious and disbelieving crowd at the Westfalenstadion, Borussia Dortmund celebrated their first Bundesliga win since 2001 – with two games to spare – after beating FC Nürnberg 2-0. The goals were scored by the club's top scorer Lucas Barrios and the following season's top scorer, Robert Lewandowski, symbolising a passing of the baton between these two strikers. Klopp was showered with giant beers, flares were set off in the stadium, Dortmund partied, and they weren't even awarded the trophy. That came at the final game of the season at home to Eintracht Frankfurt.

The 2011/12 title was far from a stroll but was a convincing defence by a team at its peak. Sadly the very best of it would depart over the following two seasons but it is to the club's great credit that they were able to keep this team together for the time they did. This season they were further enhanced by the arrival of Ivan Perišić who joined from Club Brugge. The Croatian forward scored some lovely goals in his two seasons at Dortmund, including a belter against Arsenal in the Champions League. Perišić has since found fame at Inter Milan and Bayern, and for his national team in the World Cup, but he also made a telling contribution to Dortmund's successful defence of the Bundesliga. Highlights of the season were the satisfying wins home and away against Schalke and Bayern. Dortmund completed a hat-trick against the Bavarians in the DFB-Pokal final.

With a club that has as rich a history as Borussia Dortmund there can be no single greatest or defining moment. However, the 2012 double win definitely sits alongside the other great moments like the 1966 European Cup Winners' Cup win, the 1989 DFB-Pokal triumph, the Cobra's strike to save the club from oblivion, and the great days of the mid-1990s when Dortmund dominated nationally and across the continent.

Looking back this was another of those nearly moments where it looked like Borussia would eventually overtake Bayern to be the pre-eminent force in German football. This seems naive in hindsight but at the time Dortmund were so good and had the right back office combination in Hans-Joachim Watzke as CEO and Michael Zorc, converted from former captain and club legend to Sporting Director, overseeing the club's finances and recruitment with an assuredness hitherto lacking in Niebaum and Meier. As evidence to support this view I present one Marco Reus.

When I took the tour of the Westfalenstadion we were allowed into the first team dressing rooms. Each player has his own hook with his name and photo underneath. This was in 2018 and I eagerly sat in my compatriot Jadon Sancho's seat. Everyone was huddled around and taking selfies underneath the hooks of the club's captain and arguably best player, Marco Reus. The attacking wide player played in the same Rot Weiss Ahlen team as Kevin Großkreutz. Like Big Kev, Reus is a Dortmund lad. He played for the youth team but did not make it through the ranks. Reus became the player he is at Borussia Mönchengladbach, learning to carve out goals and goalscoring chances in what was mostly a poor Gladbach team. That he was destined to move to a bigger club was beyond doubt; the surprise was that he chose Dortmund, or rather that he could choose Dortmund. In any other season, Bayern would have automatically snapped him up but in that moment Dortmund had the money, the prestige and the ambitions to match the expectations of a young professional ready to step up to the big time.

However, as it turns out, the optimists were wrong. It couldn't and didn't last. The following season Bayern Munich galvanised themselves to a sensational domestic double and Champions League win. They punished Borussia's impudence by thwarting their attempts to win a third successive title and illustrated their return to the ascendancy by beating Dortmund in front of the world at Wembley. The fact that it was a close game matters little. It is now history.

The seeds for Klopp's departure were not exactly sown on that day but what followed was a continued period of dominance for Bayern with which Klopp and Zorc could not compete, partly because Bayern nabbed two of their best players, but also because the new players that came into the squad did not lift the club as their predecessors had. For example, Ciro Immobile was a hard-working and clearly talented striker whose record at Torino suggested that he could do a job. Sadly the Italian never truly settled and did not stay long. There were however some genuinely wonderful players. The Armenian Henrikh Mkhitaryan was and is a gorgeous player to watch, and not ineffective. Pierre-Emerick Aubameyang joined from Saint-Étienne more as a winger than an out-and-out striker. He went on to become the sixth highest goalscorer of all time at Borussia. It is lamentable that he only counts a DFB-Pokal win among his honours for the five years he served the club.

His final season began disastrously for Dortmund, who conceded the fastest goal in Bundesliga history just nine seconds into the match against Bayer Leverkusen, courtesy of Karim Bellarabi. A series of terrible results followed including losses to Mainz, Schalke, Köln, Hertha and, of course, Bayern Munich. In November, during a 2-2 draw with newly promoted SC Paderborn, Marco Reus ruptured his ankle ligaments and was out for the rest of the season. Borussia sank to the bottom of the table and struggled to get out of the bottom three for the entirety of the Hinrunde. Hopes were high that Klopp would rally the squad during the Winterpause but they were dashed when the team were beaten at home 1-0 by Augsburg. At this point the fans on the Südtribune snapped. They expressed their fury at the team after the game and Roman Weidenfeller had to go in and try to calm them down. Klopp stood and watched on from just outside the tunnel with a look of shock and, perhaps, realisation. His decision to resign came the following April. Klopp announced to the media that he would depart. Subsequent to that decision results took a turn for the better. The club finished the season in seventh, causing the coach to say, "If I'd known before the start of the season that we'd put such a winning run together, I'd have announced my departure back then."

In what was an anticlimactic and entirely unfitting end for one of Borussia Dortmund's greatest coaches, there was a silver lining in the form of that DFB-Pokal run. In an emotional semi-final against Bayern, BVB managed to squeeze past the champions on penalties to set up that ultimately disappointing final against Wolfsburg in Berlin. And with that Klopp was gone...

...only to return the following season, this time wearing the red tracksuit of Liverpool FC. Nearly 50 years after the two played in the Cup Winners' Cup final in Hampden, they were drawn in the semi-final of the Europa League. The first leg in Dortmund finished 1-1 and when Borussia went 2-0 up at Anfield it looked for all the world like it would prove to be an unhappy reunion for Klopp. However, Liverpool are not the sort that take kindly to getting rolled over in their own home. They stormed back and won the tie 5-4 on aggregate thanks to a last minute header from Dejan Lovren. This madcap, knockabout goal-fest served as the ideal postscript to the Jürgen Klopp era, a period of the club's history that may never be rivalled. Borussia Dortmund may yet go on to more Bundesliga and European glory but the image of the blond-haired and bespectacled showman parading the dugout with his baseball cap on his head and heart on his sleeve is not just characteristic of Borussia Dortmund's success, but of its very nature. Whatever was to come next, it was unlikely things would ever be the same again.

2016-17

What Happened Next

"I can't forget the faces. I will never forget those faces in my life. When I saw Marc [Bartra] there and when I saw Schmelle's face. It was unbelievable."

These were the words of Nuri Şahin in an interview with Jan Åge Fjørtoft just after a Champions League match. However, these words were not about the game. They didn't describe the great joy of a decisive goal or the emotion of a dramatic finale to another great European night under the lights at the Westfalenstadion. These were the words of a young man who had been through one of the most traumatic experiences of his or anyone's life.

"It's hard to talk about. It's hard to find the right words," Şahin continued. "Until I was on the pitch in the second half I didn't think about football to be honest." That second half was Borussia's postponed Champions League quarter-final in Dortmund the day after the home side's team coach was subjected to a bomb attack on the way to the stadium on 11th April 2017. There were two bombs that were exploded shattering one of the windows of the bus and injuring Borussia centre back Marc Bartra. Mercifully no one was killed and Bartra sustained only a broken wrist. However, the ferocity of the attack is not something that you can simply shrug off.

"The pain, the panic and the uncertainty of not knowing what was going on, or how long it would last… were the longest and hardest 15 minutes of my life," the Catalan defender said in an Instagram post while recuperating in hospital. "I think that the shock is decreasing more and more and, at the same time, it adds to the desire to live, to fight, to work, to laugh, to cry, to feel, to love, to believe, to play, to train, to continue to enjoy my people, loved ones, companions, my passion, to defend, to smell the grass as I do before the game starts and motivate me."

"The only thing I ask," he wrote, "is for everyone to live in peace and to leave behind the wars."

But this attack was not about war. This wasn't a politically motivated attack, as had been suspected. Indeed, the real perpetrator left false notes taking responsibility for the attack from Islamic terrorists. The man responsible was just a crook looking to make a quick buck. Had this crime taken place in the UK then Sergej W would not have been the beneficiary of German privacy laws. His full name would have been plastered all over the popular press, as would the full details of his life and his family. In Germany he is still referred to under his alias but elsewhere he is reported as Sergej Wenergold.

The 28-year-old German-Russian placed three homemade pipe bombs stuffed with pins on the roadside and remotely detonated them as the team bus passed by. Thankfully the third did not explode. Wenergold left three notes near the scene purporting to be from Islamic terrorists. He posted another message on an independent news website, *Indymedia*, claiming to be from an anti-fascist organisation who were known to be critical of the club not taking a tough enough stance against fascist and Nazi activists within the supporter base. Another was emailed to a Berlin newspaper claiming to be from a far right organisation and taking responsibility for the crime, the motivation being the rise of multiculturalism.

In Dortmund, as in any mass supported institution, interventions from extremists and in particular from fascists is a fact of life. As *The Guardian* reported shortly after the bombing, "Borussia Dortmund's management has in recent weeks distanced itself from a far-right contingent of supporters, some of whom had attacked fans of RB Leipzig, including children, when the two sides met in February. Graffiti containing a death threat against the Dortmund chief executive, Hans-Joachim Watzke, signed by the fan group '0231 Riot' was discovered in the city days after the incident."

Part of the consequence of that attack was a forced closure of the Südtribüne for one game against Wolfsburg later that season. For that one game, the famous "Yellow Wall" was torn down. This punishment was particularly tough to take for the many thousands in the South Stand who have worked hard to present a unified front against Nazis. To be punished by the actions of those they oppose was frustrating. However, it would be naive to play down the problem. In November

2018 *Deutsche Welle* reported that Block 13, the area in the Südtribüne that contains the hardest of the hardcore who support the club home and away and devise the spectacular choreos that have come to symbolise the club, was infiltrated by known Nazi hooligans.

As real as these issues are, they were not the driving motivation behind the attack on the Dortmund bus. In fact these serious and indeed urgent matters were exploited to create a smokescreen to hide the perpetrator's true intent: money. At the same time, however, this ruse proved to be his downfall. That and a lack of understanding of how the internet works.

On the day of the attack Sergej W acquired 15,000 Put Options from a German Bank. Put options are a warrant that allows the buyer to sell shares at a predetermined price on or before a specific date. The intention was that after the bombing, Dortmund's share price would plummet and Sergej W would then sell his put options and clean up. *The Guardian* reported that, "Had the explosives killed a member of the team and the club's share price dropped, the value of his put option would have increased significantly."

The plot failed. In short, Borussia Dortmund's share prices did drop but not sufficiently for Wenergold to make the nearly €4 million that was anticipated. Also the police did not accept the various claims of responsibility as authentic. Initially a 26-year-old Iraqi was arrested but soon released. What did for Sergej W was that he bought the put options online, from his room in the same hotel in which the Borussia team had been based. According to the *Daily Telegraph*, "Wenergold reportedly drew attention to himself at the hotel, first by insisting on a window room facing the front and then, in the chaos after the blasts, by calmly walking into its restaurant to order a steak."

His purchase of the put options had drawn the attention of the online broker, Comdirect, who in turn informed the police. As the prospect of a terrorist plot thinned, they lent more credence to this outlandish example of late capitalism and eventually arrested Wenergold on his way to work. The trial lasted 11 months and he was sentenced to 14 years in prison on 28 counts of attempted murder.

During the trial Borussia Dortmund's then coach Thomas Tuchel was among the witnesses. He was on the team bus during the attack but by this point the coach who replaced Jürgen Klopp in 2015 after a fantastic six years had also left the club. Krumbach-born Tuchel is said to be something of an intense character and it has been suggested that his relationships with Aki Watzke and Michael Zorc were never as good as they could have been. However, Tuchel's frustration with the club hierarchy and indeed with UEFA was entirely understandable after the decision was made to play the Champions League quarter-final with Monaco only 24 hours later in spite of the objections of the coach and players.

If you spend too much time on social media then you may remember the images of generous Dortmunders welcoming Monaco fans into their homes and offering them a bed for the night. The thousands of fans who had travelled from the principality to the Ruhr were left with the choice of either going home or spending a night in Dortmund that they did not plan for. Locals opened up their homes in their droves, demonstrating the true nature of most people who support the club and indeed the true nature of most of us. It was an aspect of this whole incident that kept your faith in humanity.

From UEFA, and from the club's point of view, the issue was a logistical one. What had happened was shocking but the show must go on. A Champions League quarter-final is one of the biggest games in the European calendar and almost everyone had turned up. In the immediate aftermath of the attack there were thousands of people in the stadium. What on earth do you tell them? To go home and come back tomorrow or next week or even next month? From that point of view it is not difficult to understand the decision. The problem was that no one who took the decision seemed to ask the players.

During the trial both Tuchel and midfielder Sven Bender said that it was a mistake to play the game. Tuchel was also angry with the way he was informed of the decision: "We were informed by text message that UEFA was making this decision," he said, as reported in *The Independent*. "A decision made in Switzerland that concerns us directly. At that time, we did not know the reasons for this attack. There is a feeling of helplessness. The date was imposed on us. What we think has not interested anyone. We weren't asked about playing the game. A few minutes after this attack, the only question that was asked was, 'Are you ready to play?' As if we had had a beer can thrown at our coach."

The lack of consideration towards the players from UEFA caused a great deal of resentment and Tuchel in particular was unhappy with the lack of support from his boss, Watzke. "Aki has already said publicly that there was a major discrepancy," Tuchel said during the trial. "This is true. The essence of the discrepancy is that I was sitting on the bus and Aki wasn't. That's why there was a major discrepancy about how to go about things – without wanting to hold it against Aki."

It is also difficult to escape the conclusion that there are so many commercial considerations involved in a game of this profile that postponing the game would have created a considerable financial cost. Reconciling this sentiment with the lives and wellbeing of a group of young men is tough but unfortunately necessary. As Nuri Şahin said in that interview with Fjørtoft after the match, "I know football is very important. We love football, we suffer with football. I know we earn a lot of money. We have a privileged life. But we are human beings and there is so much more than football in this world."

Borussia Dortmund are the only Bundesliga club to be listed on the stock market, a decision taken, as we know, at the turn of the century, and one that set in motion a chain of events that nearly destroyed the club. Although no one at Borussia is in any way responsible for this bizarre crime it was a crime that could only have been committed against Dortmund precisely because of their stock market listing. Perhaps, and this is pure speculation on my part, among the many reasons why Watzke thought it was best to press ahead with the game is the same reason why Wenergold devised the caper in the first place: that Borussia's share prices might drop to a level that could cause long-term damage to the club. While it is not uncommon for football matches to be postponed, the reasons are usually a little more straightforward. To postpone this match for longer than a day may, it could be argued, send a signal that the club was vulnerable to such attacks and in the longer term a bad investment.

In any event the game was played and Dortmund lost 3-2. The second leg finished 3-1 to the Ligue 1 side. Tuchel stated during the trial that the experience had affected the players and contributed to their performance and subsequent defeat. Under the circumstances it is difficult to argue with that belief. This was an outstanding Monaco team under Leonardo Jardim and featuring the stellar talents of future World Cup hero Kylian Mbappé. While it is entirely likely that this team could have prevailed over Borussia irrespective of their traumas, we will never truly know. I suppose it's not very important after all.

Tuchel also said that the defeat contributed to his departure as BVB boss at the end of the following season. The disappointment Tuchel felt towards his bosses may well have soured the relationship between them. That said, it has been suggested that relations were not exactly cordial before the bombing and that the incident just made a bad situation worse. Anyone who is across the European football scene will know that Thomas Tuchel is an outstanding coach, destined to have a crack at the top jobs in club football. At the time of writing he is the coach of Chelsea in the Premier League after having very nearly delivered the Champions League to the Qatari state-run club Paris Saint-Germain. Despite the disappointment of losing in the final to Bayern in 2020, it is widely reported that the reason for his dismissal was due to his deteriorating relationship with the club's sporting director, Leonardo. By the time of his departure from Dortmund there were reports about members of the team wishing that he was gone already and it may even be that Watzke and/or Zorc would have been happy for him to go sooner. This is, of course, speculation. We may only know the truth years from now.

The decision to appoint Tuchel as Borussia Dortmund coach was an obvious one. Like his predecessor he was a Mainz alumnus. Tuchel had fashioned a team supplied by his sporting director, Christian Heidel, that was talented, tactically astute, pleasing to watch and – by the standards set by a club of Mainz's size – successful. By the time that Klopp announced his departure, Tuchel had left Mainz and was pondering numerous offers from big Bundesliga clubs including Schalke and Hamburg, the latter of which was at a late stage of negotiations before the call came from Borussia. Once Klopp gave that press conference announcing his departure in April 2015 the die was cast. Tactically, Tuchel was cut from the same cloth as Klopp and seemed like the ideal replacement. Indeed, while Tuchel's tenure was relatively short-lived it was objectively successful.

Borussia Dortmund finished the 2015/16 season with 78 points. That's three points more than when they won the title in 2011 and only three points fewer than when they lifted the Meisterschale in 2012. It was even eight points more than when they were champions in 2002. In fact, in 11 of the seasons from the turn of the century, Dortmund's 2015/16 record would have been enough to win the

Bundesliga. Unfortunately, Tuchel's team were playing during a period of particularly empathic dominance for Bayern Munich. Pep Guardiola's team finished the season on 88 points and completed the league and cup double by beating Borussia on penalties in the DFB-Pokal final. This was Dortmund's third consecutive trip to Berlin for the showpiece event and their third defeat.

The Tuchel period also gave supporters of the club the chance to see more top class talent week in and week out. Henrikh Mkhitaryan really blossomed that season at Dortmund before he left for Manchester United. Julian Weigl offered remarkable composure in the midfield for a man of only 18, alongside the silky skills of İlkay Gündoğan, who also moved at the end of that season to Manchester but as a part of the revolution at City rather than United. Then, of course, there was Pierre-Emerick Aubameyang, the Gabonese international striker who electrified the Westfalenstadion with his pace, finishing and his exuberance both on and off the field. In the four and a half seasons Auba played in the Ruhr he scored 141 goals in all competitions. Only Timo Konietzka, Lothar Emmerich, Michael Zorc, Manni Burgsmüller and Adi Preißler have scored more. The only sadness is that he did not win the Bundesliga medal his contribution merited and in most other seasons would have been his due. Emerging too was the young Christian Pulisic who by now is a Chelsea player.

Which leads us to the key aspect of modern Borussia that is both a source of great pride and profit for the club but also a great source of frustration. Already Borussia fans were disappointed with the drain of talent to Bayern Munich in the shape of Robert Lewandowski, Mario Götze and, after eight years of service, Mats Hummels in 2016. However, the selling off of young players now seems to be very much the business model.

In the two years under Tuchel Dortmund lost Gündoğan, Mkhitaryan and Hummels. After his departure, Pulisic and the mercurial if impatient Ousmane Dembélé have also gone. With the exception of Hummels all of these players have gone abroad. Traditionally it was Bayern that would buy Dortmund's best players, but now it seems that the talent is good enough for the superclubs of Europe. The sale of these players must have been deeply frustrating for Tuchel, who knew that if he could retain this talent and add to it then great things were possible. Sadly, however, Borussia Dortmund do not roll that way. The lessons of financial extravagance of the past appear to have been learned and as a consequence moving players on at a profit to keep the club going is very much part of the plan. In fact, it is written into the DNA of the club.

Borussia's training camp is located in nearby Brackel. It is a state-of-the-art facility which was described by Murad Ahmed of the *Financial Times* as a "football finishing school". From there the club recruit the best young players in Europe and beyond. The proposition: Complete your football education, get plenty of minutes for a top Bundesliga and European team in front of 80,000 fanatical supporters, and then, when the time and the price is right, move on. Sometimes it works, such as with Pulisic, whose departure was well timed. Others it doesn't, such as Alexander Isak. The Swedish striker arrived in Brackel with ridiculously high expectations which were not met. In other cases it nearly works. The aforementioned Dembélé probably needed another year at Borussia but was unable or unwilling to resist the lure of Barcelona in 2017. In terms of the bottom line, the model works. After the transfer of Christian Pulisic to Chelsea, Dortmund had earned €132.07 million more than they had spent on the transfer market in the last five years, according to *Bild Zeitung*.

So this is the way of things at Dortmund and any coach must understand that when taking on the job. Success is still possible but for the foreseeable future at least the window of opportunity to work with some of the best young players is brief. This still means that there is plenty of talent to go round and Dortmund will still be able to compete for top players such as Paco Alcácer and Axel Witsel, but it is important for modern Borussens to understand this. Given the club's past and its frequent fallow periods current fans can count themselves fortunate to be supporting a BVB that can and does win silverware, as indeed did Thomas Tuchel when his team beat Niko Kovač's Eintracht Frankfurt 2-1 in Berlin. On the road to the capital, Borussia exacted a modicum of payback over Bayern by beating them 3-2 in an emotional semi-final in Munich.

In the wake of Tuchel's departure it was becoming apparent that things needed to change. The losses had taken their toll, particularly at the back where Sokratis Papastathopoulos and Ömer Toprak were not providing the basis for a solid unit. Marc Bartra had left the club for Real Betis, almost certainly prematurely but not unsurprisingly given his terrible experience. The squad was creaking and unable to cope with the glorious yet suicidal tactics of Peter Bosz. The Dutchman had won many friends taking Ajax to the Europa League final in the previous season.

Despite a blistering start to the campaign, winning six of their first seven matches, it all went south after an exhilarating 3-2 defeat to Rasenballsport Leipzig. Without mustering a single win in the following seven games and after tumbling out of the Champions League, Bosz was sacked and replaced with interim coach Peter Stöger. The Austrian former 1. FC Köln coach steadied the nerves and safely navigated Borussia to fourth place and a Champions League spot. Stöger will not win any artistic awards for his style of football. However, he did give a debut to another exceptional young player.

Born in South London, Jadon Sancho received his football education in the cages of Kennington and later the youth system at Watford FC in Hertfordshire. A World and European champion at Under-17 level for England, Sancho was on the fringes of Pep Guardiola's Manchester City side when he instead opted to join Borussia Dortmund in 2017. By the 2018/19 season, Sancho was a vital attacking component in the BVB side that so narrowly missed out on the Bundesliga title, and was a scorer in the Revierderby. Some may argue that, had he stayed at City, he would have a Premier League, FA Cup or League Cup medal. But to what extent he would have featured in those winning teams and developed as a player, given the competition for places, is open to question. It is hard to imagine that the young Englishman would have matched the 13 goals and 19 assists that season wearing the colours Manchester City. It was those kinds of numbers that must have earned him his debut for the senior England team in October 2018.

Sancho's decision to walk away from one of the richest clubs in the world to play for Dortmund is a testimony not only to his courage but also to Borussia Dortmund's appeal. In a landscape where elite football is financed by seemingly bottomless wells of cash, it is reassuring that relatively modestly funded clubs can still attract the best young players and give them the step up they need. In the end, though, Sancho will almost certainly move on, as others have done before him.

That is not to say that Borussia is a frugal club. At the end of the 2018/19 season they spent €127.5 million on Nico Schulz, Thorgan Hazard, Julian Brandt and the return of Mats Hummels, plus the permanent acquisition of Paco Alcácer, with, presumably, a significant increase in the club's wage bill. The intention was to take advantage of perceived weaknesses of Bayern Munich under Nico Kovač. If Dortmund could catch the champions in a rare period of transition, perhaps they could go one better than second. The following winter the experienced and dynamic midfielder Emre Can and the phenomenal Erling Braut Håland swelled the ranks.

There is a note of caution to strike, however. Knowing what we know of the club's history, overspending in the pursuit of silverware is risky and can have calamitous consequences. Borussia Dortmund needs to tread a narrow path, knowing when and when not to invest. Do we want to see a repeat of the dark days where the club is driven to the edge of bankruptcy? Has BVB really learned from the mistakes of the past?

As it turned out, Bayern's transition was barely a wobble in terms of form and the holders retained their title once again. It transpired that the biggest threat to Bayern's championship came from another much more serious source. The 2019/20 season turned out to be a historic and memorable one, but not for what happened on the pitch.

2019-20

Clash of Civilisations

As we know, it is perfectly normal for fans of one club to hate another. In truth it's normal for them to hate two, three, or even more clubs, usually for irrational reasons. In the house built by football supporter culture, club rivalry is a load-bearing wall. Another side of that house is a club's supporters railing against an idea, principal or ideology. The most obvious example of that would be FC St Pauli, a football club with left-wing politics baked into its very constitution.

Almost all clubs in Germany have an 'ultra' scene – groups of supporters with a specific identity that are affiliated to their club. These days you would be tempted to refer to them as stans: fans that display obsessive or overzealous behaviour that approaches the unhealthy. A significant part of their activity is to support the team on a matchday. However, for many, that is just the beginning. Ultra groups throughout Europe are involved in their local communities and have a say in their local football clubs. Ultras are political. They both stand for stuff and are against other stuff. They campaign to make stuff happen, or to stop it from happening. Ultras are not spectators. They are engaged.

While ultra groups may be separated by their narrow club interests, many of them share the same values. Chief among them is the preservation of football tradition and the 50+1 rule, the system of ownership which means that 50% + 1 of the shares in a football club must be owned by the club itself and, therefore, its fans. As club members, supporters are given a significant stake and say in what happens to their club. Any threat from an institution or individual to 50+1, whether it be perceived or real, is challenged. In recent years a number of threats have emerged. Martin Kind is the club president of Hannover 96. He successfully lobbied to have the rule changed so that any shareholder who can demonstrate that they have made significant investments into a club for 20 years can purchase a majority share of that club. Dietmar Hopp was the first individual to take advantage of that rule. Rasenballsport Leipzig are essentially owned by Red Bull and circumvent the rule by restricting the members to a very small number of employees of the Austrian energy drink concern. However, the most high profile example is Hopp, chief financial backer of TSG Hoffenheim.

Dietmar Hopp is a billionaire software magnate and philanthropist. He grew up in Hoffenheim and, as a young man, played for TSG when they were a so-called 'village club'. In 1972 he co-founded the software giant SAP-SE and made his fortune. In the early 1990s he began to invest in TSG. These investments were stepped up in 2005 as he decided to propel his beloved hometown club into the Bundesliga. He hired Ralf Rangnick as coach and gave him the resources to build a football club. In 2008, Hoffenheim's journey from the regional leagues to Bundesliga was complete. However, the sight of a club from a small town with fewer than 4,000 inhabitants rising through the leagues caused disquiet and criticism among their rivals. Can and indeed should a football club be allowed to grow at the rate Hoffenheim has based on the financial backing of one man? Is this fair and is it sustainable? The further Hoffenheim climbed the more criticism the club, and in turn Hopp, received. Eventually, TSG's benefactor, perhaps unused to being challenged in such a way, began to push back.

"Everyone is happy that the German Football Association and the DFL are taking rigorous measures against racism. We would like to see discrimination like Mr. Heidel be dealt with pursue the same consequence, because this infamous defamation of our club, which is supposed to deliberately stir up hatred of Hoffenheim, is also suitable for triggering violence against us."

This was part of the content of a fax sent from TSG Hoffenheim to FSV Mainz in 2007 as reported in the *Rhein-Zeitung*. The fax was signed by Dietmar Hopp. The provocation: an interview in FAZ with Mainz's sporting director, Christian Heidel, who questioned the validity of Hoffenheim's existence as a professional football club. "It is legitimate to question this concept from the perspective of a professional club."

Hopp was, and is, as entitled to his view as Heidel. Moreover, Hopp is entitled to defend himself. However, the tone of the fax and suggestion that criticisms against him should be compared with racism are, to say the least, over the top. They were also a refrain that he would use again years later and indicative of the measures he will go to crush any criticisms of him personally. Being a billionaire he has money and influential friends to back him up too.

The first time Hopp saw the by now notorious image of his face in a crosshair was in September 2008 during his team's 4-1 win over Borussia Dortmund. Displayed with the banner were the words "Hasta la vista, Hopp", an expression well known to anyone with even a passing interest in popular culture. Arguably the phrase is more of a light-hearted riposte than an unambiguous threat. The banner could be construed as levity, albeit with a serious message behind it: Hopp's vision for club ownership and management threatens to undermine what makes German football great and it is he who will be the symbol of that threat.

There is an argument to be had about the rights and wrongs of football club ownership. The much vaunted 50+1 rule is cherished among the overwhelming majority of ultra groups in Germany and is the envy of many socially engaged fans beyond its borders. The rule that just over half a football club must be owned by its supporters gives them a level of influence that would not be possible in England, for example. This does not mean that fans make decisions. The club president and supervisory board is elected and given the authority to do what they feel is necessary to make the club successful, and that success is measured by the expectations of the electorate. This means that issues that are more important to fans, such as low ticket prices, are usually high up the agenda. Team results matter a great deal, especially to the bigger clubs who, like anyone else, will have an expectation of success. However, club decision makers walk between two worlds where on-pitch success is expected, and expected to be affordable.

There is a downside, of course, and that is money. Moneybags English clubs can and do attract huge investment from super-rich owners or bad actors looking to clean up their reputations. In Germany this is much harder. For instance it would be almost impossible for the Saudi Arabian royal family to buy a controlling stake in a German football club under the strict interpretation of 50+1. That said, there are some clubs – whether by exemption like Bayer Leverkusen and Wolfsburg or through circumventing the rule like Rasenballsport Leipzig – who can spend vast sums of money on a club that under normal conditions would not be able to exist at its current level. And then there is Dietmar Hopp, who as the club's chief financial backer effectively gives his money to the club. One day, when Hopp passes on, he may leave TSG Hoffenheim in a position where it's able to sustain itself as a Bundesliga team, but if he does then it will have been thanks to a level of spending that most other professional clubs can't match.

So therein lie the issues. These so-called 'plastic' clubs – Hoffenheim, Rasenballsport and to a lesser extent Leverkusen and Wolfsburg – threaten the very principle of ownership that gives supporter groups the influence they enjoy, and by doing so they create for themselves a sporting advantage. Two very good reasons for taking a thorough disliking to these clubs and the symbol of this wave of interlopers is Hopp. He is the target of the fans' ire but he is not a defenceless one and is not without allies. The individual responsible for that first crosshair banner found himself in the sights of Hopp's lawyers. He was forced to publicly apologise for its use to avoid being sued. The following season, before the two teams played again in November, Hans Joachim Watzke, who had previously badmouthed Hopp and referred to Hoffenheim as a "test tube club" in a shareholder's meeting, wrote an open letter to fans the same week asking them not to repeat the banners from the season before.

Watzke's appeal fell on deaf ears and the campaign against Hopp continued. In 2011, a Hoffenheim employee attempted to drown out the sound of BVB fans' anti-Hopp chants during the two teams' fixture at Hoffenheim's stadium in Sinsheim by playing artificial background sounds. As the protest's momentum grew, so did the intensity with fans regularly chanting that Dietmar Hopp was a "son of a whore". In combination with the crosshair image, it is understandable that Hopp himself and outside observers may feel that the fans were crossing a line. Despite repeated warnings and occasional prosecutions of Dortmund fans chanting or holding the offending banners, the protests continued. After the game at Sinsheim in May 2018, where a number of BVB fans were arrested and charged after singing "Dietmar Hopp you son of a whore", the DFB warned Dortmund that if the banners weren't furled and the chanting stopped then they would go back on their previous promise to end collective punishment for fans and ban BVB supporters from the stadium in Sinsheim. The protests did not stop and a year later the DFB made good on their promise and banned

Borussia Dortmund fans from away trips to Hoffenheim for two years.

Meanwhile, the Dortmund anti-Hopp protests were not happening in isolation. Clubs all across Germany staged their own protests when Hoffenheim came to town or when they travelled to Sinsheim. Among them were Bayern Munich, and it was because of an incident during Bayern's game at Hoffenheim in March 2020 that the conflict between the club owners and their fans escalated. Or perhaps I should say it was the reaction that caused the escalation. After 77 minutes, with Bayern 6-0 up, their fans in the away section unfurled a banner calling Hopp a "son of a whore". The game was stopped while attempts were made to persuade the fans to remove the banner from sight. The Bayern fans did not relent and the referee removed the players from the pitch. While some of the players stayed to talk to the fans, the rest remained in the tunnel for 20 minutes. Eventually, the teams returned, led by Bayern chairman Karl-Heinz Rummenigge hand in hand with Dietmar Hopp as a show of solidarity with their wounded friend. The game was played out uncontested and finished 6-0.

If you're not a regular football fan or are someone who doesn't go to football matches very often, you might be asking how it's possible to defend or take up a position sympathetic with anyone who would aim such insulting language to an individual. Part of the answer to that lies in the context in which the insults are made; that being a football match. In the UK, if you watch a game on the TV the production team do their best to drown out insulting chants using abusive language. This presumably is in response to complaints from viewers either direct to the broadcaster, or via the regulator, that TV companies don't do enough to prevent singing and chanting that is offensive to families watching on their TVs at home. The issue from a broadcast regulatory point of view is that the TV viewer does not have sufficient informed choice when it comes to being exposed to offensive chanting. On the other hand, when you go to a football match you do have that choice. The assumption is that you know or have a good idea that you are going to hear swearing, off-colour humour and angry words imparted. It is in this context that any defence of insulting chants needs to be understood. For many there is no justification for this sort of behaviour and that is fine, because those people have the option to never attend football matches. In theory, then, the insults against Hopp are acceptable in such an arena because Hopp does not need to stick around to listen to them. He could leave his seat and go to a part of a stadium where his company will be welcomed. I'm not suggesting he should, but the argument is that he could. More pertinently, a football match is a forum in which abusive and angry chanting is expected and accepted. As Stefan Witte, a defence attorney for Borussia Dortmund Fanhilfe (an organisation that provides legal representation for BVB fans) told *Schwatzgelb.de* in 2019, "Nobody would come up with the idea of calling Dietmar Hopp a 'son of a whore' in the supermarket if they happened to meet them there."

There is an important line to be drawn here marking the difference between insults aimed at an individual and the racist, homophobic, transphobic, misogynistic abuse aimed at people of colour and the LGBTQ community. In my view insulting a billionaire because he is perceived as an existential threat to an institution which you love and strongly identify with is a world away from abusing and bullying a group of people for being who they are, especially groups that are in a minority and are in many cases emotionally, socially and economically vulnerable.

Later in the weekend, after the incident at the Hoffenheim v Bayern game, Hopp was interviewed by *Sport1*. He said, "If I remotely knew what these idiots wanted from me it would be easier for me to understand. I can't explain why they are so hostile. It reminds me of very dark times."

The 'dark times' comment was seen as a clear reference to Germany's Nazi past with the ultras as the oppressor and Hopp as the innocent victim. The justification for the stoppage during the match was UEFA's three-step protocol devised for racist incidents in football stadiums, the inference being that the treatment of Hopp is comparable to those who suffer racist abuse. The hypocrisy of this is apparent in view of what happened the previous month, during a DFB Pokal game at Schalke involving Hertha BSC. A black player, Jordan Torunarigha, was subjected to monkey chants during the match. UEFA's three-step protocol was not used in the wake of that incident. In fact, Torunarigha was given a second yellow card for showing his fury in reaction to the chants. The inference could not be clearer. If you are a black football player who has been racially abused then you'd best mind your manners. However, if you are a white billionaire with influential friends, then the full weight of the law will be behind you.

Conflating protest against Hopp with the abuse of minorities is, to my mind, a greater offence, particularly in view of the work that is done by socially engaged ultras in Germany to end racist, sexist and homophobic chanting in football stadiums, and in keeping Nazis from infiltrating the terraces. And yet that is what German football's establishment has been doing in order to justify its position towards those fans and the unfair penalties that they receive.

It must also be acknowledged that there is an entirely justifiable argument that, irrespective of context, any sort of abusive behaviour, action or language used in a football stadium should no longer be acceptable. Whether you are a fabulously wealthy and influential man at the top of the ladder, a working class Muslim who wants to go to a football match, or indeed a black footballer just doing your job, you should be entitled to attend or work at a football match without abuse or fear of abuse. I am in no doubt that people stay away from football grounds because they don't feel welcome and the game is poorer for it. The perception of the football-going public is that it is dominated by white men and there are huge sections of society that feel excluded from what is one of our civilisation's greatest pastimes. However, if things are going to change then it must be done by discussion and adopting a new consensus agreed upon by and involving all stakeholders, including the match-going public.

There is another aspect of this controversy: that Hopp, used as a symbol by those seeking to defend 50+1, also symbolises a movement to end it, that the ramping up of the rhetoric, threats to impose further stadium bans and stiffer punishments is part of a broader campaign on the part of club administrators to change the ownership rules to allow further outside investments. To do this, it could be argued, you need to break the power of the ultra groups, and to do that you must discredit them in the eyes of the broader public. The ultras' campaign against Hopp could be being used against them and Hopp may, willingly or otherwise, be a totem in both sides of that conflict. To what extent this is true is a topic outside the scope of this book. Certainly more evidence would need to be gathered. Indeed, it's possible that the whole subject is moot because at the very height of the crisis, in the early part of 2020, the dispute that threatened to destroy the consensus running German football was interrupted by something far worse.

The final few paragraphs of this chapter are being written in June 2020, five months after the World Health Organisation declared COVID-19 a public health emergency and three months after the disease was classified as a pandemic. A deadly airborne virus with no vaccine is the biggest global public health crisis since the Spanish Flu in 1918. With a few notable exceptions, countries all over the planet went into lockdown with all public events, including football matches, closed. As those of us who could retreat into our homes to escape the virus, the character of our public life altered from one of leisure to one of survival and mutual aid.

In Dortmund the north side of the Westfalenstadion was converted to an outpatient facility, providing care and treatment for people with symptoms of the disease. Borussia Dortmund's ultra groups put down their banners and helped vulnerable or at risk members of the community with their shopping. The community and club response on display in Dortmund was happening with clubs all over Germany. Dietmar Hopp, primary investor in a German biopharmaceutical company, was at the forefront of the development of a vaccine for the virus. At this moment, earlier disagreements seemed trivial. COVID-19 has changed the world. The question as to how much it changes back is a concern for the future of this book and the past for its readers.

The last Bundesliga match before the lockdown was on 10th March, a postponed Rheinderby game between Borussia Mönchengladbach and FC Köln that was played in an empty Borussia Park. Plans to play the next round of fixtures behind closed doors were scratched at the last minute by the DFL and the season was suspended. The season resumed on 16th May with the Revierderby as the headline act. Dortmund beat Schalke 4-0 in front of a select group of coaches, officials, journalists and board members, and under strict social distancing. Players were regularly and routinely tested for the virus and placed into isolation for the duration of the season.

The morality of the decision to restart football while people were still suffering the consequences of the disease and with no fans in the stadiums was and is highly disputed. Most ultra groups across the country have made their view clear: football is nothing without fans in the stadium and the activity of playing games while still in the grip of the virus was inappropriate. The counter-argument from the DFL was unambiguous. The Bundesliga was due millions of euros from broadcasters for completing the season and without that money no fewer than 13 clubs from the Bundesliga's two divisions could have faced insolvency. Among the clubs facing the precipice was Schalke 04. Who knows, by the time this is published the Gelsenkirchen club could be playing in the Regionalliga West.

In terms of the football, for Borussia Dortmund it was a season of what might have been, the title race effectively ended on May 26th when referee Tobias Stieler blew the whistle on an entertaining Klassiker between Borussia and Bayern which ended in a 1-0 win for the visitors. Jadon Sancho started from the bench, Axel Witsel and Marco Reus were injured, and Erling Braut Haaland limped off in the second half. Dortmund huffed and puffed but Bayern's house was too strong. Referee Stieler and the VAR team made a decisive contribution to the match by refusing to give a penalty for a pretty obvious handball in the box by Bayern's Jerome Boateng. The defeat extended the gap between Borussia and Bayern to seven points with six games left, mathematically possible but psychologically – not so much.

The decision to push the boat out during the summer and re-sign Mats Hummels to join Julian Brandt and Nico Schultz – plus Haaland and Emre Can in the winter – had not paid off. Lucien Favre could not take advantage of Bayern's perceived transition and break their seven-season streak as Bundesliga champions. Objectively, Bayern's squad was much bigger and deeper. Dortmund should congratulate themselves for keeping pace for so long. However, the Rekordmeisters' early-season wobble and Dortmund's mid-season collapse resulted in a feeling that an opportunity had been missed. That said, Borussia Dortmund could look forward to continued competition in the Champions League. While the sublime Ashraf Hakimi departed after his two-year loan from Real Madrid, Thomas Meunier joined from PSG. Sancho, who was the club's top scorer in 2019/20, may well have left by the time you read this, but Gio Reyna, at 17, looks like a worthy replacement.

On the management side few eyebrows were raised when Michael Zorc extended his contract. The sporting director's relationship with Borussia Dortmund is almost symbiotic. It's hard to imagine him leaving the club except in a pine box. A few more eyebrows were raised when the club confirmed that no changes would be made in the dugout and Lucien Favre would remain as coach. There is a narrative surrounding the former Nice, Hertha and Gladbach coach that his football, while exhilarating to watch, is lacking the tactical balance to win a league title. His team was also accused of not rising to the occasion when it mattered. Perhaps that's true, but it is a fact that only Mönchengladbach, Leipzig and Bayern conceded fewer goals in his last season than Favre's team and that included the atrocious 4-0 defeat to Hoffenheim on the last day. It is also a fact that, according to *Transfermarkt.com*, Borussia Dortmund were averaging 2.04 points per match under Favre. This compares very favourably to Jürgen Klopp's average 1.9 and Ottmar Hitzfeld's 1.86 points per match. With that in mind you can easily see why the club stuck with the likeable Swiss coach and considering the season they were having, you have to conclude that his eventual dismissal in December 2020 did not really change the club's immediate fortunes. Just as this book is being sent off to the printers, BVB are looking far from certainties to finish in the top four.

In any event Borussia Dortmund, like many other clubs and indeed like many of us, face an uncertain future as they and we step forward into a Coronavirus future. When the 2020/21 season kicks off it will be with significantly fewer fans in the stadium. The reduction in matchday revenue and domestic incoming TV revenue, and the overall effect of the inevitable shrinking of the economy both in Germany and around the world, will create new risks and more uncertainty. It is vital, then, that Borussia Dortmund stick to their plan and the people who can carry it out. If they keep plugging away, keep bringing in the best young players, eventually that Bundesliga title will once again be held aloft, all being well in front of a jubilant and sold out Westfalenstadion.

Postscript

The image started travelling down the algorithmic byways of Twitter the following day. A man, probably in his late twenties, with a Borussia Dortmund scarf tied around his neck, standing in the foreground surrounded by thousands of other Borussens, on one of the vast terraces at Berlin's Olympiastadion. The occasion was the DFB Pokal Final in 2012. The young man was Edin Terzic.

The image was posted on Terzic's Instagram account along with another photo taken nine years later, on 13th May 2021. Now 38, Edin is back at the Olympiastadion for another cup final, but he is not standing in the terraces. Instead, he is standing on the winner's podium, having coached Borussia Dortmund to their fifth DFB Pokal win.

The first picture was taken two years after Edin's career as a Regionalliga player ended. At the time he was involved in the youth set up at Borussia Dortmund as assistant coach to Hannes Wolf's under 17s team. He was also working for the club's chief scout, Sven Mislintat. That year he submitted an analysis of the Republic of Ireland national team to the Croatia manager Slaven Bilic, with whom he had developed a friendship. The Irish were group stage opponents for Croatia in Euro 2012. Aware of Edin's talents, Bilic eventually hired Edin as part of his coaching staff when the Croatian took charge of Beşiktaş the following year.

Edin followed Bilic to West Ham United and it was in England that he took the 18-month UEFA Pro Licence course from the FA. It is a measure of how things have changed in the European football scene that a trainer with an English coaching education succeeds in Germany, the home of the *Fußballlehrer*.

After Bilic was sacked from West Ham, Edin returned to Germany and to Dortmund, this time not just as a fan but as assistant to the incoming head coach, Lucian Favre. Initially, the plan had been for Hannes Wolf to be Favre's number two but they couldn't make it work so Edin got the nod.

Despite Favre's impressive points average, the club lost patience with him after a 5-1 defeat to Stuttgart in December 2020. Favre's style of football was exhilarating but the lack of balance in the team was shipping goals and it looked, to me at least, like the team could not function adequately without the phenomenon that is Erling Braut Haaland. Favre was fired, and a new coach would be hired in the summer of 2021.

Between them, Michael Zorc and Aki Watzke saw enough in Edin to entrust him with the keys to the dressing room until the end of the season and to get Borussia into the top four of the Bundesliga and in turn the Champions League. It was a risk because. not for the first time in their history, the club were feeling the financial pinch, this time thanks to COVID rather than financial prolificacy.

If you're reading this book shortly after publication then the chances are you will remember that for a time it looked like the wrong decision. Dortmund did not enjoy the dubious and unscientific benefits of the new coach bounce. Borussia slumped as low as seventh in the table. However, as the season reached its climax, the team revived, helped by a barnstorming run to the quarter finals of the Champions League (a campaign that partially cemented the 17-year-old Englishmen, Jude Bellingham as a big game player and a bonafide Dortmunder) and a run to the final of the DFB Pokal.

For the latter they had some help in the shape of a relatively kind draw in the semi-final. Second division Holstein Kiel, who knocked Bayern out in the second round, were drawn out of the hat and Bremen (soon to be a Bundesliga 2 side themselves) and Rasenballsport Leipzig were avoided until the final.

In the meantime, the team's Bundesliga form started to improve. In April and May they only lost once in the league, to Eintracht Frankfurt, their principal rival for one of the coveted top four spots. After the cup final spot was secured, Borussia went on to beat their fellow finalist's Rasenballsport and then FSV Mainz, who under new coach Bo Svenson had gone from one of the worst teams in the Bundesliga to one of the best. With that and thanks to a late season slump from Eintracht, Edin's primary task was complete. Borussia had qualified for the Champions League with all the glamour and money that goes with it. What was needed to cap off the season was the completion of a fairy-tale for Edin and his team: A trophy win.

Normally, the DFB Pokal final takes place at the end of the season. However, the 20-21 season has been like few others and due to scheduling conflicts the final happened on a Thursday with two more league fixtures still to play. So the players took to the field at the Olympiastadion knowing that there was still work to do. The omens weren't great. Yes, it's true that they had beaten the Leipzig team only the previous weekend but that could have worked against them. Also, Leipzig, under the young coaching phenom Julian Nagelsmann were comfortably the second-best team that season. This was a match RB easily could have won.

However, Borussia Dortmund were triumphant, and victory was achieved by the force of their own narrative. Or to use a cliche, they wanted it more.

The Borussia players swamped their opponents in a first half of breath-taking pace and energy. Better still the players took full advantage of their control of the match by scoring three goals and putting the match beyond Rasenballsport by the time they were heading up the escalator for the interval. Two goals by Jadon Sancho, by this point an almost complete footballer, committed to his team and his players. Supported with one more by the perennial scorekeeper-botherer, Haaland.

Rasenballsport gathered themselves for the second half and had the better of the game. When they got a goal back in the 71st minute I started to panic, remembering the way in which the team almost threw away their Champions League round of 16 tie against Sevilla, only the previous month. However, there was to be no collective defensive brain-fart and for good measure Haaland grabbed a classic late goal against the run of play. You know the sort: the type of goal that always makes the result look more one-sided than it was. Fantastic!

The emotion at the end of the game was almost too much. Edin celebrating an unlikely and unexpected rise from fan to coach. Club legend Łukasz Piszczek breaking down in tears, knowing this was his last season for the club. Marco Reus who put in a signature performance to win the match finally lifting a trophy as Captain. Here was a player that, fitness notwithstanding, could have won everything there was to win, had he chosen the red of Bayern over the yellow and black of Borussia. It is gratifying to know that the image of Reus holding aloft the DFB Pokal seals his fate as one of Borussia Dortmund's greatest captains.

It is probably too early to say but the 2021 Cup win may prove to be the clubs most significant since 1989. The club were in a much healthier position than when the one-and-a-half legged Nobby Dickel crashed in his hattrick on the summer evening in Berlin over three decades earlier. However, the COVID crisis plus the disappointment that the club has not been able to keep pace with Bayern since the days of Klopp and Tuchel, mixed with the special togetherness of this squad, overcoming adversity with an untried coach has made this cup win extra special.

Inevitably this group of players will disperse. That is how professional football works. Some retire, others are sold on for vast sums of money. The 21-22 season starts under new coach Marco Rose. What happened under the former Mönchengladbach coach is your past and my future. Perhaps, he will still be the coach when you are reading these words. Perhaps he'll be gone by the following Christmas. Who knows?

What we do know is that for at least one season, Borussia will live without one of the foundation stones that define the club's character and culture. After years of mismanagement its hated rival Schalke 04 succumbed to relegation at the end of one of the worst seasons in any club's history.

The schadenfreude of seeing *Herne West* in the second division is something to savour. But Borussia Dortmund and its fans must now face the immediate future without the bi-annual nerve shredding emotion of the Revierderby. I suspect that once the fixture list for the season ahead is published, the implications of derby's absence will be deeply felt. It is, after all, a fixture that almost every football fan in Germany and increasingly beyond takes an interest in and will be missed by fans, clubs, sponsors and by the DFL. Of all the significant changes that will occur after COVID-19, the loss of the Revierderby may be among the greatest, unless Schalke can find their way back into the Bundesliga's first division soon.

Will Borussia Dortmund prosper or wilt without Schalke. And how will they face the challenges presented by a world, changed by Coronavirus? There is literally only one way to find out.

About the Author

Terry Duffelen has written about German football since 2006. He is a regular panellist on the Sound of Football and Talking Fussball podcasts. He also co-founded the long-running Yellow Wall, Borussia Dortmund podcast.

Terry is a son of Croydon (and a Crystal Palace fan) but fell in love with Borussia Dortmund in 2004 and is now a club member. He lives in Sussex.